GAINSHARING

Plans for Improving Performance

GAINSHARING

Plans for Improving Performance

Brian Graham-Moore
Timothy L. Ross

with contributions by
Ruth Ann Ross
Paul S. Goodman
James E. Jarrett
James W. Dean, Jr.
Larry L. Hatcher

The Bureau of National Affairs, Inc., Washington, D.C. 20037

Second Printing, March 1991

Library of Congress Cataloging-in-Publication Data

Graham-Moore, Brian E., 1935–
  Gainsharing : plans for improving performance / Brian Graham-Moore
and Timothy L. Ross, with contributions by Paul S. Goodman . . . [et al.].
    p. cm.
  Includes bibliographical references.
  ISBN 0-87179-625-2
  1. Gain sharing. 2. Gain sharing—United States. I. Ross, Timothy
L., 1938–   . II. Goodman, Paul S. III. Title.
HD4928.G34G7 1989
331.2'164—dc20   89-48299
                                                                   CIP

Published by BNA Books, 1231 25th St., N.W.
Washington, D.C. 20037

Printed in the United States of America
International Standard Book Number 0-87179-625-2

Foreword

An acquaintance once described an uncle of his as the essence of the traditional, the unchanging. The uncle would urge his nephew to hold fast to the old, tried, and true ways of life and thought and to shun deviations from established custom and practice. "Take me, for instance," the uncle would say: "My father and grandfather were cabinet makers and, as you know, so am I. That's tradition. My father and grandfather always voted conservative and so do I. That's tradition. My father and grandfather always bowed before the wisdom of their superiors, and so do I. That's sound tradition. And my father and grandfather were bachelors, and, as you know, so am I!"

Obviously, not all tradition is worthy of rigid preservation!

It is heartening to witness the changes, the departure from tradition, which are spreading gradually within the field of labor-management relations.

The Tayloristic concept of the authoritarian work organization is losing its luster as, increasingly, it is recognized that employees as individuals and in groups often put management and engineers to shame, once afforded the opportunity to apply to the work force their knowledge, experience, and their bent for innovation. Experimentation in participative management processes has taken many different forms, with varying degrees of success. When emphasis has been directed toward enhancing the role of the employees in the decision-making process, and toward creating the climate for improved job satisfaction, the workplace traditions that inhibit creativity become discarded. New approaches to solving old problems displace the tired habits of the past. An excitement runs through the organization as it enjoys renewed vitality. When the emphasis, however, is directed essentially toward producing more for the sake of increased profit, this process becomes a management gimmick, co-opted to its advantage with but limited benefit to the work force that makes improvement possible.

Gainsharing plans have a unique role to play in bringing about rational change in the organization of work—and even in the management of enterprises. It is all the more urgent that they not become a gimmick designed just to fulfill management's objectives, but that they represent a mutually beneficial pact in a joint action process. True, gainsharing programs are anchored in the opportunity to win larger paychecks and enhance profitability. The driving force, nevertheless, should be based on producing a work climate which will advance the dignity of the employees as the adult human beings they are and ensure that they will not be treated as mere cogs in a machine.

In the final analysis, the most potent protection against management co-optation of gainsharing programs is the co-equal status with management of the employees' collective bargaining representative in planning, designing, implementing, and administering the program. The joint union-management structure promises assurance against undue advantage being taken by management. It provides a necessary voice for the work force in promoting the most desirable qualities of gainsharing. It guarantees joint effort in all aspects of its operation—in a genuine mode of cooperative endeavor.

Whether the gainsharing takes the form of Scanlon as its initiator originally envisaged its implementation, or of Rucker or Improshare, which are more directly related to production standards as the base for reward, the ultimate test is whether the work force will be recognized as true co-partners in the operation.

This vital point is incorporated, although not outrightly expressed, in the authors' finding that institutionalization of gainsharing programs is best achieved when there are common goals. Fulfillment of common goals is best accomplished when the factors leading to institutionalization are jointly managed. Joint commitment, joint training, jointly devised allocation of reward, joint examination of feedback, joint diffusion of the process throughout the organization, joint alteration of the program as the need for change becomes evident—these are the elements for a sound initiative and continuing success. And, success within this scenario makes absolutely imperative the commitment to depart from tradition and create a mind-set, a culture which "thinks anew and acts anew."

The authors' study of gainsharing judiciously analyzes the features that more likely assure success for gainsharing plans and the overall enhancement of job satisfaction. While their treatment does not dwell on the importance of union involvement as I would view it, the basic elements which are the firm foundation for gainsharing as an instrument for the economic viability of organizations are carefully explored and are presented with clarity. Their work should give added impetus to the expansion of the use of gainsharing programs, with the studied explanation of the procedures for success and the reasons for failure. Management and unions alike would do well to note the findings and give heed to the recommendations.

Irving Bluestone
Professor of Labor Studies
Wayne State University
Retired Vice President, UAW

Introduction

Interest in gainsharing continues to grow. In a 1987 study, The American Productivity and Quality Center predicted that some form of gainsharing will become one of the fastest growing strategies in the country during the 1990s. Articles on pay for performance and contingent/variable compensation are commonly found in a wide range of publications. Major sectors of the economy, such as the steel and auto industries, now have broad forms of gainsharing integrated into pay and union contracts. Why? The answers to this simple question are the reasons for this book.

Although "traditional" gainsharing practitioners may be disturbed by current trends, gainsharing is meeting the strategic needs of many different kinds of organizations. For example, one firm may use it to help save itself from bankruptcy; another may use it to phase out an obsolete individual incentive system; others may use gainsharing to improve labor relations, whereas still others may install gainsharing as a substitute for normal wage increases. Even if "purists" may find these trends disturbing, they occur nevertheless.

More ideal applications are also found in very successful organizations that see gainsharing as just an expansion of already successful techniques. These firms use gainsharing for integrating improved communications and cooperation, enhancing existing employee involvement, and increasing their competitiveness. Cost control, quality, and customer service combined with the shared financial benefits of gainsharing help to mutually reinforce existing systems of quality organizations. Also, these organizations see sharing financial gains as a fair practice. One thing is certain, adding financial rewards adds a powerful ingredient to the change and identity variables of organizational success.

In this book, we attempt to explain why gainsharing works and why it sometimes does not. Theoretical underpinnings are discussed in Chapter 1 with the understanding that no one model is likely to explain gainsharing success. It may lead to organizational change in one situation, or it may reinforce positive organizational change in another. In these situations, different and appropriate models are needed to match organizational requirements with their environments.

Other conceptual issues are discussed in the remainder of Part One. Chapter 2 discusses the extensive literature on gainsharing; Chapters 3 and 4 cover most of the important measurement issues that, without becoming overly complex, must be considered; and Chapters 5 and 6 delve into why plans fail or succeed in the long run.

Part Two provides much practical experience, starting with a 17-year case study. In fact, companies with as many as 40 years of gainsharing experience exist. From this we know that gainsharing can last a long time. One problem is the lack of appropriate information on long-term gainsharing success. A variety of other issues are covered in subsequent chapters. Some issues regarding government sector applications are covered in Chapter 8; current union trends are outlined in Chapter 9; and a case study on a transition of an individual incentive system to gainsharing is discussed in Chapter 10.

Research studies of apprehensions and change processes underlying gainsharing are presented in Chapters 11 and 14. If an organization is planning a major change process with much employee involvement, Chapter 12 provides some useful educational outlines. The growing area of service sector organizations is reviewed in Chapter 13. Most good professionally oriented books should also provide some predictions of future expectations. This is done in our Chapter 15.

No book is solely the result of the author's efforts. This is particularly true in our case since the fruits of this book would have been impossible without the tremendous support of numerous firms and individuals who allowed us to learn at their expense. Without this cooperation, certainly this book would never have been written. Fortunately, this is the great thing about gainsharing—companies that successfully practice it really do believe in the concept. This makes our research and writing activities immeasurably easier because these firms want to share their knowledge and experience.

A special acknowledgment is due to our colleagues and students at Bowling Green State University and The University of Texas at Austin. They have listened to our ideas many times and provided much useful criticism. We also wish to acknowledge the contributions to this book by Robin Graham-Moore for her mastery of microcomputer text editing.

Finally, we thank our associates in this endeavor as they have generously contributed to the publication of this book.

December 1989

Brian Graham-Moore
Timothy L. Ross

Contents

Part Two. Cases and Applications

7. Seventeen Years of Experience With the Scanlon Plan: DeSoto Revisited 139
Brian Graham-Moore

Part One

Theory, Measurement, and Conceptual Issues

Chapter 1

Understanding Gainsharing

Brian Graham-Moore and Timothy L. Ross

Introduction

Gainsharing is a formal reward system that has existed in a variety of forms for over fifty years. Sometimes gainsharing is known as the Scanlon plan, the Rucker® plan, or Improshare®. The generic term, however, is gainsharing and its definition usually is made up of these three components:

1. the philosophy of cooperation,
2. the involvement system,
3. the financial bonus.

This book will continually define these components and provide examples, but a brief discussion of each of these terms follows. The philosophy of cooperation refers to an organizational climate wherein high levels of trust, two-way communication, participation, and harmonious industrial relations exist. Positive values supporting these behaviors are held by most, if not all organizational members at good installations.

The second component, the involvement system, refers to the structure and process whereby organizational productivity is improved. Most typically it is a broadly based suggestion system implemented by an employee-staffed committee structure which usually reaches all areas of the organization. Sometimes this structure involves work teams, sometimes quality circles, but usually it is simply an employee-based suggestion system. The employees involved develop and implement ideas related to productivity.

The third component is the financial bonus. This bonus is determined by a calculation that measures the difference between expected costs and actual costs during a bonus period. The word gainsharing was coined by F. Taylor in 1886 to refer to the payment of bonuses out of these differences. Some firms use expected versus actual time as their bonus calculation and others use profit improvement. Many varieties of calculations are found in practice.

These three components mutually reinforce each other. Higher levels of cooperation lead to information sharing, which in turn leads to employee involvement. Typically, this employee involvement leads to new behaviors, such as the offering of suggestions, which improve organizational productivity. This increase in productivity then results in a financial bonus (based on the amount of the productivity increase) which rewards or reinforces the philosophy of cooperation. While some forms of gainsharing may emphasize one component of this definition over the other two, or even delete one or more of these components, most gainsharing examples employ all three components.

Descriptive Model

Defining and describing gainsharing is an easier task than predicting its success. For example, developing a theory for gainsharing is very difficult because it exists in so many variations and in so many different environments. While theoretical development is a desirable goal, few comprehensive efforts have been made in this direction. Nevertheless, decision makers within organizations wish to know where and how gainsharing has failed. Presumably, they would like to avoid similar pitfalls. While this approach would imply that failure avoidance is a safe strategy, this framework doesn't predict success, just the avoidance of sure failure. This position is, in effect, only partial theory and begs for a more complete answer. Obviously, gainsharing needs more and better predictive theory.

Our approach in this chapter is to present a description of gainsharing along with some predictions as to how well it can work under various conditions. First, we present a descriptive model that describes, in part, how gainsharing works for contingent compensation strategies or the traditional gainsharing strategy, i.e., the self-managed work force[1] (see Exhibit 1.1). This model permits us to list and defend what we do know about gainsharing. While this is useful in the same way as failure avoidance, the descriptive model doesn't permit full prediction and validation of those propositions

Exhibit 1.1 Gainsharing Descriptive Model

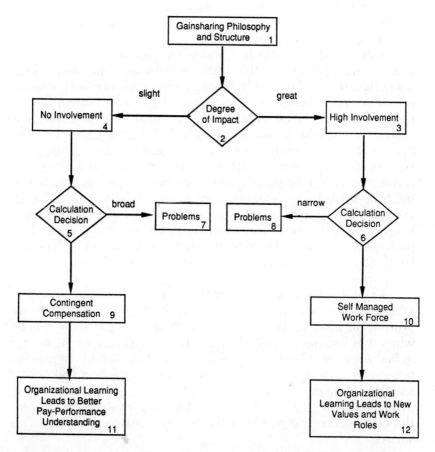

which make gainsharing success possible. Later in this chapter, some elements of predictive gainsharing theory will be introduced. For now, let's turn to Exhibit 1.1 and the descriptive model.

As we can see, box 1 refers to all of the knowledge that goes into and supports what we perceive to be true concerning gainsharing. The first decision diamond (no. 2) raises the question concerning the degree of impact gainsharing is intended to have on the organization. In cases in which the intended impact is slight, we can honestly say that these organizations use gainsharing in a fashion contrary to what the literature reveals in Chapter 2. Very clearly, the near past has seen concessionary bargaining and takeaways of pay and fringe benefits. As compensation experts redesign their reward packages, they wish to avoid those policies which tend to feed inflation. Also, they are drawn toward innovative reward systems that adjust for economic realities, i.e., variable pay, two-tiered pay, and, even, gainsharing.

Exhibit 1.1 indicates box 9 as contingent compensation, one gainsharing strategy. In this instance, base pay may be slightly lower than the market, but bonuses are employed to meet or exceed prevailing rates when they are justified by commensurate human performance. As box 4 shows, no or low involvement of the gainsharing philosophy is associated with this strategy. Based on the degree of involvement, the calculation decision (part of the gainsharing structure) can be either narrow or broad. If narrow, the result (box 11) can be that the most significant organizational learning is better knowledge of pay-performance relationships. That is, the human resource, or the work force, learns that high quantity leads to high bonuses. This outcome differs from that created by individual incentives because the gainsharing bonus is typically contingent on the quantity produced by *all* employees, not just one person.

Exhibit 1.1 also accounts for those organizations that combine a broad calculation with no or low involvement. This is perfectly possible to do since the organization chooses to pay more money when it is making a profit. In good times, bonuses are high, and in bad times problems (box 7) will occur. For example, employees become frustrated because they have no control over bad times, and there is no mechanism in place to help the organization become more profitable or avoid deficits. Without an involvement system, the intelligence and power of the human resource has no way to surface.

Looking at Exhibit 1.1 again, if the degree-of-impact decision is to adopt high involvement and the calculation decision is to develop a broad calculation, then successful gainsharing must be associated with a self-managed work force (box 10). The organizational learning includes new work values and work roles, and the organizational culture is markedly changed. Chapters 3 and 4 delve into the intricacies of calculation development. These chapters specify the trade-offs required in the use of various calculations to reinforce appropriate organizational strategies. The degree of impact desired does not always produce the predictable results seen in Exhibit 1.1. For example, decision makers could offer a narrow calculation to employees in combination with a high involvement system. That is, high involvement with a narrow calculation could lead to feelings of frustration and inequity as indicated by box 8. Why does this occur? Successful gainsharing culture shows the human resource how to work smarter, cooperate, and participate in ways which lead to a self-managed work force. A narrow calculation reinforces only part of those behavioral changes. Self management isn't partial. It is a real commitment to influence *all* of the factors associated with an organization's success—if they are under the control of the work force. A narrow calculation excludes many factors that are under work force control.

It is clear that gainsharing exists in a variety of forms and stages of development. Virtually all of the literature reviewed in Chapter 2 is concerned with traditional gainsharing. The traditional view suggests that the only goal of gainsharing is a self-managed work force. Obviously, there are other strategies, such as contingent compensation, which are not being evaluated and researched. Nevertheless, numerous examples exist where gainsharing has been used to further a contingent compensation strategy, and these economic facts of life cannot be ignored.

Traditional Gainsharing and Organizational Fit

The conditions which favor traditional gainsharing have been "known" for some time.[2] We say known because recognition of these conditions has been achieved through various types of research. Exhibit 1.2 lists four broad categories of conditions and variables which affect the success of gainsharing. For example, Exhibit 1.2 denotes organizational size, as measured by total number employed at one location, as an important factor. Since part of the gainsharing philosophy is to share information, cooperate, and have an influence on one's working environment, it is not surprising that increasing organizational size works against gainsharing. A national survey taken in 1987 reported that gainsharing companies ranged in size from fewer than 250 employees (22 percent of the gainsharing companies) to more than 20,000 employees (6 percent of the gainsharing companies). The reported median was a surprisingly high 954 employees.[3] However, 60 percent of the organizations reported 500 or fewer employees. Therefore, size is a factor, yet it would appear that larger organizations are attempting gainsharing than has been previously thought.

Organizational climate and communication must be conducive to the acceptance of traditional gainsharing philosophy. That is,

Exhibit 1.2   Conditions That Affect the Success of Gainsharing Plans

ORGANIZATIONAL FACTORS

Size
Climate
Communication

FINANCIAL/MARKET FACTORS

Financial measures
Market for output
Product stability
Seasonal nature
Capital investment

TECHNOLOGICAL FACTORS

Type
Technological uncertainty
Work flow/cycle

LABOR FORCE FACTORS

Work force characteristics
Union relations
Supportive services
Overtime history

sufficient trust and open communication must exist within an organization before gainsharing can have an impact. If there are no norms and values reinforcing the sharing of information, the institution of a gainsharing plan alone would not effect this change.

Exhibit 1.2 lists technological factors that can affect gainsharing success. For example, if there is a high degree of task interdependency, then sharing and rapid movement of information is needed to achieve task success. Thus, the way work is organized can either help or hinder gainsharing success. If each work station is concerned only with its own output, then gainsharing may not have general appeal. In the same way, if the technology is well understood, highly programmed, and tightly controlled by the machine process with few variances, then opportunities to "work smarter" are limited. Reciprocal workflows and longer work cycles help the gainsharing process because they require sharing information, teamwork, and coordination. Indeed, these are new sources of intrinsic satisfaction which can lead to higher levels of participation.

Financial and market factors should not be overlooked. As will be explained in Chapters 2–5, the degree of sophistication of financial information systems will work either for or against gainsharing. Organizations that cannot assemble accurate historical cost data should not entertain the idea of gainsharing. In addition, a series of economic factors needs to be assessed. For example, will there be a market for increased output? Is product stability likely or will there be many changes to the product line that in turn change the accuracy of historical costs? Does the seasonal nature of the production cycle influence the measure of productivity? Do very long runs reflect the same patterns of efficiency? In reference to financial-market factors, will planned capital investments change the amount of value added by labor? Chapters 3 and 4 explore some of these questions.

The last category on the list of conditions affecting gainsharing (Exhibit 1.2) regards the characteristics of the labor force. For instance, levels of job satisfaction and employee motivation must be sufficiently high for gainsharing to be perceived as an instrumental link to even higher levels of human performance. By the same token, if union relations with management are poor, gainsharing would be expected, as a structure, to lead to better levels of industrial relations. It should be obvious that gainsharing can reinforce harmonious relations more easily than it can change an adversarial climate. Also, an organization's supportive services (e.g., maintenance, supply, etc.) will be strained under a gainsharing program because new demands will be placed upon them by the involvement system. Therefore, these supportive services should be flexible and capable of expansion.

The last condition listed in Exhibit 1.2 is overtime history. Case studies discussed in Chapter 2 have indicated how overtime practices, if poor, can undermine a gainsharing program. For example, in a case in which overtime is not justified, a gainsharing bonus will make this unfair difference in pay even larger. Therefore, overtime practices which are perceived as fair are a favorable condition for gainsharing, because dollars earned is typically used as the basis for calculating a gainsharing bonus.

Organizational Variables: The Degree of Fit

Our ability to predict how well gainsharing will fit into organizations with favorable conditions comes from understanding what the research has told us so far. Chapters 3 and 4 outline many of these relationships as they affect the gainsharing calculation. Most typically, decision makers who have opted for gainsharing programs in the past fifty years have had to consider conditions associated with success and failure and then compare them to their own situation. The patterns of conditions that have emerged as most important are listed in Exhibit 1.2. Throughout this book, these conditions are explored theoretically and then tested empirically with survey and case study data. For example, in Chapter 2, Review of the Literature, early literature on the subject is separated from more current studies and clear patterns of contemporary conditions which favor gainsharing begin to emerge. These clear results are obtained partly from the use of theory driven research, but mostly because of the improvement of research techniques in recent years.

One contemporary approach to considering a gainsharing program is to immerse oneself in the literature, compare the characteristics of one's organization to the characteristics which are known to favor gainsharing, and then begin a task-oriented assessment. Exhibit 1.3 depicts this process and presents the five steps which are involved. The first is to review the available literature and to make a judgment, perhaps based on many of the conditions listed in Exhibit 1.2, as to whether to assemble people for staff meetings.

The second step would be to develop a task force and pursue an educational effort to see if a consensus on gainsharing can be reached. If the employees of the organization have a union, union representatives should become involved early in the process. Also, employee surveys may be useful in order to acquire more information on the chances of gainsharing success. Step 3 marks the assessment of the calculations which may be used for gainsharing. At some point the committee or task force must decide on the best calculation formula for the organization. This decision and the review of the organization's climate (via survey data) leads to the formulation of a gainsharing plan. After a trial of one year, the program is typically evaluated. If the plan is deemed a success and if conditions remain favorable, gainsharing is usually retained for a much longer period of time.

This sequence of five steps represents the prototypical stages of development for traditional gainsharing. At every step, rejection of gainsharing is clearly possible. Most of the people who are involved in the gainsharing program should want it to continue as a measure of their commitment to the value of gainsharing. However, it is better to reject the program rather than force the philosophy and structure on all concerned. This notion expresses the idea that gainsharing *lags* behind the organization's particular profile of conditions. If gainsharing is to *lead* the organization to better conditions, rather than lag behind, then it must serve to build higher levels of trust and cooperation. A pattern of large bonuses which are perceived as fair[4] will gradually create a change in attitude. Either way, lag or lead, gainsharing is new to the organization and represents organizational change. The organizational learning required in adopting a traditional gainsharing plan will be less if it assumes a lagging role and considerably more if it leads.

Exhibit 1.3   Steps of Gainsharing Assessment

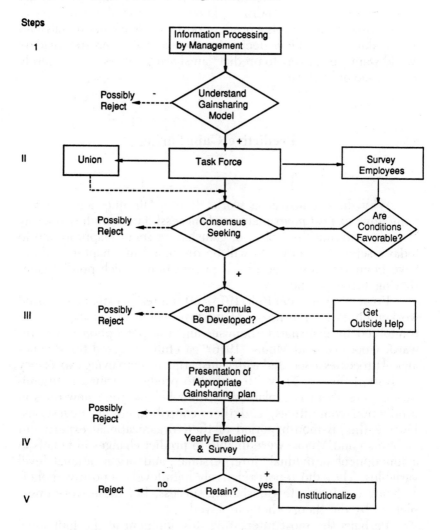

Our concern in this chapter has been to raise the issues involved in understanding gainsharing. One approach has been to separate contingent gainsharing from traditional gainsharing. To improve our understanding of how gainsharing might fit into any particular organization, we specified those conditions (Exhibit 1.2) which influence gainsharing success. Then, we introduced the prototypical steps involved in installing a gainsharing plan. Most organizations deliberately go through these steps while comparing their situation to the conditions known to bring about success in gainsharing. While this is a prudent posture, we cannot be satisfied with it alone. We believe decision makers and all interested readers would want a clear way to predict gainsharing success—not merely a way to avoid failure.

Predictive Gainsharing

Why does gainsharing work? It is a fair question to raise. Somehow, *ex post facto* analyses of successful case studies as a way of understanding the "why" of gainsharing seem inappropriate in today's scientific world. As will be discussed in Chapter 2, there have been very few theoretical specifications which predict gainsharing success or failure.

Frost, Wakely, and Ruh (1974)[5] attempted to explain increased worker effort by the assumed intrinsic value of participation as reinforced by gainsharing bonuses and the perception of fair reward. Goodman and Moore (1976)[6] carefully assessed the psychological processes associated with gainsharing by employing expectancy motivation theory. They attempted to predict learning of organizational members as explained by their beliefs, their new roles in production committees, and their contributions of suggestions. During the six-month period of their organizational experiment Goodman and Moore were unable to predict changes in beliefs as a function of individual, interpersonal, and organizational level variables. They did report relatively high levels of positive beliefs as being conducive to gainsharing success, but these were unexplained by the theory they employed.

Perhaps the most interesting development at the individual and role level of analysis is by Tove Hammer (1988).[7] She hypothesizes that both bonus payments and participation are important for gainsharing success and has stated that much previous research has stressed intrinsic factors such as participation more than the use of bonuses. As indicated by Hammer, see Exhibit 1.4, bonuses reinforce participation twice—once when they are promised and again when they are regularly received. Given this, participation has three hypothesized outcomes:

Exhibit 1.4 Worker Role Outcomes Under Bonus Conditions

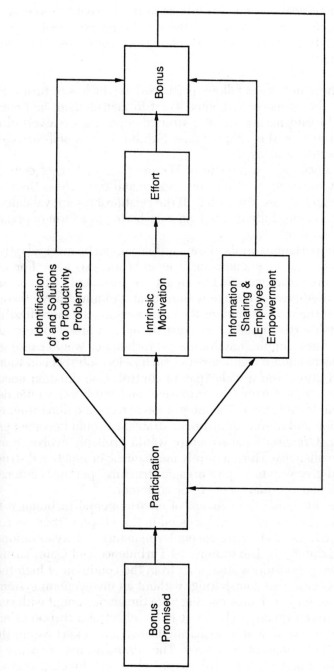

Adapted from T. Hammer, "New Developments in Profit Sharing," in J. Campbell, R. Campbell, and Associates, *Productivity in Organizations* (San Francisco: Jossey-Bass, 1988).

1. identification of and solutions to productivity problems,
2. intrinsic motivation increases due to changes in job design,
3. information sharing and feelings of employee empowerment.

Each of these outcomes follows participation which is in turn reinforced by the gainsharing bonus. Trust in management and commitment to gainsharing are also strengthened. As we asserted at the beginning of the chapter (see Exhibit 1.1), a self-managed workforce then emerges.

The advantage to the use of Hammer's model is, of course, the ability to specify variables in advance and then assess them as Goodman and Moore attempted. If the relationships are validated, then we can more fully understand gainsharing as a form of organizational learning.

It is important to predict how gainsharing can be more adaptive or responsive at an organizational level of analysis also. For example, if organizational environments are turbulent, what structures are predicted to change within them? Administrative theory argues that the more turbulent the environment, the more flexible and adaptable the organization must become in order to respond properly. For example, environmental turbulence would cause organizations to choose characteristics such as low job specialization, decentralization, and a wide span of control. Coordination needs of the organization would be extensive, and the bureaucratic use of rules would give way to the integration of roles and departments. Cooperation and mutual adjustment strategies would become very important. Organizational structure would probably evolve to accept these changes. Thus, a purely mechanistic or functional structure could give way to a more organic structure, perhaps centered on a particular product, service, or customer.

If we introduce the concept of environmental turbulence to the two types of gainsharing discussed in this chapter, then we can explore the tradeoffs that are encountered in terms of organizational change. Exhibit 1.5, Environmental Turbulence and Gainsharing, depicts two propositions stemming from the condition of high turbulence. Contingent gainsharing, without an involvement system, faces the sources of change coming from the environment with staff and managerial quality. The most likely effect of a turbulent environment on contingent gainsharing is increased effort within the boundaries of organizational rules. The administrative response is fixed, at least partly because of the presence of a directed or com-

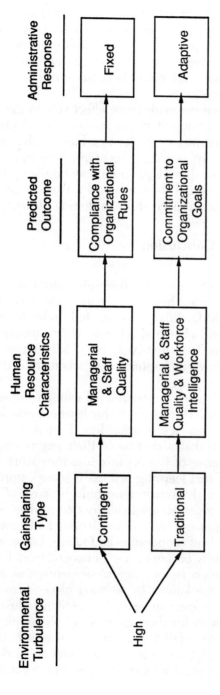

Exhibit 1.5 Environmental Turbulence and Gainsharing

Environmental Turbulence	Gainsharing Type	Human Resource Characteristics	Predicted Outcome	Administrative Response
High	Contingent	Managerial & Staff Quality	Compliance with Organizational Rules	Fixed
	Traditional	Managerial & Staff Quality & Workforce Intelligence	Commitment to Organizational Goals	Adaptive

pliant work force. Conversely, traditional gainsharing, because of involvement, adds work force intelligence to its resources in addition to staff and managerial quality. The most likely outcome that can be predicted is further commitment to organizational goals. The administrative response is adaptive, because of the presence of a self-managed work force.

Organizational structure responds more effectively to the dynamic demands of the environment if the structure is adaptive. Optimal organizational structures are easier to achieve with a committed work force. Conversely, in a situation of low environmental turbulence, a contingent gainsharing program may be the optimal choice, given low environmental demands and a fixed organizational structure which has been successfully exploiting its markets.

Conclusion

This chapter introduces the reader to the philosophy and structure of gainsharing. Gainsharing has been a part of the incentive and industrial relations field for fifty years, yet full understanding of why it works has eluded behavioral science. How gainsharing works in certain situations has, however, been adequately researched. Indeed, the following chapters will demonstrate these accomplishments well.

Both contingent gainsharing and traditional gainsharing reinforce organizational learning. The result of this learning may be a sharpening of the pay/performance relationship. That is, all employees begin to recognize that a portion of their pay is clearly connected to the performance of the organization they work for. In traditional gainsharing, this learning process is more complex. We want to understand its dynamics more fully because of the immense value of the new organizational culture that evolves from it. Employees begin the process by working harder and smarter and then reach higher levels of cooperation and identification with organizational goals, eventually becoming a self-managed work force. While it is true that employers become more competitive, mature gainsharing organizations are known to be good places to work. That is, these organizations appear to be leaders in their industries for many reasons—not simply for their gainsharing philosophy.

Of all the conditions associated with success in gainsharing, perhaps a positive organizational climate and a strong network for communication stand out as most important. Climate is a catch-all word referring to virtually all the behavioral aspects of work. However, the level of trust in management, the perceptions of the quality of supervision, the overall level of job satisfaction, to name but a few climate factors, are critical to the adoption of the new ways exemplified by gainsharing. Communication is equally basic to the success of the process. For example, some organizations have no system for communicating to all of their employees except through the supervisory structure and, maybe, through the use of a public address system. It's not surprising that messages with any content become distorted when they move down the hierarchy. It's nothing short of miraculous when messages are accurately transmitted up through the same system! Traditional gainsharing adds an additional structure for communication to the organization, and underlying this structure is the increased value of performance information. Because communication now benefits all concerned, cost and performance information flows rapidly up and down the hierarchy.

The remaining chapters review what is known about gainsharing. Chapters 3 and 4 provide excellent insight into the method of gainsharing calculations, the area which is initially of greatest interest to employees. Over time, the bonus calculation diminishes in importance because gainsharing, if it succeeds, becomes a way of organizational life. One visit to a company employing traditional gainsharing proves this point to even the most disinterested observer. The long term effect of traditional gainsharing is a strong change in behavior and values concerning organizational performance and a commitment to organizational learning.

Notes

1. Contingent gainsharing is a form of variable compensation since the fixed rate of pay is less than the fair value for any given job. This fixed rate *plus* the gainsharing bonus brings the total pay up to a competitive pay level. Traditional gainsharing computes bonuses on top of the fair rate of pay. Nonbonus months are not perceived as inequitable because the fixed rate of pay reflects the organization's compensation strategy to lead or meet the market in terms of pay.

2. R.J. Bullock and E.E. Lawler III, "Gainsharing: A Few Questions and Fewer Answers," *Human Resource Management* (1984) 5, 197–212.

3. C. O'Dell and J. McAdams, *People, Performance, and Pay* (Houston: American Productivity Center, 1987).

4. E.E. Lawler III, "Gainsharing Theory and Research: Findings and Future Directions," Technical Report no. 85-1(67), CEO, University of Southern California, 1985.

5. C.F. Frost, J.H. Wakely, and R.A. Ruh, *The Scanlon Plan for Organizational Development: Identity, Participation, and Equity* (East Lansing: Michigan State University Press, 1974).
6. P. Goodman and B. Moore, "Factors Affecting Acquisition of Beliefs About a New Reward System," *Human Relations*, 1976, 571–588.
7. T. Hammer "New Developments in Profit Sharing" in J. Campbell, R. Campbell, and Associates, *Productivity in Organizations* (San Francisco: Jossey-Bass, 1988).

Chapter 2

Review of the Literature

Brian Graham-Moore

National interest in gainsharing has increased in the 1980s because of declining levels of productivity. However, what seems like a new reward system probably began with the program instituted by the Nunn-Bush Shoe Company of Milwaukee on July 2, 1935. One other firm was involved in organizationwide gainsharing near that time, according to H.L. Nunn (1961), but published records are difficult to trace.[1]

In the management literature of the 1930s, the name Joseph Scanlon immediately surfaces. A former cost accountant, steelworker, union official, and, finally, lecturer at the Massachusetts Institute of Technology, Scanlon has been so important to the gainsharing movement that it was suggested that a generic term for gainsharing be the "Scanlon plan".[2] Scanlon himself never attempted to put his name to the plan, but his support of gainsharing had a strong influence on a generation of managers, labor leaders, consultants, and academicians. These individuals have kept gainsharing alive to this day, even to the point of institutionalizing it in the form of the Scanlon Plan Association.

This chapter reviews the literature covering gainsharing in order to present the background and history of the field. The Scanlon plan has received so much attention in the early gainsharing literature that other contributions are often overshadowed. Of particular interest is one of the newest and most successful forms of gainsharing—Improshare®. It may prove to have more impact in 5 years than Scanlon plans have had in 40.

What Is Gainsharing?

Gainsharing involves a measurement of productivity combined with the calculation of a bonus designed to offer employees a mutual share of any increases in total organizational productivity. Usually all those responsible for the increase receive the bonus. Total productivity is an all-encompassing term when we consider that outside forces also affect a firm's productivity. For example, the lack of financial productivity can eliminate the gains of performance productivity. Nationally, productivity has been defined by most economists as output per hour of all persons. As this ratio of output to the cost of labor increases, real economic growth occurs. With such a broad definition of productivity, many factors could be considered influences on it, not the least of which could be the level of technology, the quality of the work force, and the amount of capital investments. With so many forces influencing productivity, our understanding of aggregate economic behavior does not easily elucidate the behavior of specific firms. Each firm must study its own economic behavior. The relationship between sales value of production and the labor cost required to produce the product can be remarkably stable for many industries.[3] Any company can refer to the U.S. Department of Commerce for reports on its industry's average value added per $1.00 of plant payroll. It is estimated by the Eddy-Rucker-Nickels Company, a consulting firm, that 9 out of 10 manufacturers demonstrate these stable co-variations between sales value of production and labor cost.[4]

Of the many variables used to measure total productivity, one significant variable is labor productivity. Thus, the term gainsharing is sometimes more easily understood when it is described as labor gainsharing. Although nonlabor factors influence labor costs, many firms probably will base their bonus sharing on gains in productivity out of the decrease in expected labor cost.

Requirements of Gainsharing Formulas

Whatever the particular gainsharing plan, virtually all plans require that a historical standard of expected labor costs be computed. Any increase in output combined with the same or lower actual labor cost creates a bonus. Most gainsharing plans split this bonus between the company and the total work force.[5] The mechanics of establishing the historical standard are not necessarily simple. The method for constructing the bonus calculation denotes the variant of gainsharing—be it Improshare®, Rucker®, or a Scanlon plan. However, the keys to all successful gainsharing formulas are as follows:

1. the normal, average, or standard labor cost is measurable,
2. the ratio of either sales value of production or units of production value to labor cost is relatively stable, and
3. the policy established for sharing true increases in labor productivity is fair.[6]

Gainsharing formulas that meet the objectives listed above should be able to produce motivating bonuses. In fact, this statement can be validated retrospectively with data from the firm's own experience. Gainsharing formulas can be calculated with historical accounting data. "Estimated" bonus calculations can be modeled and reviewed using historical data. Questions that management can ask include the following—What if we had a bonus (that week or month)? Would there have been greater gains? Would productivity have been higher? Would quality improve, turnover and absenteeism decrease? Would we, as managers, have had more flexibility to achieve improved methods, or, perhaps, greater volume to exploit our markets? The answers to these questions are derived, initially, from the combined judgment of management personnel. Management ought to know if a 5 percent to 30 percent gainsharing bonus would cause the work force to increase productive behavior.

Conditions Necessary for a Scanlon Plan

Complete answers to the questions above require introduction of the rest of the description of gainsharing—the behavioral and philosophical elements. Here, the literature has been extensive. One of the best sources is *The Scanlon Plan for Organizational Development* by Frost, Wakely, and Ruh.[7] Carl Frost capped many years of successful Scanlon experience by collaborating with former students to produce this book, which undertakes a comprehensive exposition of the philosophy of Scanlonism. For example, they delineate what they call the three conditions for a Scanlon plan— identity, participation, and equity.

By identity, Frost and his associates mean a clear statement of organizational goals and intended achievements. Furthermore, this identity of organizational goals and intended achievements should meld with personal goals that each employee would like to achieve through his or her role in the organization. If organizational and personal goals are congruent, then the perceived identity of both is a very powerful form of organizational development. While organizations may strive to communicate their objectives, clarifying *how* the individual can match personal goals with these objectives requires a constant educational process.

The second condition is participation. Frost and his associates quite simply assert that participation is defined as the opportunity provided to the employee to be involved while exercising responsibility. Increasing the employee's awareness of his or her responsibility for achieving a fiscally sound and competitive organization is essential if both the employee and the firm are to fulfill themselves. Clearly, increased participation reinforces individual commitment to and identification with the firm.

The third condition is the mutual commitment to equity—by both the employee and the firm. In effect, the firm strives to create a return to all employees in exchange for their participation and increased responsibility. The financial basis for this return is expressed by the gainsharing formula. Thus, the investment of all employees in identity and participation is enhanced by a fair method for sharing the value of increases in productivity. The increased interest in the firm and its reliable performance, as well as mutual trust are exchanged via a formula for sharing that is equitable according to Frost *et al.*

Initial interest in gainsharing often focuses on the formula, the payout, or the bonus because managers do not want to create a giveaway. Once the exercise of researching, constructing, and testing a gainsharing formula is completed, however, it becomes apparent that many gainsharing formulas may work, but not optimally, as Chapter 3 explains. The philosophical and behavioral differences associated with the various gainsharing formulas need careful understanding as they will become more important over time. While it fails to deal with the philosophical issues surrounding gainsharing formulas, the Frost book is quite useful because it delves into the behavioral issues more than any other source. Frost's book is unique in that it reveals so well the human side of gainsharing. The only other book dealing with gainsharing before this time was edited by F.G. Lesieur in 1958. Both books are difficult to find except in good libraries. Neither of these books, however, explained how to develop a gainsharing plan, test the formula, install the involvement system, and maintain gainsharing over time.

Moore and Ross addressed this area in 1978 in *The Scanlon Way to Improved Productivity.* R. Doyle's book, *Gainsharing and Productivity*, which appeared in 1983, is also a detailed and orderly accounting of how to implement a gainsharing plan. It does not review the literature of the time as the Moore and Ross (1978) book does, yet it clearly draws on the experience of well-known consultants. All of the books on gainsharing tend to be organized around the central themes of the gainsharing literature—industrial cooperation and involvement as reinforced by a particular gain-sharing formula. This chapter will employ those themes as part of its organizational structure in order to unfold the early literature. Later in the chapter, the emphasis shifts to the burgeoning new literature that focuses on organizational goals, union issues, service industry issues, and issues of variable compensation. To begin, we will look at some generic types of gainsharing plans: (1) Scanlon-simple, (2) Scanlon-complex, (3) Rucker, and (4) Improshare.

Scanlon Calculation—Simple

The original Scanlon plan was developed by Joseph Scanlon when he helped to save the Empire Steel and Tin Plate Company. President of his union local and trained in cost accounting, Scanlon was convinced that his own union's demands would force the company into bankruptcy. Through his leadership, management and labor made a strong effort to improve labor-management cooperation. Scanlon believed that the average worker was a great reservoir of untapped information concerning labor-saving methods. Workers needed a mechanism permitting them "to work smarter, not harder." This following excerpt epitomizes Joe Scanlon's belief in labor-management cooperation:

> One of the greatest advantages of this kind of collective bargaining from the worker's point of view is the knowledge that it gives him of the business. When a slump is coming, he knows it. He is even given a chance to combat it, in the sense that if he can devise a cheaper way of turning out his product, perhaps the company will be able to take away business from somebody else. In a number of instances the Lapointe workers have actually done this, the most spectacular example being that of an order from a big automotive concern in December, 1942. The workers had been pressing management to accept orders even at the break-even point so as to tide over a bad period. Mr. Prindiville, who sometimes sits in on the screening-committee meetings, had given in to the pressure some months previously to the extent of taking an order from this firm for

100 broaches at $83 per broach. But Lapointe had lost 10 percent on the deal, and Mr. Prindiville now put his foot down. If this business was to be taken again the price would have to be raised. In view of new competition, it meant that Lapointe almost certainly would not get the business—at a time when work was scarce. The gloomy gathering that listened to Mr. Prindiville's pronouncement was then electrified by a question from Jimmie McQuade, skilled grinder and one of the most outspoken members of the screening committee. Who says we can't make those broaches at that price for a profit? Mr. McQuade wanted to know. If you'd give the men in the shop a chance to go over the blueprints before production starts and to help plan the job, there are lots of ways of cutting costs without cutting quality. The idea grew, and the next day the suggestion ran around the shop like wildfire. The order was taken at the old price, this time with a profit of 10 percent—a total gain in efficiency of 20 percent. The truth is that the Scanlon Plan has generated a competitive spirit throughout the factory: one hears as much about competition from the workers as from management itself. If there is a question of struggling for existence the whole company struggles collectively, and all the brains available are focused on the fight. The worker is no longer a pawn in a game he does not understand. He is a player. He enjoys it. And his contribution is worth money to all concerned.[8]

This kind of story is common to most contemporary Scanlon companies. Such companies enjoy a very high degree of employee involvement. In a word, they have teamwork. One measure of this involvement is the high percentage of suggestions received that are put into use.[9]

While sentiments about cooperation, participation, teamwork, and unleashing the knowledge of the worker depicted the original Scanlon plan, the first plan had no bonus calculation.[10] Joe Scanlon ultimately designed a bonus system to reinforce these philosophies. By that time he was working for the production-engineering department of United Steel Workers. The Adamson Company in East Palestine, Ohio, was the first company to try a bonus calculation constructed by Scanlon. In many ways, this calculation is the most imitated—at least in principle. The most commonly applied formula is generally expressed as follows:

$$\text{Base ratio} = \frac{\text{Labor costs}}{\text{Sales value of production}}$$

Scanlon's idea was to focus the attention of everyone on those variables within the control of the firm and its human resources. Because of its apparent simplicity, the calculation was quickly adopted into use. At the same time, the Scanlon plan became the darling of the industrial relations literature focusing on labor-management cooperation. Most industrial relations personnel textbooks include a section on the Scanlon plan. However, in terms of the bonus calculation, there is no one Scanlon plan.[11]

Scanlon Calculations—Complex

In instances in which Scanlon plans have failed, this failure has been attributed to the formula.[12] In almost all cases, simple Scanlon formulas, i.e., the single ratio were used. Multiple products create a complex situation which may render the simple ratio inaccurate. Firms with many product lines that vary in labor content, such as produced labor or buy-out labor, were either overvaluing or undervaluing the expected labor cost. Thus, the split ratio formula grew out of necessity. Controllers developed a base ratio for each product line, which could more accurately reflect a fair measure of labor input.[13] The split ratio formula deals more equitably with problems of product mix. A single ratio formula mentioned in Chapter 3, Exhibit 3.6, Assumed Bonus Under Single and Split Ratios, for example, overpays by $40,000 when there is no true increase in productivity. The allowed labor formula, as discussed extensively in Moore and Ross, demonstrates a crucial difference between this calculation and "traditional" Scanlon calculations in that it excludes sales and bases its measurement on direct labor productivity only.[14] This calculation is very similar to Improshare, which will be reviewed below. The rationale is to decrease problems associated with product mix *and* variations in selling price. This formula assumes that accounting data or engineered time standards are available for all or most direct hours. Then, allowed times are based on actual past performance. The allowed hour formula can be seen as antithetical to the Scanlon philosophy of teamwork and cooperation because it can easily become a management tool. Since allowed labor can be calculated for product line and department, this split ratio calculation could isolate problem areas for corrective action by management. Clearly, this is a goal of gainsharing, but only mature gainsharing firms can take advantage of this kind of information—for example, Lincoln Electric has the kind of human resource which actively uses cost information in order to solve problems.[15]

A more useful, sophisticated formula is the multicost ratio.[16] This formula could approach some aspects of profit sharing—which, of course, is not technically gainsharing. Incidentally, it is reported that many profit-sharing firms are inclined to use other incentives, including gainsharing.[17] Profit-sharing plans take their place alongside Improshare, Scanlon, and Rucker plans as alternate or complementary ways to bring about more productivity, as well as a mutually beneficial relationship between management and employees.

Except for its timing, profit sharing is held by some to be the ultimate in the total system incentive approach because it links motivation and reward to the final measure of corporate performance—i.e., profits.[18] Profit sharing rewards or penalizes all those who contribute to the growth of the enterprise in relation to the firm's economic productivity—as accepted by and paid for by the market place.

The idea behind the multicost ratio is to include all costs in the formula. The base ratio becomes:

$$\text{Base ratio} = \frac{\text{Labor} + \text{all costs}}{\text{Sales value of production}}$$

Assuming a firm has a comprehensive, sophisticated accounting system, this calculation can be made monthly—which, of course, makes its timing better than that of profit sharing. Most of the problems of product mix and inflation reported in case studies of Scanlon failures[19] are considerably decreased with the use of this calculation.

A firm first trying gainsharing should be discouraged from attempting this formula because of the behavioral considerations. The objectives of gainsharing are to involve everyone, at some level, with the overall goal of improving productivity.[20] If employees find the complex gainsharing formula difficult to understand, they may react with distrust or perceive it as a gimmick. Obviously acceptance and learning are then thwarted. Scanlon formulas, as well as other gainsharing formulas, have been oversimplified or completely overlooked in the early literature.

Rucker Plan

Using studies of data collected by the U.S. Census and Surveys of Manufacturers, Allan W. Rucker showed in the early thirties that economic productivity had been extremely stable from 1899 to 1929.[21] A parallel analysis for the years 1964 to 1968 was conducted by P.J. Loftus, Director of the Statistical Office of the

United Nations.[22] The results were the same. While each industry has its own pattern, the study showed a stable relationship between production value and value added by labor.

Publishing in proprietary sources, Rucker performed industry-by-industry analyses of manufacturers. He maintained that in 90 percent of the cases conditions were favorable to gainsharing. Unfortunately, few studies or evaluations of the Rucker plan exist. The primary sources of information are proprietary booklets published by the consultants. Despite this lack of data, it is known that the plan has been successful in a variety of manufacturing firms.

The concept of value added is well known in accounting circles and recently has been the focus of attention for pay systems.[23] As with all gainsharing plans, the value-added formula can be tailored to include only workers with a very close connection to the production process or all personnel in an organization. Thus, value added is defined as the difference between the value of production (sales +/− various adjustments) less outside purchases such as materials and supplies.

The following example is offered in Exhibit 2.1, The Rucker/Value-Added Formula. Step 1 reflects the difference between the selling price and price adjustments for seasonality. Step 2 reflects subtractions for outside purchases such as materials, supplies, and energy. Step 3 is value added of $340,000, or 34 percent of the selling price. Now, Step 4 applies the historical average of labor value added to the product. This is called the Rucker Standard. In this example, 41.17 percent, or $140,000, is the allowed (or expected) labor costs. Step 5 shows that the actual labor cost was $130,000. Thus, Step 6 reflects a bonus pool of $10,000. A 50/50 split is a common policy (as in Improshare), and Steps 7 and 8 reflect this. Steps 9 and 10 reflect a policy of a reserve for deficit months (as in the case of many Scanlon companies). Since the participating payroll is $80,000 (Step 11), then the bonus percentage becomes 5 percent in Step 12.[24]

Many similarities exist between the Rucker and Scanlon plans, and these are both similar to some extent to Improshare. Like Scanlon, there is no one Rucker Plan. In principle, the different gainsharing plan formulas vary in subtle yet profound ways. Subtle, because the measurements all attempt to capture the ratio of labor input to production outputs. Profound, because the sensitivity of the measurements can be magnified by environmental and product mix factors in ways which could be a problem if left unchecked.

Exhibit 2.1   The Rucker Value-Added Formula

VALUE-ADDED CALCULATION METHOD—MONTH X

1. Value of production (sales +/– various adjustments)		$1,000,000
2. Less outside purchases (materials, supplies, energy)		
Material and supplies	$500,000	
Other outside purchases, nonlabor costs	160,000	660,000
3. Value added (#1 – #2)		340,000
4. Allowed employee costs (from diagnostic historical analysis) #3		
× 41.17%)		139,978
5. Actual labor (employee costs)		129,978
6. Bonus pool (#4 – #5)		10,000
7. Company share (50% × #6)		5,000
8. Employee share (#6 – #7)		5,000
9. Reserve for deficit months (20% × #8)		1,000
10. Bonus Pool (#8 – #9)		4,000
11. Participating payroll		80,000
12. Bonus percentage (#10/#11)		5%

Adapted from B.E. Moore and T.L. Ross, *The Scanlon Way to Improved Productivity* (New York: Wiley-Interscience, 1978), 81.

Lastly, the differences in the formulas can result in behavioral differences which must be considered when choosing a formula. That is, no gainsharing plan will work without acceptance and some level of trust. With this in mind, it should be remembered that Rucker plans can share many similarities with Scanlon plans; therefore, much of the behavioral information to be reviewed concerning Scanlon plans can be generalized to include the Rucker plans.

Improshare

Improshare means *im*proved *pro*ductivity through *shar*ing. This plan is relatively new to the field of gainsharing. Invented in 1973, it is the creation of Mitchell Fein, an educator, consultant, and industrial engineer. Because of its overall simplicity and lack of emphasis on employee involvement, Improshare is relatively easy to install. The plan focuses on the number of work hours saved for a given number of units produced in much the same way the allowed labor calculation does. The actual hours taken to produce a given number of units are subtracted from hours required (or expected) to produce the same number of units. Savings realized by producing a given number of units in a reduced number of hours are shared equally by the firm and the worker. There are three key factors to Improshare:

1. the work-hour standard,
2. the base productivity factor (BPF),
3. the understanding by most workers of the relationship of hours worked to units produced.

By definition, a work-hour standard is the total production hours worked divided by the units produced. The acceptable standard could be set through the use of engineered standards (e.g., time studies) and/or through the use of previously generated accounting data. Either way—or both—the standard is the agreed or expected number of hours required to produce an accepted level of output.

Base Productivity Factor

The base productivity factor, or BPF, is the total production and nonproduction hours divided by the value of work in work hours. For an example, see Exhibit 2.2, The Improshare Calculation. While there is a more complete discussion on the Allowed Labor/Improshare calculation in Chapter 3. Exhibit 2.2 shows how the U.S. General Accounting office publication presents principal ideas of this calculation:

1. Work-hour standards are total production hours of "good production,"
2. Work-hour standards are normally computed for each product line, and
3. The base productivity factor (BPF) is the ratio of actual human resource hours to standard hours.

Each product line's output, at its own standard, is multiplied by the BPF to compute the expected number of total hours required to produce that output. Then, actual hours are calculated and subtracted from the expected hours (sometimes called Improshare hours). The difference, positive in this example, is 600 hours. These hours can be converted at average wage rates to create a cash value.

Simplicity of Improshare Formula

Another key factor associated with Improshare is the simplicity of the formula and, thus, its ready comprehension by the work

Exhibit 2.2   Allowed Labor/Improshare Calculation

BASE PERIOD OF ACCEPTABLE PRODUCTIVITY

Facts: 40 direct and 20 indirect employees

$$\text{Work hour standard} = \frac{\text{total production work hours}}{\text{Units produced}}$$

$$\text{Product A} = \frac{20 \text{ employees} \times 40 \text{ hours}}{1000 \text{ pieces}} = 0.8 \text{ per piece or } .8 \times 1000 = 800$$

$$\text{Product B} = \frac{20 \text{ employees} \times 40 \text{ hours}}{500 \text{ pieces}} = 1.6 \text{ per piece or } 1.6 \times 500 = 800$$

Total standard value hours 1,600 in Base Period

$$\text{Base Productivity Factor (BPF)} = \frac{\text{total production and nonproduction hours}}{\text{total standard value hours}}$$

$$\text{BPF} = \frac{\begin{array}{c}(40 \text{ direct employees} \times 40 \text{ hours})\\ + (20 \text{ indirect employees} \times 40 \text{ hours})\end{array}}{\text{actual hours}}$$

$$= \frac{2,400 \text{ production hours}}{1,600 \text{ standard value hours}} = 1.5$$

Bonus Calculation for Month X

Product A = 0.8 hours × 600 units × 1.5BPF	= 720
Product B = 1.6 hours × 900 units × 1.5BPF	= 2,160
Improshare hours (standard hours for actual units produced)	= 2,880
Less actual hours (assumed)	= 2,280
Gained hours	600

$$\text{Employee share} \left(50\% \text{ of } 600 = \frac{300}{2280} = 13.1\%\right)$$

Adapted from *Productivity Sharing Programs: Can They Contribute to Productivity Improvement?* U.S. General Accounting Office, AFMD-81-22 (March 3, 1981), 11.

force. While Fein has stated that many elements of the Improshare formula have been in use for twenty years,[25] he has assembled a formula that avoids some problems of Scanlon-type formulas. Fein's formula offers the concept of productivity to the worker in a psychologically accessible form. Americans probably think in terms of so many hours to produce so many units of work. Indeed, we are a time-conscious culture.

There is some evidence to suggest that workers in firms using Scanlon plans fail to understand the bonus formula. Many Scanlon firms spend a great deal of time educating the work force about the formula—often to little avail. Conversely, one study of an Improshare firm shows that line supervisors can readily explain what factors influence the formula to their subordinates.[26]

Fein has incorporated elements of the Halsey premium plan (which dates from 1890) into an organizationwide formula. By pooling all production and nonproduction hours from a selected base period, Fein created the BPF. This is a significant contribution. The BPF, while based on standards, is a composite measure of direct and indirect work. Since there are no standards on indirect work, a necessary assumption is that there is a constant relationship between direct and indirect work. The BPF, therefore, is constructed with data from an average period of productivity, or one that management recognizes as acceptable. This differs from a Scanlon analysis, which looks at the total budget period. Clearly, the Improshare plan seeks to increase quantity. The calculation is constructed to "beat yesterday's performance" if yesterday was a representative day. Once the BPF is computed it "represents the relationship in the base period between actual hours worked by all employees in the group and the value of the work in (work hours) produced by these employees."[27]

Aside from product mix problems cited in the literature, Fein has argued (in a similar fashion as the Value-Added/Rucker Plan) that volatility in the inputs and outputs of doing business, such as raw materials prices and the fluctuating level of sales, hurts the Scanlon gainsharing calculation. In effect, allowed labor/Improshare calculations exclude these ingredients from their formulas, using only hours required to produce.

Acceptance of Improshare

The timing of Improshare with the general acceptance of gainsharing has been impressive. The adoption of Improshare programs has been extensive—Firestone, Hooker Chemical Co., Rockwell International, Ingersoll-Rand, Prestolite, Atlas Powder Co., McGraw-Edison, and Stanley Home Products, to name but a few, have one or more Improshare installations.

While a series of educators, consultants, managers, and labor leaders have contributed to the development of Scanlon-type plans, Mitchell Fein is unique in his singular contribution to gainsharing. The following is an excerpt from "An Alternative to Traditional Managing."

Traditional work measurement established the time "it should take" to perform a given task under prescribed conditions, not how long it took to perform the work in the past. Such normal or fair day's work standards are established through performance rating with stop watch time study or predetermined standards, against a defined measurement base. This leveling or normalizing of observed data is the keystone of traditional work measurement; it must be employed.

The arguments that arise in setting traditional time standards are avoided by measuring productivity against the average level of an agreed base period. Using a method called measurement by parameters, standards are set at the average of the past, using historical data within a place of work, with no need to performance rate the work performance data. The rationale for this approach is that "yesterday's" performance is established as the Accepted Productivity Level (APL). Measurements in the future will be made against this APL base.[28]

Traditional work measurement may seem antithetical to some of the assumptions of gainsharing—namely, it might remind one of the individual incentives. However, a measure of labor productivity must start somewhere. Fein has blended many older ingredients into a newer, more successful package. However, there is no set philosophy associated with Improshare.

Mentioned earlier, for example, was the fact that no employee involvement is required to install Improshare. Technically this is true, but in practice Improshare may have almost the same advance build-up as a Scanlon plan, including, perhaps, the installation of labor-management committees. That is, an outside consultant may prepare management with a program and training so that employees have sufficient information about the plan. However, *there is no particular structure to Improshare* as there is with Scanlon. Fein, who favors a strong communications network, believes that labor-management committees under Scanlon plans are too structured.[29]

In point of fact, Improshare can be installed in firms with either autocratic or participative management styles. Labor-management committees, suggestion systems, and other examples of employee involvement may or may not be a part of Improshare. Gainsharing exists in many forms and can become a way of life in any of them. For example, Lincoln Electric has the nation's most successful incentive system and there is no commitment to a sophisticated management philosophy. Instead, Lincoln strives to maximize every day in every way the shared gains in increased productivity. There are only two known in-depth publications about Lincoln Electric,[30] and the inference to be drawn from these works is that the firm's personnel are highly motivated by pay and have a highly rational view towards productivity.

In many ways, Improshare spans the gap between those firms with no interest in participative management and concepts such as the quality of work, and those firms that do espouse those management philosophies. Therefore, Improshare is, above all, a formula which can be applied to many situations. As a formula, however, Fein argues it is a "way of life" because management obligates itself to a set of rules, yet places no limitations on the workers.[31] No memo of understanding, vote, or commitment is sought in advance from the employees. The purpose of Improshare is to make workers "bottom-line oriented."

Gainsharing Involvement Processes

While other gainsharing plans may or may not have a structure to achieve labor-management cooperation and participation, all known Scanlon organizations have a commitment to a highly structured suggestion system that requires much involvement from employees. Predating Quality Control Circles, Scanlon committees have strived to produce productivity-related suggestions. This aspect of Scanlonism has been generally impressive.

Graham-Moore (see Chapter 7) has analyzed suggestion-making at Desoto, Inc., of Garland, Texas. The pattern of results at DeSoto is similar to the pattern in many other Scanlon companies. DeSoto's experience indicates that most employees find quantity-improving suggestions easiest to make, and, thus, this type forms the majority. Suggestions regarding quality and cost-reduction are far fewer in number.

Ideally, suggestions unrelated to productivity should disappear after the first year of a Scanlon program. Apparently, this channel of communication, once opened, will always incur some suggestions motivated by discontent within the organization. Since the involvement system is not by definition a grievance procedure, these suggestions are normally referred to the appropriate channels by most firms.

Two critiques of the involvement system are a part of the literature. Gray[32] maintains that in a large English automobile body-stamping plant, production committees used more work hours than was cost effective. Fein, speaking for Improshare, favors labor-management committees or Quality Control Circles because he has less confidence in the highly structured committees of Scanlon Plans.[33]

One fact is irrefutable. Scanlon production and screening committees produce more accepted and implemented suggestions than are produced by individual suggestion systems. Typically, the average number of suggestions per employee ranges from .46 to .95 per year in Scanlon companies. In individual suggestion systems, the average per employee never exceeds .26 per year.[34] By rotating personnel through the Scanlon committee system, workers are brought into close contact with management, as both pursue problem solving. Scanlon managers clearly identify with participative management philosophies.[35] The structure of the involvement system makes these rotating assignments routine, and guarantees representation and exposure of all employees to the involvement system. (See Chapter 7 for examples.) Mature Scanlon companies have had virtually all employees serving at some time in the committee system. Peer review of suggestions reinforces suggestion-making behavior—whether suggestions are accepted or rejected.[36] The Scanlon involvement system serves as a form of organization development since it becomes a new communication structure for many firms.[37] Most literature on the Scanlon plan cites not only participation and communication but also willingness, cooperation, and acceptance of change that occur because of the structure and process of the suggestion system.[38]

Evaluation Studies

For years, the only evaluation studies of Scanlon plans came from MIT, because of its historical connection with Joe Scanlon. In the Midwest, Carl Frost has been directly responsible for the direction and leadership of the Scanlon Plan Association, originally based at Michigan State University. This association has had considerable impact on firms in Michigan, Ohio, Indiana, Illinois and elsewhere. Occasional studies by the association are published as reports but these are generally available only for association members.

In general, evaluation case studies are the type of evidence modern managers wish to see. Older literature is replete with testimonials and anecdotes, but today's decision makers and behavioral scientists want more quantitative information and they want it collected rigorously within a theoretical framework. This anecdotal, less rigorous type of case study was the predominant method of Scanlon and gainsharing study until the late 1960s. It is possible to review older case studies and newer empirical studies by organizing them around their principal findings—regardless of their methodology. The following are organizational or environmental conditions associated with early Scanlon plan research:

- Front-line supervisors may feel threatened by the suggestion system because they feel they are no longer bosses or because a high rate of suggestions makes their past behavior look autocratic.[39]
- The performance norm is difficult to adjust in the face of changing conditions.[40]
- A fair measurement of an organization's performance may be impossible.[41]
- Managerial attitudes must either favor participative management or be disposed to change.[42]
- Previous wage structures, such as individual incentive-suggestion systems, must be phased out. Compromises here are common and lead to transitional (protected) rates.[43]
- The plan can focus too intently on labor savings while not providing sufficient attention to other sources of savings.[44]
- The characteristics of the firm, such as size, management philosophy, climate, technology, sophistication of accounting systems must be considered in choosing a gainsharing program so as to make optimal use of these factors.[45]

Now that Improshare is so popular, we may begin to see evaluation studies of its use. Three hundred companies have experimented with or installed Improshare according to Fein.[46] By analogy, some of the favorable outcomes may be replicated in evaluation studies of Improshare and other forms of gainsharing—if they produce bonuses and emulate the philosophy of Scanlonism.

The literature of gainsharing, until recently, has focused on the Scanlon plan. Key features of this plan are delineated below and supporting studies are cited.

- The plan enhances coordination, teamwork, and sharing knowledge at lower levels.[47]
- Social needs are recognized through participation and mutually reinforcing group behavior.[48]
- Attention is focused on cost savings—not just quantity.[49]
- Acceptance of change due to technology, market, and new methods is greater since higher efficiency leads to bonuses.[50]

- Attitude of workers changes and they demand more efficient management and better planning.[51]
- Workers try to reduce overtime—to work smarter, not harder or faster.[52]
- Workers produce ideas as well as effort.[53]
- More flexible administration of union-management relationship occurs.[54]

What Do We Know?

In the periodical literature there are hundreds of anecdotal pieces which were written on gainsharing from 1935 to 1989. Also, there have been many published case studies, some more rigorous than others, which evaluate the impact of gainsharing on a single organization. Chapter 1 points out that describing gainsharing is relatively easy. Predicting its success from the results of carefully controlled, theory-driven research is more difficult.[55]

Organizational Size

Using available case studies of small organizations, researchers originally thought that organizational size influenced success in gainsharing. It probably does, but not to the extent once thought. In their review of the literature, Moore and Goodman reported that the median size of gainsharing organizations was 250 employees. Bullock and Lawler reviewed unpublished master's theses and doctoral dissertations of the Massachusetts Institute of Technology (where Joseph Scanlon finished his career as lecturer), as well as other sources, and fixed the median at 500. The national survey conducted by the American Productivity Center (1987) is a better indication of size.[56]

Number of Employees	Percent Responding (n = 55)
1– 250	38%
251– 500	22
501– 1,000	13
1,001– 5,000	22
5,001–10,000	5
	100%

Therefore, independent confirmation suggests the median of 500 is correct. However, it is surprising to see larger organizations with greater than 5,000 employees using gainsharing. The key factor seems to be that at some point organizationwide incentives lose impact. The larger the group the greater the difficulty workers encounter in seeing what effect a change in their performance can have on production.

Other Variables

More rigorous research has looked at variables other than organizational size. For example, technology, environment, and management style have been assessed to measure their impact on gainsharing success.[57] Goodman and Moore assessed these variables and studied the process wherein all employees developed new beliefs concerning a Scanlon Plan. The chance that an employee will make a productivity suggestion was associated with group attitudes and supervisory acceptance. Since researchers have focused their attention on the involvement system of gainsharing, the variables listed above are assessed in order to understand how they influence or moderate the processes of learning and change what have been the reported outcomes of successful gainsharing organizations. Group and supervisory approval seem to influence appropriate gainsharing beliefs.

One institutional variable that has been examined empirically is union-management cooperation. Since the philosophy of gainsharing stresses increased cooperation, one might be surprised that this factor needs assessment; however, Schuster, in a longitudinal study, assessed the impact of union-management cooperation in nine manufacturing firms over a four to five year period. Six of the nine manufacturers had either Scanlon or Rucker plans. Time series analysis in unionized gainsharing companies showed that four organizations experienced statistically significant positive changes in productivity and that two others had positive trends. Employment remained stable in eight of the nine organizations. Only one gainsharing firm fared poorly in his sample. Larger samples and longer time frames are always preferred, but Schuster drew these conclusions from this study:

> cooperation requires a stimulus to change a traditional bargaining relationship; in the present study, cooperation was stimulated by the dire financial position of one company and by adverse competitive conditions in several others. Additional stimuli were provided by factors internal to the firm, including a desire to upgrade the work-

place environment, improve communication, and replace or supplement an existing compensation program.[58]

Union and Nonunion Organizations

Graham-Moore and Rodgers surveyed gainsharing organizations to assess the relationship between institutional/organizational factors and type of gainsharing calculation. They found no difference in bonus history between union and nonunion organizations. Even though gainsharing began in the union environment, its greatest growth recently has been in nonunion environments.[59] The union/nonunion variable appears to offer no explanatory power in their study. This is an important finding when one considers the strategy of contingent gainsharing mentioned in Chapter 1. That is, even when organizations use gainsharing in a mode different from traditional gainsharing, certain basic principles still apply. That is, equity must be preserved if the mutually reinforcing components of the gainsharing definition are expected to work.

As a result of the strong interest in worker participation strategies such as quality of work life, quality circles, and employee involvement programs, Kochan, Katz, and Mower have characterized worker participation programs as a "mixed bag" full of risks for union members and union leaders. Indeed, stand-alone employee involvement programs seem to have a poor chance of becoming permanent parts of the organizational structure. Schuster's research offers some true support for gainsharing's ability to reinforce organizational cooperation with equitable bonuses. Other ideas which support the institutionalization of employee involvement systems can also be found in Chapter 6, Making Productivity Programs Last. The research indicated that process is more important than institutions or structures. That is, the way in which gainsharing is introduced and whether it is perceived as an equitable program are greater determinants of long range success than the existence of a union or nonunion environment.

Motivation and Learning Theory

Lawler's review of the same research led him to hypothesize that we know a fair amount of motivation and learning theory, an important component in the formulation of gainsharing programs. Therefore, gainsharing plans will increase organizational performance if—

1. Beliefs are established that rewards are based on organizational performance.
2. Communication of organizational performance is provided to everyone.
3. Ways or mechanisms are established for employers to influence organizational performance contingently measured by the reward system.
4. Opportunities to learn how to contribute to organizational performance are provided along with interpreting measures of performance.[60]

Participative Management

As has always been argued in the literature of gainsharing, participative management is crucial to traditional gainsharing success. Often misstated by others, the exact contribution of participative management is to clarify the connection between individual contribution and organizational performance—not just to require more effort. Lawler (1986) hypothesizes that participative management refers to those behaviors and actions which build trust during the process of improving organizational performance, a necessary precedent to the bonus. This idea is echoed in older case studies which state how important it is for the work force to understand how the gainsharing calculation works. Participative management shifts power, knowledge, and information down into the organization. If managers ask employees for intelligent input, they must exchange some power, knowledge, and information for it.

Common Sources of Gainsharing Failures

According to the literature reviewed, the most common causes of gainsharing failure were economic, the existence of wage inequities or the inability to provide bonuses. Also, the formulas used did not adequately reflect rapid changes in product mix. Those studies noting failures are Gilson and Lefcowitz,[61] Gray,[62] Helfgott,[63] Johnson,[64] Jehring,[65] and Ruh *et al.*[66] Gilson and Lefcowitz report poor plan installation, poor understanding of the formula, and a high component of secondary wage earners who preferred individual incentives. Most compelling is the fact that the product mix greatly affected the ratio of the formula. To counteract this, more complex and exhaustive methods of formula construction are now in use.[67] Gray reports large inequities in pay among departments of an English auto body manufacturer. In this case, as with other plan failures, the formula did not adequately reflect rapid changes in product mix. The usual result was that no bonus or bonuses were paid because there was no increase in true productivity. Work practices apparently conflicted with the need for reassigning workers, and conflict rather than cooperation ensued. Gray indicated that "bonuses were inadequate (and) disillusionment with participation appeared. . . ."[68] Gray challenged the motivational role of the suggestion system. He states that since the suggestion system is to be learned as an instrumental way to increase productivity, why wouldn't it work without a bonus? In another case study, however, Lesieur cites workers actually searching for ways to improve business (by suggestion making) during hard times with no bonuses.[69] Then, too, management attitudes can greatly affect the commitment to gainsharing. In Jehring's study, management decided to shift its emphasis to a profit-sharing plan when keeping the gainsharing formula accurate was perceived as too difficult.

Goodman identified 72 coal companies which have used various forms of gainsharing since 1982. While these plans appear to be in use today, their inception was caused by a general intent to increase productivity, reduce costs, and, in some plans, to reduce accidents. According to Goodman, the typical coal company is a poor choice for gainsharing. That is, their pay system values are characterized by—

1. secretive behavior,
2. decision making concentrated in top management,
3. centralized structures,
4. organizationwide performance practices for rewards,
5. standardized pay systems,
6. job-based versus skill-based pay,
7. hierarchical versus egalitarian orientation,
8. reliance on a tradition-driven system.

One wonders why so many union leaders from the United Mine Workers signed off on these plans? As Goodman points out, a secretive communication system runs counter to traditional gainsharing philosophy. His technical report makes clear that gainsharing, though existing, is a poor fit for the typical coal company. Apparently, most coal companies are poor choices for systems which require a high level of commitment, even though other reward system alternatives could be employed in coal companies. For this reason, the ideas surrounding the interaction of gainsharing calculations and organizational goals presented in Chapter 3 take on special relevance if decision makers are to avoid failure.

Gainsharing as a Way of Life

Gainsharing can become a way of life. A firm successfully embarking on the route to gainsharing begins a form of organizational development. One of the forces which drives the gainsharing process is the unleashing of the worker's intelligence.[70] It is not surprising that a Firestone manager experienced with Improshare states, "No one knows the job better than the one doing it."[71]

Given that a job incumbent knows his or her job better than anyone else, just how does an organization unleash this knowledge? The conditions stated in Chapter 1 come quickly to mind because levels of involvement and trust, and the quality of managerial philosophy become crucial. Does an organization possess these characteristics to a sufficient extent so that employees can perceive their individual growth as congruent with organizational objectives? Within the framework of the involvement system, many of the steps of a gainsharing trial year are analogous to the steps of organizational development (OD).

OD Structure and Process

French and Bell[72] have listed eight common steps or factors of the OD structure and process, which are described in Exhibit 2.3. Step 1, diagnostic activities, frequently includes measurement and assessment of opinions and attitudes. Gainsharing trial years often use the same approach in order to gauge whether to begin or to develop a baseline measure with which to compare growth. Interestingly, problem identification for OD refers to process consulting wherein basic learning situations are presented to clarify perception and understanding. These learning situations are usually handled in special training sessions. Conversely, these opportunities to learn are created within involvement systems. For example, a worker may be a member of a committee to research the usefulness of a suggestion. The particular suggestion may not be truly acceptable, yet the worker will search for ways to make it acceptable through modification and improvement rather than dismissing the suggestion. The result is that the worker offering

Exhibit 2.3   Organization Development Activities and Scanlon Counterparts

OD	SCANLON
1. Diagnostic activities: attitude and opinion measurement, including formal measurement that comprises formal questionnaires or interviewing to ascertain the state of the organization	1. Trial year evaluation methods
2. Problem identification: process consulting to help perception and understanding of individual, group, and organizational-level issues	2. At all times in the involvement system
3. Goal setting and methods achievement: planning, utilizing information from problem solving, and to compare the real versus the ideal	3. Management's direction, especially through the screening committee and through the influence of the formula
4. Communication improvement: survey feedback activities, education and training activities, to improve coordination	4. All committees improve this, plus annual questionnaire will help
5. Conflict identification and resolution: third-party peacemaking, confrontation counseling to improve cooperation	5. Peer review of suggestions in production committees is a form of open problem solving.
6. Task forces: team building intergroup activities to enhance cooperation	6. Group suggestion making is a very common outcome of the plan
7. Job design: technostructural activities to improve technical or structural aspects of work	7. One of the most common outcomes of Scanlon plans is acceptance of technical change
8. Measurement and evaluation: assessment activities to produce information on "where we are"	8. Annual survey, financial analysis, and annual Scanlon meeting

Adapted from B.E. Moore and T.L. Ross, *The Scanlon Way to Improved Productivity* (New York: Wiley-Interscience, 1978), 151.

the suggestion, the helping committee member, and the member(s) from management all gain a new understanding and respect for one another. The suggestion may be enhanced and accepted. Worker members of the committee may handle new tasks, and management acquires a new respect for the worker. The firm gains a productivity-related suggestion. None of these experiences would happen in a training session. Rather, they are real experiences which become part of the human fabric of the firm.

Analogs to Involvement System

Exhibit 2.3 illustrates many subsequent steps or factors associated with OD and gainsharing involvement. An analog for each of these factors exists in the involvement system. For example, OD Activity 3 (Goal setting and methods achievement) often occurs as part of an OD training exercise, while gainsharing firms demonstrate a natural process of positive communication through the committee system. OD Activity 4 (Communication) here again is achieved in gainsharing firms through the committee system, the give and take of suggestion making and evaluation, and of course, feedback from any annual surveys. In sum, most identifiable OD activities are found in most traditional gainsharing firms.

According to Hatcher and Ross, gainsharing provides a visible structure that leads some organizations to higher levels of organizational development. In fact, as gainsharing becomes institutionalized its functions become part of standard procedures. This structure helps the process of OD to continue. Hatcher and Ross quote a president of one midwestern manufacturing firm:

> I like the structure Gainsharing forces on a company. Without that structure, I don't know how to get participation, and I don't know how to support it. But if I've got someone telling me that we've got a Gainsharing meeting at 3:00, I'll be there, and so will everyone else. The structure is the only thing that keeps the plan from dying a slow death.[73]

Summary and Conclusion

The objective of this chapter has been to review the gainsharing literature. Other reviews[74] have focused selectively on the Scanlon plan, almost to the exclusion of other forms of gainsharing. Most reviews are purely descriptive. This chapter has attempted to provide some necessary context to the theoretical models of Chapter 1. Many of the calculations were presented, but with an eye toward their historical relevance. More extensive treatments are found in Chapters 3 and 4 as well as elsewhere in the book.[75]

Most of the early literature depicts "every man as a capitalist" and focuses on labor-management cooperation and participation. Unfortunately, much of that literature is anecdotal. Fortunately, more contemporary research broadens the scope of evaluation to most forms of gainsharing, and methods used to assess gainsharing have become more quantitative. Certain key issues, such as size, involvement, presence of a union, and sources of failure, have been identified. We now know what gainsharing is, what it isn't, and we have a good grasp of what it can realistically accomplish. Perhaps not enough of the literature addresses how gainsharing works under specific circumstances.[76] The factors associated with learning a new reward system are clearly the more interesting parts of the gainsharing literature since they offer so much promise.

The future of gainsharing as a reward system enhancing organizational development will be explained by new research which is sure to come. Understanding why gainsharing works will be the goal of this research because the current literature is full of descriptive studies that explain how gainsharing works. Prediction of gainsharing success will be the primary goal of this new research.

Notes

1. H.L. Nunn, *Partners in Production* (Englewood Cliffs, N.J.: Prentice-Hall, 1961).
2. B. Moore and T. Ross, *The Scanlon Way to Improved Productivity* (New York: Wiley-Interscience, 1978).
3. A. Rucker, *Labor's Road to Plenty* (Boston: Page, 1937).
4. C. Heyel, ed., *The Encyclopedia of Management*, 2nd ed. (New York: Van Nostrand Reinhold, 1973).
5. Moore and Ross, *The Scanlon Way*, note 2, above.
6. Ibid., 2.
7. C.F. Frost, J.H. Wakely, and R.A. Ruh, *The Scanlon Plan for Organization Development: Identity, Participation, Equity* (East Lansing: Michigan State University Press, 1974).
8. F.G. Lesieur, ed., *The Scanlon Plan: A Frontier in Labor-Management Cooperation* (Cambridge: Technology Press of M.I.T. and New York: John Wiley & Sons, 1958) 249–250.
9. B.E. Moore, *Sharing the Gains of Productivity* (Scarsdale, New York: Work in America Institute Studies in Productivity, 1982); B.E. Moore, *A Plant-Wide Productivity Plan in Action: Three Years of Experience with the Scanlon Plan* (Washington, D.C.: National Commission on Productivity and Work Quality, 1975).
10. C. O'Dell, *Gainsharing: Involvement, Incentives, and Productivity* (New York: American Management Association, 1981).
11. Moore and Ross, *The Scanlon Way*, note 2, above.
12. Moore, *A Plant-Wide Productivity Plan*, note 9, above.
13. Moore and Ross, *The Scanlon Way*, note 2, above.
14. Ibid.
15. J.F. Lincoln, *Incentive Management* (Cleveland: Lincoln Electric Company, 1951).

16. Moore and Ross, *The Scanlon Way*, note 2, above.
17. B.L. Metzger, *Profit Sharing in Perspective*, 2nd ed. (Evanston, Ill.: Profit Sharing Research Foundation, 1966).
18. Moore and Ross, *The Scanlon Way*, note 2, above.
19. J.J. Jehring, "A Contrast Between Two Approaches to Total Systems Incentives," *California Management Review*, 1967, 7–14.
20. Frost, Wakely, and Ruh, *The Scanlon Plan For Organization Development*, note 7, above; F.G. Lesieur, ed., *The Scanlon Plan: A Frontier in Labor-Management Cooperation* (Cambridge, Mass.: Technology Press of M.I.T. and New York: John Wiley and Sons, 1958); Moore and Ross, *The Scanlon Way*, note 2, above.
21. Heyel, *Encyclopedia of Management*, note 4, above.
22. P.J. Loftus, "Labor's Share in Manufacturing," *Lloyd's Bank Review*, April 1969.
23. G. Copeman, "Wages and Added Value," *Management Today*, June 1977, 45–46; B. Cox, "Formulas for Value Added Incentives," *Accounting* (UK), February 1980, 113–116.
24. Moore and Ross, *The Scanlon Way*, note 2, above.
25. M. Fein, "An Alternative to Traditional Managing," in *Handbook of Industrial Engineering*, ed. Gavriel Salvendy (New York: Wiley, 1981).
26. R.S. Alanis and B.E. Moore, "Organizational Learning of New Incentive Systems: Improshare" (manuscript, The University of Texas at Austin, 1981).
27. Fein, "Alternative to Traditional Managing," note 25, above.
28. Ibid., 481.
29. Ibid., 41.
30. Lincoln, *Incentive Management*, note 15, above; R. Zager, "Sharing the Wealth: HRD's Role in Making Incentive Plans Work," *Training*, January 1979, 30–31.
31. Fein, "Alternative to Traditional Managing," note 25, above.
32. R.B. Gray, "The Scanlon Plan—A Case Study," *British Journal of Industrial Relations*, 9, 291–313.
33. Fein, "Alternative to Traditional Managing," note 25, above.
34. J. Short and B.E. Moore, "Preliminary Findings of a Multivariate Analysis of Suggestion Systems Impact on Productivity" (working paper, Graduate School of Business, The University of Texas at Austin, 1975).
35. E.E. Lawler, *Pay and Organizational Development* (Reading, Massachusetts: Addison-Wesley, 1981); J.K. White, "The Scanlon Plan: Causes and Correlates of Success," *Academy of Management Journal*, 22, June 1979, 292–312.
36. White, "The Scanlon Plan," note 35, above.
37. Lawler, *Pay and Organizational Development*, note 35, above; Moore and Ross, *The Scanlon Way*, note 2, above.
38. Lawler, *Pay and Organizational Development*, note 35, above; F.G. Lesieur and E.S. Puckett, "The Scanlon Plan—Past, Present, and Future" (Proceedings of the 21st Industrial Relations Annual Winter Meeting, 1968) 71–80; T.L. Ross and G.M. Jones, "An Approach to Increased Productivity: The Scanlon Plan," *Financial Executive*, February 1972, 23–29; R. Ruh, J.H. Wakely, and J.C. Morrison, "Education, Ego Need Gratification and Attitudes Toward the Job" (manuscript, East Lansing, Michigan State University, 1972); J.N. Scanlon, "Adamson and His Profit-Sharing Plan," Production Series no. 172 (New York: American Management Association, 1947) 10–12;

G.P. Shultz, "Worker Participation on Production Problems: A Discussion of Experience with the Scanlon Plan," *Personnel*, November 1951, 209–11.
39. Frost, Wakely, and Ruh, *The Scanlon Plan for Organization Development*, note 7, above; Lesieur, *The Scanlon Plan: A Frontier*, note 8, above; William F. Whyte, *Money and Motivation* (New York: Harper and Brothers, 1955).
40. Jehring, "Contrast Between Two Approaches," note 19, above; R.B. Mc-Kersie, "Wage Payment Methods of the Future," *British Journal of Industrial Relations*, June 1963, 191–212; T.L. Ross, et al., "Measurement Under the Scanlon Plan and Other Productivity Incentive Plans" (manuscript, Bowling Green State University, 1975).
41. W.J. Howell, Jr., "A New Look at Profit Sharing, Pension and Productivity Plans," *Business Management*, December 1967, 26–42; G. Strauss and L.R. Sayles, "The Scanlon Plan: Some Organizational Problems," *Human Organization*, Fall 1957, 15–22.
42. Frost, Wakely, and Ruh, *The Scanlon Plan for Organization Development*, note 7, above; Ruh, Wakely, and Morrison, "Education, Ego Need Gratification," note 38, above.
43. T.O. Gilson and J.J. Lefcowitz, "A Plant-wide Productivity Bonus in a Small Factory—Study of an Unsuccessful Case," *Industrial and Labor Relations Review*, 1957, 284–96; Gray, "The Scanlon Plan—A Case Study," note 32, above; McKersie, "Wage Payment Methods," note 40, above.
44. McKersie, "Wage Payment Methods," note 40, above.
45. P.S. Goodman, "The Scanlon Plan: A Need for Conceptual and Empirical Models" (Symposium, 81st Annual Convention, American Psychological Association, 1973); O'Dell, "Gainsharing," note 10, above; White, "The Scanlon Plan: Causes and Correlates of Success," note 35, above.
46. M. Fein, "An Alternative to Traditional Managing," note 25, above.
47. Lesieur, *The Scanlon Plan: A Frontier*, note 8, above; McKersie, "Wage Payment Methods," note 40, above; B.E. Moore and P.S. Goodman, "Factors Affecting the Impact of a Company-Wide Incentive Program on Productivity" (Final Report submitted to the National Commission on Productivity, 1973); Scanlon, "Adamson," note 38, above; Joseph N. Scanlon, "Remarks on the Scanlon Plan" (Proceedings of the Conference on Productivity, June 4, 1949) 10–14; S.H. Slichter, J.J. Healy, and E.R. Livernash, *The Impact of Collective Bargaining on Management* (Washington, D.C.: The Brookings Foundation, 1960).
48. Frost, Wakely, and Ruh, *The Scanlon Plan for Organization Development*, note 7, above; R. Ruh, R.H. Johnson, and M.P. Scrontino, "The Scanlon Plan, Participation in Decision Making and Job Attitudes," *Journal of Industrial and Organizational Psychology* 1, 1973, 36–45; Whyte, *Money and Motivation*, note 39, above.
49. McKersie, "Wage Payment Methods," note 40, above; Moore and Goodman, "Factors Affecting the Impact," note 47, above.
50. Lesieur, *The Scanlon Plan: A Frontier*, note 8, above; McKersie, "Wage Payment Methods," note 40, above.
51. Lesieur, *The Scanlon Plan: A Frontier*, note 8, above.
52. A. Anderson, "Devising Real Incentives for Productivity," *American Machinist*, June 1978, 115–30; Scanlon, "Adamson," note 38, above; Scanlon, "Remarks," note 47, above.
53. Lesieur, *The Scanlon Plan: A Frontier*, note 8, above; Slichter, Healy, and

Livernash, *Impact of Collective Bargaining*, note 47, above; Whyte, *Money and Motivation*, note 39, above.

54. R.B. Helfgott, "Group Wage Incentives: Experience with the Scanlon Plan" (New York: Industrial Relations Counselors, Industrial Relations Memo, 1962).

55. T. Hammer, "New Developments in Profit Sharing," in J. Campbell, R. Campbell, and Associates, *Productivity in Organizations* (San Francisco: Jossey-Bass, 1988).

56. C. O'Dell and J. McAdams, *People, Performance, and Pay* (Houston: American Productivity Center, 1987).

57. R.J. Bullock and E.E. Lawler III, "Gainsharing: A Few Questions and Fewer Answers," *Human Resource Management* (1984) 5, 197–212.

58. M. Schuster, "The Impact of Union-Management Cooperation on Productivity and Employment," *Industrial and Labor Relations Review*, Vol. 36, No. 3, April 1983.

59. B. Graham-Moore and R. Rodgers, "Productivity Gainsharing and Organizational Fit," unpublished manuscript, The University of Texas at Austin, 1986.

60. E.E. Lawler III, "Gainsharing Theory and Research: Findings and Future Directions," Technical Report no. 85-1 (67), CEO, University of Southern California, 1985.

61. Gilson and Lefcowitz, "Plant-Wide Productivity Bonus," note 43, above.

62. Gray, "The Scanlon Plan: A Case Study," note 32, above.

63. Helfgott, "Group Wage Incentives," note 54, above.

64. R.B. Johnson, "The Scanlon Plan: Criteria for Success in Non-Union Plants" (Master's thesis, School of Industrial Management, M.I.T., 1959).

65. Jehring, "Contrast Between Two Approaches," note 19, above.

66. R. Ruh, R.L. Wallace, and C.F. Frost, "Management Attitudes and the Scanlon Plan," *Industrial Relations*, 1973, 282–88; Ruh, Johnson, and Scrontino, "The Scanlon Plan, Participation, and Attitudes," note 48, above.

67. Ross et al., "Measurement Under the Scanlon Plan," note 40, above.

68. Gray, "The Scanlon Plan—A Case Study," note 32, above, 242.

69. Lesieur, *The Scanlon Plan: A Frontier*, note 8, above.

70. Scanlon, "Adamson," note 38, above; Whyte, *Money and Motivation*, note 39, above.

71. *Hamilton* (Ontario) *Spectator*, November 18, 1980.

72. W.L. French and C.H. Bell, *Organization Development: Behavior Science Interventions for Organization Improvement* (Englewood Cliffs, N.J.: Prentice-Hall, 1973).

73. L.L. Hatcher and T.L. Ross, "Organization Development Through Productivity Gainsharing," *Personnel*, October 1985, 49.

74. Moore, *A Plant-Wide Productivity Plan*, note 9, above; Moore, *Sharing the Gains of Productivity*, note 9, above; White, "The Scanlon Plan: Causes and Correlates of Success," note 35, above.

75. Moore, *Sharing the Gains of Productivity*, note 9, above; Moore and Ross, *The Scanlon Way*, note 2, above.

76. Goodman, "The Scanlon Plan: A Need for Models," note 45, above; P.S. Goodman and B.E. Moore, "Factors Affecting Acquisition of Beliefs About a New Reward System," *Human Relations*, June 1976, 571–588.

Chapter 3

Formulas for Developing a Reward Structure to Further Organizational Goals

Brian Graham-Moore

For too long, the means for developing a gainsharing reward structure has been "hidden" from view. Some gainsharing formulas are held to be proprietary; yet in their generic form none are. Possibly this area of our knowledge has been obscured because consultants have held this information close to the vest. Just as responsible, however, may be the general ignorance that prevails in any area of financial analysis. Put simply, the decision maker of the 1990s can no longer be held in the dark. Selecting an appropriate gainsharing formula should be an informed decision. Instead of selecting just one formula, perhaps several should be chosen and tested so that the tradeoffs can be fully understood.

Formula determination is the leading cause of disagreement among corporate officials, local management, human resource, and outside consultants. Proper formula determination consists of making a series of informed judgments in a rational way. This chapter presents a diagnostic tool for organizations to use in developing a gainsharing formula which will reinforce the positive properties of the organization specified in Chapter 1 (Exhibit 1.2). As a first step, organizations should address all of the issues in this chapter before implementing a gainsharing plan.

This chapter reviews the goals that should be specified when gainsharing is considered. Also, five generic formulas are presented to illustrate how these organizational goals interact with the strengths and weaknesses of each formula. Then, assessment of selected formulas is delineated so that the decision maker can install a gainsharing formula with few surprises. This assessment portion of the chapter introduces the fact that hybrid gainsharing formulas can be developed once key decision makers specify the profile goals and understand the fit between goals and their organization. Gainsharing formula selection is not easy; however, it is definitely a rewarding process. A clear understanding of how gainsharing fits within an organization creates a clearer understanding of the organization's culture and its policies.

The Decision-Making Approach

The sequential decision-making process recommended here reflects the concerns raised in the literature describing gainsharing failures, discussed in Chapters 2 and 5. Probably the estimated one-third of gainsharing installations that failed did so in the first year. Typically, the blame is placed on the formula. To avoid a poor selection of formula, a rational decision-making model should be followed. The sequential steps are these:

1. goal specification,
2. formula selection,
3. assessment of fit between the organization and the formula.

All organizations need to address the three steps listed above. Otherwise, failure to specify the objectives and carefully consider the formula and the organization's needs will result in intraorganizational conflict. Consider the following scenario: An individual in the organization hears of a way to improve productivity, possibly at a conference. A renowned consultant is brought in providing empirical evidence that her or his method has proved to increase productivity. In fact, the consultants can even provide examples showing great success in improving productivity. Who can argue with results? A gainsharing program is quickly adopted. What were the specific goals that the organization wanted to achieve? Was a serious search given to alternative gainsharing plans? Proper evaluation of gainsharing is unlikely since organizational goals weren't specified. The organization may have adopted a gainsharing plan that works but the reason for the selection was not well considered. The comparative approach specified above makes more sense.

In 1978, Moore and Ross presented the most comprehensive

known discussion of (1) formula calculation, (2) alternative formulas, and (3) measurement problems in the context of gainsharing.[1] This chapter goes beyond the issues they raised and attempts to examine a set of issues that build on this previous work. Specifically, this chapter outlines a framework for theoreticians, practitioners, and other decision makers that addresses the following issues:

1. What does the organization expect to gain from a gainsharing program formula?
2. Which criteria help an organization to select among alternative formulas?
3. What are the tradeoffs between the various formulas?
4. How does an organization select a formula that will survive in a turbulent environment and permit institutionalization?

Goal Specification

Goal specification sounds like such an obvious step, yet gainsharing organizations often exhibit symptoms months after gainsharing implementation that suggest poor clarification of their goals. If a key manager says "I thought gainsharing would reduce scrap and waste and that hasn't happened," very likely the formula selected is a poor fit with organizational goals.

Goals

Goal specification centers on honestly addressing all the goals listed here along with the theoretical issues discussed in Chapter 1. These goals and issues appear in many forms and in many combinations. Key decision makers need to understand these combinations in order to make optimal use of their organization's particular profile. Clearly, one choice is to reject gainsharing as inappropriate for the company in question. In all cases, decision makers must attempt to select a program that fits best with the organization's technology and culture.

Process

The process of goal specification is also very important. That is, an obvious goal of gainsharing is to make organizational goals common across the entire organization. Often overlooked are ways to involve all the constituencies that make for successful gainsharing. Early task forces can include union representatives, staff members, and hourly wage earners. Key individuals who can and will influence gainsharing implementation, and later institutionalization, need to be a part of the goal specification process.

Clarification

Clarifying what the organization means when it says it wants to improve productivity is often a fascinating exercise. Most people agree that productivity refers to the ratio of inputs to outputs. Taken to a deeper level, however, organizational productivity can be viewed as the comparison of profits (outputs) to investments (inputs). If an organization wants to assume this financial definition of productivity, a profit-sharing program may fit best. In contrast, productivity can be viewed as the amount of output produced by a certain amount of labor. Using this definition of productivity, a direct efficiency formula such as allowed labor can be implemented.[2] This type of formula, however, ignores overhead and offers no incentive for efficient management of resources. There are other gainsharing formulas that measure the ratio of goods produced to strictly labor inputs. One must remember that rewarding efficient management may weaken the relationship between pay and performance. Also, the broader the formula the more it will be affected by economic fluctuation, unless it is adjusted for these fluctuations.

Organizational Factors

The various gainsharing formulas express different behavioral and organizational objectives. It is a good idea for firms to establish that these gainsharing objectives "fit" with the organization's objectives. Once this has been accomplished, firms should adopt a rational approach for selecting a formula. All gainsharing formulas can be evaluated against most of the following seven behavioral and organizational factors:

1. strength of reinforcement,
2. scope of the formula,
3. motivation of harder work,
4. motivation of smarter work,
5. motivation of behavior to produce nonlabor savings,
6. ease of administration,
7. economic flexibility.

As indicated in Chapter 1, our purpose is not to support one kind of gainsharing plan, rather we suggest that a formula can be constructed to best achieve the goals of a firm, whatever its current status. Goals should require a firm to stretch, but should not be so high that they contribute to frustration. Those firms embarking on a gainsharing program should specify their organizational goals. The firm should view these goals within the theoretical framework suggested in Chapter 1 so that it can select and evaluate a gainsharing formula against the factors discussed here.

Decision makers must first specify what they mean by productivity. How extensive will the definition be? Who contributes to productivity? Each gainsharing formula has a different impact on the subgoals of productivity, as the reader will see. Therefore, strategic planning in gainsharing should contemplate all relevant behavioral and organizational factors given the common understanding of the firm's view of productivity.

Elaborated below is the list of seven behavioral and organizational factors that affect the attainment of the goals of gainsharing. This list should provide organizations with a starting point, but they may want to add additional factors or goals as they progress with the plan.

Strength of Reinforcement

The amount of the bonus can be small or potentially very large. Lincoln Electric has paid total bonuses equal to annual pay. Just how much the work force will be influenced by extrinsic rewards can vary as a function of compensation philosophy, cultural values, and individual differences. Annual average gainsharing bonuses range from 0 to 30 percent.

Scope of the Formula

Does the organization want a formula to capture broad areas of productivity or to focus narrowly on, say, output? The ability of the formula to assist decision makers and any participating employee groups in isolating evolving problems is often overlooked. For example, if quality of product or service is a desired goal, a narrow cost reduction gainsharing formula might work toward this objective. A more broadly based gainsharing formula that includes all controllable costs in the numerator and the market value of output in its denominator encourages all to share the final test of the marketplace.

Motivating Harder Work

Is the organization trying primarily to get its workers to work harder? While it seems organizations always want to encourage employees to work faster, it may not be possible to get a large increase in speed. In addition, other factors, such as safety, may prohibit attempting to achieve this apparently obvious goal. Organizations should seriously evaluate the desire and potential for harder work.

Motivating Smarter Work

Does the organization want to encourage workers to try to come up with better ways to produce goods? While all organizations like to find better ways to produce goods, encouraging workers to make this type of contribution does not come without costs. Obtaining ideas from workers involves administration costs. In addition, supervisors may feel threatened when workers try to act smarter. Thus, organizations should assess the viability of this pursuit before undertaking such a program. The inability to implement employee-authored improvements will deter gainsharing success.

Motivating Nonlabor Savings

To what degree is it possible for workers to create savings on expenses (e.g., materials, equipment) other than labor? To the extent that such savings are possible, the organization may want to select a formula to reward expense savings that go beyond labor savings. Organizations should be aware that complex formulas can cause additional costs—e.g., problems with measurement, communication, and understanding.

Ease of Administration

While gainsharing plans offer the potential for dramatic increases in productivity, they do require administrative work. Different formulas require different amounts of administrative work. Consequently, organizations need to specify how important it is to minimize administrative complexity. For example, bonuses can be reported and paid weekly or monthly. Information must be collected, processed and managed. Also, some gainsharing plans involve supervisors heavily. They must explain the formula and related policy to employees and, thus, must receive special training in order to be effective.

Economic Flexibility

During economic downturns, a number of gainsharing firms have had to cut production dramatically. These cuts, unfortunately, may have an unexpected impact on the appropriateness of the standards used in a gainsharing formula. If organizations anticipate that economic fluctuations will affect the required level of production, a formula should be chosen that (partially) buffers the gainsharing plan from such changes. Seasonal variations can also affect the bonuses and deficits in ways which are independent of human endeavor. Simple gainsharing formulas do not offer the same opportunities to buffer these swings that a more complex formula can provide.

Generic Formulas

An organization typically begins the mechanics of gainsharing formula determination by developing the expected (standard) amount of labor cost necessary to produce a given amount of goods based on historical data. Once the plan is completed, actual labor costs are compared to standard costs for each bonus period (e.g., a week, a month) and the bonus is based on labor cost savings. The five generic formulas outlined below vary in terms of what goes into the production costs. Each formula influences the behavioral and organizational factors in different ways. Sufficient information is presented to allow you the opportunity to understand and evaluate each of them. Before implementation, however, it is appropriate and necessary to examine a more detailed description of the mechanics of the desired formula via spreadsheet analysis.

To evaluate each formula with respect to a given organization, it is important to realize that the advantages and disadvantages of a given formula are only relevant to the extent that they affect that particular organization. Some of the considerations listed below would not have a serious effect on many organizations. Thus, an

Exhibit 3.1   Five Gainsharing Formulas—A Comparison

TRADITIONAL SCANLON	EXPANDED SCANLON RATIOS		IMPROSHARE/ ALLOWED	RUCKER/ VALUE-
SINGLE RATIO	SPLIT RATIO	MULTICOST RATIO	LABOR	ADDED
HR Payroll Costs	HR Payroll Costs by Product	HR Payroll, Material, Overhead by Product & Department	Actual Labor Hours by Product & Department	Direct Labor
Net Sales or Production Value	Net Sales or Production Value	Net Sales or Production Value	Production Standard	Value Added

organization must attempt to select the formula with the most advantages and least disadvantages, since there is no perfect way to measure productivity.

Exhibit 3.1 displays the similar and dissimilar aspects of five generic gainsharing formulas. Each formula varies considerably in the construction of a balance sheet of items that go into making the formula operational. Focusing primarily on the behavioral and organizational factors, each generic gainsharing formula is reviewed below.

Impact of the Single Ratio Scanlon Formula

The mechanics of the single ratio formula dictate determining expected labor costs from historical data, preferably over a relatively long time frame. This is done by calculating the percentage of sales that has been used to pay labor expenses. This relationship of historical human resource cost to sales or output cost is termed the base ratio. Once this percentage is set, a bonus is earned in any period in which actual labor costs are less than the allowed (expected) rate.

Exhibit 3.2, Developing a Single Ratio, depicts the basic ingredients and typical steps followed in calculating a Scanlon single ratio. All human resource costs under the control of the worker for a year are totaled and then divided by either net sales or the production value for the year. Usually, three year's data are captured. Then, the stability of the base ratio is reviewed. In this case, the expected human resource cost ranges from 19 to 21 percent. Therefore, the historical base ratio of expected human resource cost is a value ranging from 19 to 21 percent.

Exhibit 3.2 Developing a Single Ratio

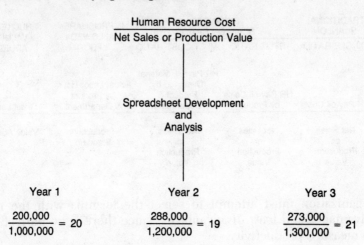

$$\frac{\text{Human Resource Cost}}{\text{Net Sales or Production Value}}$$

Spreadsheet Development
and
Analysis

Year 1	Year 2	Year 3
$\frac{200,000}{1,000,000} = 20$	$\frac{288,000}{1,200,000} = 19$	$\frac{273,000}{1,300,000} = 21$

Therefore, the historical base ratio of expected human resource cost is a value ranging from 19 to 21 percent.

Now consider a subsequent bonus period (e.g., a month) in which sales value of production is equal to $1,200,000 and labor costs are $210,000. The bonus pool would be equal to $30,000 (line 8) of Exhibit 3.3, Single Ratio Scanlon Monthly Report. This is merely the difference expected between payroll costs (line 6, $240,000) and actual payroll costs (line 7). The allowed or expected percentage on line 6 was selected from Exhibit 3.2, wherein the choice ranged from 19 to 21 percent.

In actuality, a typical single ratio bonus calculation is very straightforward. Exhibit 3.3 illustrates how most Scanlon companies report their monthly bonus in the form of a balance sheet.

Even this simple (and original) Scanlon formula has its policy implications. In Exhibit 3.3, for example, line 9 reduces the bonus pool by 25 percent. If this deduction is taken by the firm, it serves as a hedge against future productivity improvements that are not a result of efforts by the labor force. Thus, by taking a share of each bonus pool the company is less likely to adjust the base ratio for each technological improvement.

Line 10 of Exhibit 3.3 shows a reserve for deficit months, a similar hedge for leveling out cyclical variations. In this way, a deduction for periods of very high productivity can be applied to the deficits incurred in periods of very low productivity. One of its purposes is to build long-term attitudes.

Exhibit 3.3 Single Ratio Scanlon Monthly Report

1. Sales	$1,100,000
2. Less sales returns, allowances, discounts	25,000
3. Net Sales	1,075,000
4. Add: increase in inventory (at cost or selling price)	125,000
5. Value of production	1,200,000
6. Allowed payroll costs (20% of value of production)	240,000
7. Actual payroll costs	210,000
8. Bonus pool	30,000
9. Company share (50%)	15,000
Subtotal	15,000
10. Reserve for deficit months (25%)	3,750
11. Employee share—immediate distribution	11,250
12. Participating payroll costs	168,750
13. Bonus percentage ($11,250/$168,750)	6.7%

Adapted from: B.E. Moore and T.L. Ross, *The Scanlon Way to Improved Productivity* (New York: Wiley-Interscience, 1978) 71.

Line 11, reflecting employee share, is $16,875 which is divided by the participating payroll costs for the period. The result is a 10 percent bonus applied on top of the actual pay earned during the period. Thus, the bonus is differentially applied in terms of absolute dollars. That is, all employees—from the plant manager to the lowest paid worker—receive 10 percent of their respective monthly earnings. All gainsharing plans are not intended to change the regular reward structure, but rather to stimulate productivity. Therefore, the bonus is calculated on actual earnings in most gainsharing companies. Notice also that line 7, actual payroll costs, is greater than line 12, participating payroll. Normally, there are some exclusions to the participating payroll, i.e., the sales force, key management positions, and so forth. The participating payroll may be a lower value, yet total human resource cost is appropriately found on line 7.

Because of its simplicity, the single ratio calculation is easy to understand. However, its impact on the organization is not so simple. Exhibit 3.4, Effect of Single Ratio Formula on Behavioral and Organizational Factors, illustrates how this formula affects meaningful factors in gainsharing. For example, of the seven behavioral and organizational dimensions, the single ratio has a significant impact on strength of reinforcement, motivation of hard work, and ease of administration.

Note that the scope of the single ratio is relatively narrow for most organizations. That is, overhead, materials, and to some ex-

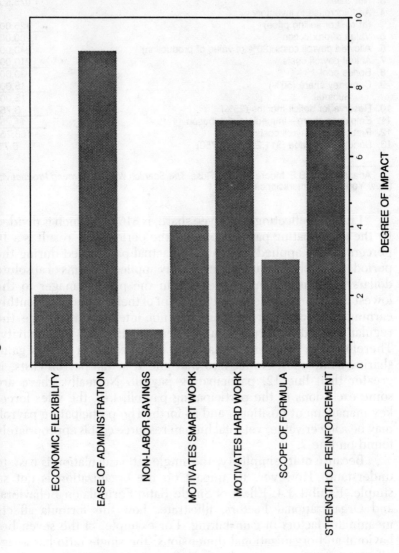

Exhibit 3.4 Effect of Scanlon Single Ratio Formula on Behavioral and Organizational Factors

tent waste are not specifically covered by this labor-only ratio. However, if an organization were very labor intensive and had low overhead, this ratio might have more appeal. Perhaps, in some service industries, such as cable television, the single ratio could be a reasonable choice (see Chapter 13 for service industry examples).

As Exhibit 3.4 shows, nonlabor savings are virtually nonexistent. Methods which provide suggestions that actually save raw materials in Scanlon companies affect the bonus in *labor* efficiency. True, if gains in labor-saving methods were translated into increased sales or output, then the decrease in labor is also associated with an increase in the profit realized from the output. This increase would help to produce bonuses. Generally, it is fair to say that since single ratio plans do not calculate and transfer gains from nonlabor savings into bonus dollars, there is no direct relationship. If the scope of the calculation were broad, as in the multicost formula, then gains in nonlabor savings are shared more directly.

Sudden and significant changes in prices for raw materials can cause the denominator of the single ratio formula to reflect bonuses incorrectly if adjustments are not made for these changes. The single ratio does not have to account for inflation, effects on changes in product mix, technological change, or capital investment. Rapidly peaking cycles of production cannot be easily smoothed by this formula either. None of these consequences of the single ratio are necessarily bad, if decision makers are aware these facts.

Impact of the Split Ratio Formula

Exhibit 3.5, Effect of Split Ratio Formula on Behavioral and Organizational Factors, indicates the impact of the split ratio formula on the organization. This calculation develops the base ratio by product line or other functional cost category. Since this improvement overcomes the problem of changing product mix encountered with the single ratio formula, the split ratio formula can deal more accurately with economic flexibility and cyclical variations. Ease of administration does suffer somewhat, since more information must be processed and evaluated. And while this formula is inherently fairer, it is more complex. While this formula does reward all employees, it also demonstrates that some product lines contribute more to overall productivity than others. This identification of differing product performance may lead to conflict among

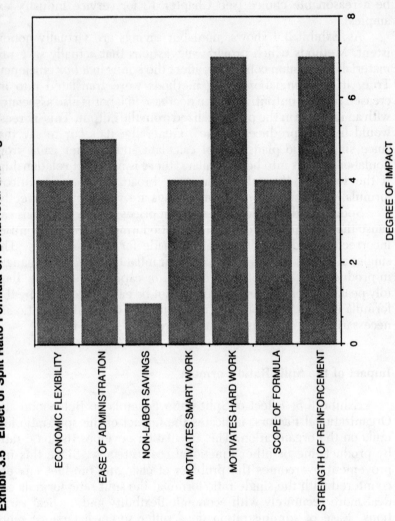

Exhibit 3.5   Effect of Split Ratio Formula on Behavioral and Organizational Factors

areas of the firm. Some competition may be beneficial. However, if the conflict is not well managed, lack of cooperation and inter-departmental harassment can result. In spite of the above, improvements in measurement with the split ratio formula, the motivational factors are about the same as the single ratio formula.

Finally, it is important to understand exactly why the split ratio can be a choice for those firms with sufficient product mix to affect the bonus calculation. Exhibit 3.6, Assumed Bonus Calculation Under Single and Split Ratio Methods, illustrates why the split ratio could be useful. In this example, the single ratio calculates a bonus pool of $60,000. Under the split ratio, the bonus is $20,000. Thus, the single ratio overpaid by $40,000. The true increase to productivity was reflected only in the Product B line.

Exhibit 3.6 Assumed Bonus Calculation Under Single and Split Ratio Method

TYPICAL SINGLE RATIO PERIOD 1		SPLIT RATIOS		
		PRODUCT A	PRODUCT B	TOTAL
Sales value of production	$1,800,000	$1,200,000	$600,000	$1,800,000
Allowed payroll costs:				
Single ratio: 20%	360,000			
Split ratio: 10% product A 30% product B		120,000	$180,000	300,000
Actual payroll (assumed)	300,000	140,000	160,000	300,000
Bonus pool	$ 60,000	$ (20,000)	$ 20,000	$ 0
Assumptions:				

Period 0
Two products (A and B) are produced with equal quantities and selling prices.
 Sales of product A = $600,000; sales of product B = $600,000
 Labor costs allowed = 20% in total; A actually = 10%, B = 30%

Period 1
 Sales of A increase by 100% ($600,000 + $600,000); B's remain the same ($600,000).
 Total sales now equal $1,800,000.
Split ratio calculation
 When determining the original allowed amounts, indirect payroll costs were allocated to products based on sales and this continues for actual costs in subsequent periods.

Source: B.E. Moore and T.L. Ross, *The Scanlon Way to Improved Productivity* (New York: Wiley-Interscience, 1978) 75.

Impact of the Multicost Split Ratio Formula

Exhibit 3.7, Effect of Multicost Split Ratio on Behavioral and Organizational Factors, depicts how the profile of behavioral and organizational factors changes under this formula, especially when compared to the Scanlon formulas previously described. Scope of the formula has a very high degree of impact since the formula is so comprehensive. Nonlabor savings can now be reinforced since the formula is almost a monthly total performance calculation. Previously described formulas cannot reinforce for nonlabor savings. This formula also provides necessary adjustments for economic flexibility and cyclical variations. For example, utility prices which fluctuate wildly can be budgeted or normalized so that only their usage is reflected in the formula and not their great swings in actual price. Also, costs which tend to run above the standard are identified for problem solving. If these costs are under the control of the worker, the information system which supports the multicost calculation points to areas for productivity improvement. Obviously, the motivation of smarter work gets a boost—see Exhibit 3.7.

Overall, the impact of most of the behavioral and organizational factors increases favorably. However, this is a sophisticated formula requiring excellent accounting and information systems that some firms simply do not have. Firms may also encounter difficulties in administering this formula—especially if trust is not high. By way of contrast, the single ratio formula has often been called the simple ratio. Its ease of communication is heightened by its simplicity. When one looks at the multicost split ratio formula, it appears that its reinforcement value is less than that of the Scanlon ratios. This is because it more accurately reflects all the forces impacting on productivity. Therefore, this formula tends to level payments while Scanlon ratios reflect labor productivity only and run the risk of over or underpaying. Since reinforcement is one of the primary reasons for choosing a gainsharing plan, this is no small consideration.

Looking more closely at the multicost ratio formula (see Exhibit 3.8), we see that it includes all production expenses (labor, materials and supplies, energy, and so forth) in the base ratio. This ratio is determined on historical data. In similar fashion as specified in the single ratio formula above, the base ratio is determined as follows:

$$\frac{\text{Production expenses by product or department}}{\text{Sales value of production}}$$

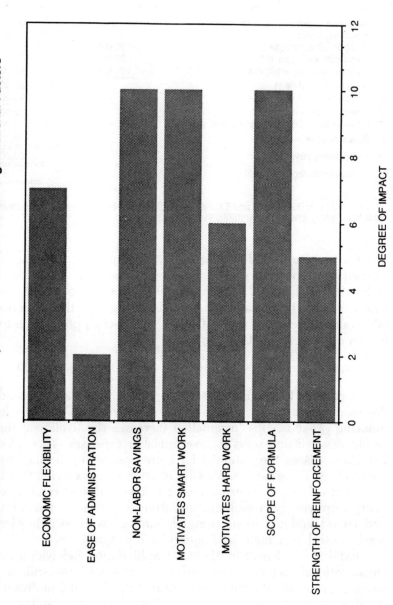

Exhibit 3.7 Effect of Multicost Split Ratio on Behavioral and Organizational Factors

Exhibit 3.8　Multicost Split Ratio Monthly Report

1. Value of production (sales ± inventory, allowances, etc.)		$1,000,000
2. Allowable expenses (80% of #1)		800,000
3. Actual expenses:		
Labor (all employee costs)	$120,000	
Material and supplies	500,000	
Other costs (energy, etc.)	160,000	780,000
4. Bonus pool (#2–#3)		20,000
5. Company share (50% × #4)		10,000
6. Gross bonus (#4–#5)		10,000
7. Reserve for deficit months (40% × #6)		4,000
8. Bonus pool (#6–#7)		6,000
9. Participating payroll		80,000
10. Bonus percentage (#8/#9)		7.5%

Adapted from: B.E. Moore and T.L. Ross, *The Scanlon Way to Improved Productivity* (New York: Wiley-Interscience, 1978), 79.

During any period in which actual expenses are less that the allowed rate, a bonus is earned. For example, assume that for every $1,000,000 of sales value of production, $800,000 of production expenses were historically incurred. If during a particular period sales value were equal to $1,100,000, while actual production expenses equaled $780,000, then

Bonus pool = ($1,000,000 × .80) − $780,000 = $20,000.

In contrast to the single ratio formula, this formulation extends the scope of expenses that the work force receives rewards for reducing. That is, this formulation increases the likelihood that employees will find ways to save nonlabor expenses. This calculation also places the potential for more bonuses in the hands of the workers. For example, working smarter includes trying to conserve virtually every controllable cost. The multicost ratio, however, requires greater administrative expense, is harder to understand, and may frustrate and de-motivate workers if they lack much control over materials, energy, and so forth.

Exhibit 3.7, Effect of Multicost Split Ration Behavioral and Organizational Factors, correctly shows that the multicost split ratio formula has maximum impact on scope of the formula, motivating smart work, and nonlabor savings. The factor which suffers, of course, is ease of administration. Also, as discussed in Chapter 1, there is a greater tendency by management to overcontrol with this calculation. In effect, there is a risk it will become a control system rather than a reward system.

Again, referring to Exhibit 3.7, the strength of reinforcement is an interesting tradeoff between magnitude and frequency of the gainsharing bonus. Single ratio calculations tend to pay higher bonuses in good months, but the multicost plan appears to pay bonuses more frequently. For example, a company with a single ratio Scanlon plan may report six deficit months while the same company using a multicost formula is more likely to report nine bonuses plus a year-end bonus, although all of these bonuses will be smaller. In terms of learning, more frequent, but smaller bonuses have higher reinforcement value.[3]

The multicost formula can also obtain the benefits of the split ratio formula by calculating a sub-bonus pool for each product based on multicosts and adding the sub-bonus pools to obtain the total bonus pool. These advantages, however, give rise to the problems of sensitive information systems and their understanding by all employees.

Moore and Ross strongly recommend that a company new to productivity gainsharing should not start out with a multicost formula.[4] They argue that the formulation is too confusing for employees to relate to and understand. They suggest that organizations desiring a multicost formula should use a two-stage implementation plan, whereby a single ratio is implemented, accepted by the work force, and then modified to a multicost format some years later.

Impact of the Allowed Labor or Improshare Formula

Exhibit 3.9, Allowed Labor/Improshare Calculation, shows how Improshare computes the Base Productivity Factor or BPF. In many ways it looks different from other gainsharing calculations. Invented by Mitchell Fein in 1976, it is an organizationwide bonus based on the individual-level Halsey Premium Plan. By aggregating this measure and folding in nonmeasured work, such as staff, Fein has created a very useful variant of gainsharing which has numerous advantages and disadvantages.

Let's deal with Exhibit 3.9, Allowed Labor/Improshare Calculation, first, then evaluate this calculation against the behavioral and organizational factors. Step 1 in Exhibit 3.9 indicates that our example is a small firm with a total of 100 employees. Of that 100, let's say that 75 are hourly wage earners and the remainder are staff and managers. Their hours worked in the previous year totaled

Exhibit 3.9   Allowed Labor/Improshare Calculation Steps

1) 100 Employees produced 50,000 units in 50 weeks for a total hours worked of 200,000 or (100 employees × 50 wks × 40 hrs = 200,000)

2) Average time per unit produced:

$$\frac{200{,}000 \text{ hours}}{50{,}000 \text{ units}} = 4.0$$

3) Standard hours to produce 50,000 units is 105,000.

   In the past 50 weeks the engineered standards account for 105,000. Total hours are higher because not all produced hours are in the standards, e.g., shipping, maintenance, set up, overhead, staff, etc.

4) Total hours   200,000

5) Convert engineered standards to reflect 50 weeks of productivity and to factor in all non-productive time

$$BPF = \frac{\text{Total hours worked}}{\text{Total standard hours produced}}$$

   or,

$$BPF = \frac{200{,}000}{105{,}000} = 1.905$$

6) Multiply all standard output by 1.905 to create the *base ratio*.

   For Example:
   If actual hours = 105,000 × 1.905 (BPF) = 200,000
   Then, there is no change or bonus

   If actual hours = 100,000 × 1.905 (BPF) = 190,500
   Then, bonus hours = 9,500 (200,000 − 190,500)

7) Divide 9,500 by 2 since company share is one-half.

8) Bonus Distribution = $\dfrac{4750}{200{,}000}$ = 2.38%

Note: The BPF measures total hours required in an acceptable base period to produce 1.0 standard hour of product. Obviously, this BPF can be multiplied by each standard for a product line and then be aggregated to give the total BPF, i.e., the expected hours.

200,000. Step 2 merely divides total hours worked by the output, which is 50,000 units. Thus, the average time required to produce one unit is four hours. Step 3 shows that "standard hours" to produce 50,000 units were 105,000. Standard hours simply refers to the engineered standards or work measurement done by industrial engineers, e.g., Motion-Time Analysis (MTA), Methods-Time Measurement (MTM), Master Standard Data (MSD). Conceivably, these standards could come from less direct methods of industrial engineering such as an empirical analysis of time records. Nevertheless, Allowed Labor and Improshare require specification of a standard. Step 4 reminds us that total hours are not the same as standard hours. Indeed, fixed and variable payrolls can present problems in gainsharing calculations because the fixed payroll is unmeasured and is assumed to co-vary with the variable payroll. If staff, as overhead, are added at a value greater than the assumed (via organizational change, growth, etc.), then this variable payroll "eats up" real productivity gains made by the variable payroll group, i.e., the hourly wage earners.

Step 5 shows how the Base Productivity Factor (BPF) of Improshare is calculated. Its purpose is to gather production and nonproduction related costs (both variable and fixed) into one statistic. BPF is analogous to the Base Ratio in other gainsharing plans. In our example shown in Exhibit 3.9, this BPF equals 1.905. Step 6 shows that if we multiply 1.905 times our "standard hours" we can convert that product to a bonus/nonbonus statistic for *any given interval of work*. This feature is important because many Improshare companies can pay the bonus weekly because of the ease of this conversion factor. Step 7 demonstrates the policy, very common among Improshare companies, of dividing the bonus in half. Obviously, the company favors this policy since it gets one-half of all labor productivity gains. Valuing the hours according to average wage rates leaves dollars available for distribution. This distribution policy is similar to other gainsharing plans in that the bonus is contingent on the value of hours worked, i.e., dollars earned. Where the Improshare system differs greatly is in frequency of payout. It can, and, in contemporary practice, does pay a weekly bonus. Typically, however, a four-week rolling average is used to smooth out the highs of a bonus and the lows of the deficits. There is no reserve account as seen in Scanlon and multicost calculations. All of the bonus and all of the deficit are included in the four-week rolling average.

Improshare calculation is associated with many policy recommendations of its inventor. For example, Fein has suggested that Improshare programs include these essential stipulations:

- Work-hour standards should be frozen at the average of the base period.
- Standards should not be changed except when new capital equipment is acquired and changes are made in technology.
- An agreed-upon ceiling should be established on productivity sharing. The excess over the ceiling is to be carried

forward to future time periods, i.e., banked. If appropriate, standards may be "bought back" with a single cash payment.[5]

Whereas these descriptions of Improshare's calculation and policies are correct, this gainsharing plan, more so than any other, takes many shapes. For example, it can be tailored to serve a group, such as hourly wage earners, or subdivisions of the organization, such as departments. This plan is often installed as a financial incentive program only; however, it is also found as an organization-wide bonus system and combined with an involvement system such as Quality Control Circles or labor-management committees. It is clear that Fein favors an organizational culture that fosters clear communications and productivity suggestions similar to the philosophy espoused in Scanlon companies.

Exhibit 3.10, Effect of Allowed Labor/Improshare on Behavioral and Organizational Factors, displays the impact of this calculation. This profile is remarkably different from the three previous profiles. The reason for this great difference is that *there is no comparable denominator in the Allowed Labor calculation*. Sales bring about productivity, but their volatility can influence the Scanlon-like calculation in inequitable ways. This calculation reduces this source of instability. It's fair to say reduced since the Allowed Labor and Improshare formulas pay a bonus on acceptable finished goods—in the case of manufacturing. Without controls in the form of good sales forecasting and good inventory control, the reality of the marketplace is absent in the calculation. The positive side of this, of course, is the ability to pay the bonus weekly. For that reason, the Allowed Labor/Improshare formulas get high marks when it comes to strength of reinforcement. Bonuses can be more frequent than in other gainsharing plans and can be as high as 30 percent. If they exceed 30 percent (which is 160 percent of base productivity), certain controls are employed to bring them in to the 160 percent range.

Equally affected by this type of gainsharing calculation is the motivation for harder work. There is no question that this calculation places its emphasis on quantity of output. This is the most direct way to influence the bonus since the value of the output is not factored into the calculation. Conversely, the scope of the formula is very narrow, i.e., it encompasses labor only. Therefore, the factors of working smarter and making suggestions, which can affect other gainsharing plans, are usually omitted in these plans.

Exhibit 3.10 Effect of Allowed Labor/Improshare Formula on Behavioral and Organizational Factors

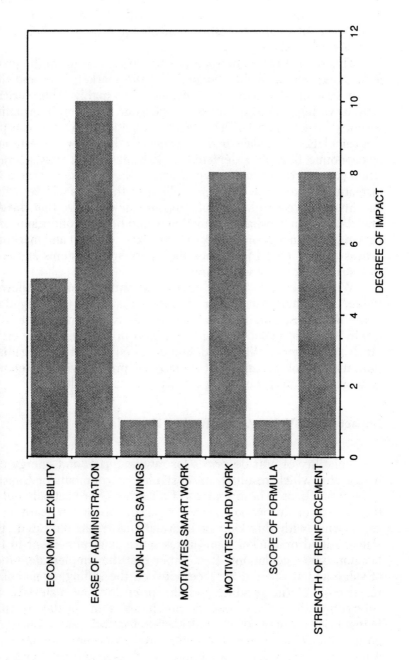

Since these are forms of nonlabor savings, why make suggestions in that direction when the labor-only calculation excludes their potential bonus value? Quality controls must be good before acceptance of finished goods.

This type of calculation was created to avoid some of the problems associated with the economics of the marketplace, and that is why ease of administration is evaluated so highly. Those organizations with good industrial engineering and excellent information systems, which, in turn, drive good budgeting practices, can put this calculation into place in days. Ironically, however, the estimate of economic flexibility depicted in Exhibit 3.10 is only average when compared to Scanlon-type calculations because the same information systems have to be excellent in the areas of forecasting and inventory control. It would appear, for example, that the Allowed Labor/Improshare calculation would benefit continuous process manufacturing companies with low labor content and machine-processed and paced jobs since the information systems and controls are of necessity well planned.

When one looks at the obvious advantages of the Allowed Labor/Improshare calculation, it is clear that a full understanding of the behavioral and organizational factors is very important. This is why the theoretical positions reviewed in Chapter 1 take on so much significance. Without defining the culture of the organization, its technology, and what is meant by productivity, the choice of an appropriate gainsharing calculation can be risky.

Impact of the Value-Added/Rucker Formula

Volatility of outside prices for raw materials and energy can be a factor which results from unstable environments or transfer pricing practices. These sources of uncertainty are actually out of the control of the worker, so why burden his or her learning of gainsharing with this kind of information? When indicated, the Value-Added or Rucker plan makes sense as a refinement to the Scanlon-type calculations. Remember that the simplest definition of value added is the difference between the selling (or manufactured cost) of the product and the price for raw materials. By subtracting the price of outside purchases, some of the volatility in that price is removed. The outside purchase price does, however, go into the selling price or manufactured cost—our denominator. Therefore, the employee has influence of usage and gets rewarded

Exhibit 3.11   Value Added/Rucker Monthly Report

VALUE-ADDED CALCULATION METHOD—MONTH X

1. Value of production (sales ± various adjustments)		$1,000,000
2. Less outside purchases (material, supplies, energy)		
Material and supplies	$500,000	
Other outside purchases, nonlabor costs	160,000	660,000
3. Value added (#1–#2)		340,000
4. Allowed employee costs (from diagnostic historical analysis) #3		
× 41.17%)		140,000
5. Actual labor (employee costs)		130,000
6. Bonus pool (#4–#5)		10,000
7. Company share (50% × #6)		5,000
8. Employee share (#6–#7)		5,000
9. Reserve for deficit months (20% × #8)		2,000
10. Bonus pool (#8–#9)		3,000
11. Participating payroll		80,000
12. Bonus percentage (#10/#11)		3.75%

Adapted from: B.E. Moore and T.L. Ross, *The Scanlon Way to Improved Productivity* (New York: Wiley-Interscience, 1978) 81.

for it if it is less than the standard. See Exhibit 3.11, Value-Added/ Rucker Monthly Report.

Step 1 of Exhibit 3.11 reflects the difference between the selling price and price adjustments for seasonality. Step 2 reflects subtractions for outside purchases such as materials, supplies, and energy. Value added of $340,000, or 34 percent of the selling price, is made up of outside purchases. At Step 4 the historical average of labor value added is applied. This is often called the Rucker Standard. In this example, 41.17 percent ($140,000) is the allowed (or expected) labor cost. Step 5 shows that the actual labor cost was $120,000. Thus, Step 6 exhibits a bonus pool of $20,000. A 50/50 split is a common policy and Steps 7 and 8 reflect this. Steps 9 and 10 show a policy of a reserve for deficit months (as in the case of many Scanlon companies). Since the participating payroll is $80,000 (Step 11), then the bonus percentage becomes 10 percent in Step 12. The exclusion of outside purchases (Step 12) permits adjustments for inflationary pressures. Also, cyclical variation in other outside purchases and nonlabor costs are kept out of the formula. Thus, Exhibit 3.11 accurately reflects how these two factors are well handled by the value-added formula.

Exhibit 3.12, Effect of Value-Added/Rucker on Behavioral and Organizational Factors, illustrates how the Value-Added, or Rucker formula interacts with these factors. The relative strength of its reinforcement value is equal to the single and split ratio formulas. In fact, most of the behavioral and organizational factors have similar profiles to those in the single and split ratio formulas. The key differences are in the area of economic flexibility. Most Scanlon formulas do not deal well with the inflationary effects on the sales value of production and have to be adjusted. Double-digit inflation can undermine the appropriateness of the base ratio used in most Scanlon calculations.

Value-added formulas subtract outside purchases (material and supplies, energy, etc.) from the sales value of production to determine the value added by the production process. Based on historical data, allowed labor costs are computed as a percentage of the value added. This makes the Value-Added/Rucker calculation very similar to the Scanlon single and split ratio calculations, yet certainly not as simple nor as understandable. The scope of the formula is slightly more comprehensive than the simpler formulas (it deals with usage of materials), but not as comprehensive as the multicost. Its ability to motivate hard work is similar to the Scanlon ratios.

The Value-Added/Rucker rates slightly higher on its impact on working smarter than Scanlon or Allowed Labor/Improshare since its involvement system rewards the efficient usage of outside purchases. For the same reason, nonlabor savings are improved by this calculation, but not as greatly as by the multicost formula. Ease of administration is rated below the levels shown in the Scanlon and Allowed Labor formulas, but higher than in the multicost. For example, Value-Added/Rucker plans don't pay weekly bonuses as the Improshare plan does. Assembling price and cost data requires time, and there are necessary pulses and flows to this process. All of these factors, make the Value-Added/Rucker plan more similar to the multicost where ease of administration is concerned; however, less manipulation of price and cost data is required than there is in the multicost formula.

Lastly, but most importantly, economic flexibility is rated highly because of the one significant difference of this calculation—separating out volatility of outside purchase prices. Since gainsharing asks employees to take more control of their work and become more responsible, the gainsharing calculation that buffers those

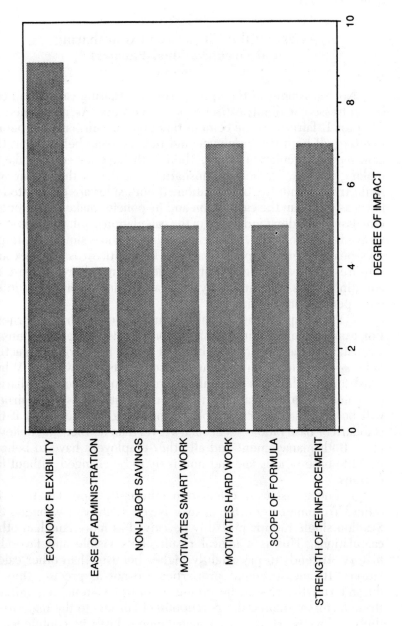

Exhibit 3.12 Effect of Value-Added/Rucker on Behavioral and Organizational Factors

factors outside of the control of most employees has greater motivational force.

Assessing the Fit Between Gainsharing and Organizational Fairness

No assessment of the appropriate gainsharing calculation can be addressed without a discussion on fairness. As mentioned in Chapter 1, fairness is the cement that holds a gainsharing program together. If both the employee and the company believe that the gainsharing calculation is fair, then both have an equal stake in making it work. In fact, a gainsharing calculation that is fair will build trust within the organization. If both sides are committed to fairness, how can the calculation and its policies make a difference? One issue is understandability of the calculation itself, perhaps even its availability for audit. The Scanlon single ratio is simple. It simply says beat yesterday's performance. The multicost is complex and requires some aptitude, if not knowledge, in the area of cost accounting. Thus, the simplicity of a gainsharing formula can influence perceptions of fairness.

Gainsharing policies can also influence perceptions of fairness. For example, most gainsharing companies distribute the bonus as a constant percentage of pay, but that means it is variable in actual dollars—depending on pay classifications and hours worked. When a task force undertakes the challenge of assessing which gainsharing plan meets the organization's needs, an honest discussion of fairness will be revealing. For example, gainsharing will not work if the standard or base ratio is set at such a level than neither side believes in it. Both management and all other employees have to believe that the base ratio is fair and not likely to be changed without fair reasons.

Is one gainsharing calculation inherently more fair than another? To some extent, the answer is yes. Rightly or wrongly, the Scanlon single ratio is probably perceived as more fair than other calculations. This is a logical result of its visible and favorable history. It tends to pay slightly higher bonuses than other calculations. Its measurement properties are not as precise; thus, it doesn't run the risk of becoming a control system. So, initially these factors reinforce the perception of fairness to the majority of the employees. However, if management loses its confidence in the Scanlon ratio because of its poor measurement properties, then they feel that fairness to the stockholders is being jeopardized. As always, fairness is a two-way exchange. If a balance is not struck gainsharing will fail.

Scenario Generation

Five generic gainsharing formulas have been presented with their respective behavioral and organizational profiles. Critical issues surrounding choice of each gainsharing formula have been examined. The key decision makers should accept the responsibility to consider the differences between the gainsharing formulas as they fit into their own organizational culture and technology. As Chapter 1 indicated, this process requires a thorough understanding of the organization's status and climate, what beliefs its people espouse, and how the organization expects to achieve its objectives.

Comparisons of Formulas

The best way to make a rational choice is, after thorough discussion, to select at least two formulas, build a database of relevant historical data, and create spreadsheets to generate "what if" scenarios. This exercise will accomplish many things—

1. It will structure a discussion concerning how gainsharing policies fit into the organization's goals.
2. It will clarify and make operational the working knowledge of the key decision makers.
3. It will permit empirical testing of different gainsharing formulas under normal and "stressed" business constraints.
4. It will build confidence in any appropriate gainsharing calculation—particularly if it has to be sold or defended to higher level decision makers.
5. It will lead to a judgment on selecting a fair standard.

If a rational plan of gainsharing formula assessment is pursued, then management may choose to tailor a calculation to the organization. For example, Exhibit 3.13 reflects gainsharing calculations that evolved within an integrated steel company. After much study and review of the five generic formulas discussed in this chapter, this company developed two different "hybrid" gainsharing formulas for two substantially different parts of its organization, rather than imposing one uniform gainsharing calculation throughout. Exhibit 3.13 displays one year of a base period spreadsheet for the

Exhibit 3.13   Hybrid Multicost Formula of Blast Furnace Cost Data by Quarters, 1987

	JAN.	APR.	JUL.	OCT.	YEAR-END/ AVERAGE(X)
1. Net tons produced	181,669	171,185	148,494	159,144	1,971,784
2. Equivalent employees	309.4	306.5	321.2	318.7	3760.2
3. Total all hours	0.295	0.310	0.374	0.347	0.330(X)
4. Distribution standard = 0.330					
5. Workhours @ standard	59,951	56,491	49,003	52,518	650,690
6. Actual workhours	53,523	53,027	55,560	55,142	650,516
7. Workhour savings (loss)	6,428	3,464	(6,557)	(2,624)	174
8. Save (loss @ $12.50	$80,350	$43,300	($81,963)	$32,800	$2,175
9. Operating cost per net ton produced	($2.91)	($4.73)	($3.36)	($1.08)	($2.85)(X)
10. Standard per ton	($2.85)	($2.85)	($2.85)	($2.85)	
11. Savings (loss)/ton	$0.06	$1.88	$0.78	($1.77)	
12. Total savings (loss)	$11,213	$321,614	$116,139	($282,137)	$8,081
13. Average 1987 yield	61.47	61.47	61.47	61.47	61.47
14. Actual yield	61.52	60.61	62.33	61.96	
15. Gain (loss)	0.05	−0.86	0.86	0.49	
16. 1% effect per ton	$0.536	$0.536	$0.536	$0.536	$0.536
17. Total savings (loss)	$4,869	($78,909)	$68,450	$41,798	$5,970
18. Total savings (loss) all combined	$96,432	$286,005	$102,626	($273,139)	$16,226

blast furnace operation of this large, integrated steel company. As discussed earlier, the formula used is a multicost ratio, in that labor, operating cost, and yield are the three parts of this comprehensive calculation. As such, it is designed to achieve the behavioral and organizational objectives found in Exhibit 3.7. That is, have medium reinforcement, comprehensive scope, motivate hard, but especially smart work, share nonlabor savings, and have good economic flexibility.

Obviously, the plan will be complex and difficult to administer. For that reason, key decision makers chose to use the best known measure of labor productivity in steel, work-hours per net ton. This measure is more similar to the Allowed Labor/Improshare calculation since it is based on engineered standards for most hourly jobs. There is great continuity to this measure since it is found in government reports, industry reports, annual reports, and the union contract. Comparisons of work-hours per net ton can be made over very long periods of time and can be made with foreign competition. Therefore, combining this statistic with operating costs and yield makes sense.

Thus, this hybrid gainsharing formula measures the blast furnace productivity by measuring the mean of 1987 for work-hours per net ton at .033 (see line 3, Year-End Totals or Average). This weighted average for the entire facility of around 325 employees reflects total work-hour per ton at this location. The year 1987 was considered to be representative of a good year of productivity; 1985 and 1986 were not thought to be as good.

Line 4 of Exhibit 3.13 reflects the distribution standard or mean of all work-hours divided by net tons produced. It is .33 and is the distribution standard being tested in this spreadsheet. Here again, the message of gainsharing is to beat yesterday's productivity. Applying the mean against actual 1987 data, we can see that line 8 reports seven bonus months and five deficit months with a total annual payout of $2,175, but only four months are shown on the exhibit. Since deficits are shared equally in this example, a total labor-only payout of $2,175 divided by some 325 employees wouldn't have much impact.

Now, there are two other components to this calculation— operating cost and yield. Line 9 of Exhibit 3.13 shows actual operating cost while line 10 applies the standard which is based on the mean of twelve good months. Line 11 reflects increases or decreases when this standard is applied. Line 12 shows that efficiencies in operating cost contributed to seven bonuses and five deficits in the full spreadsheet with year-end savings of $8,081. Fifty cents of each dollar saved below the expected operating cost would be shared under this plan.

Finally, the third component of this calculation is yield. This reflects the efficiency of the blast furnaces throughput. That is, low work-hours per ton and low operating cost could still lead to a poor finished product. Therefore, this company wishes to share the gains of high quality output. Again, 1986 was a year wherein all decision makers agreed that product quality was never higher. The average yield of this year is 61.47 (line 13). When applied to 1987 actual yield, only six months produce a bonus in the full spreadsheet. Notice that the statistics from these months do not co-vary perfectly with the labor and operating parts of the calculation. In April, for example, line 8 shows labor produced a modest bonus (3,464 hours below the expected hours). Operating costs in April were excellent (see line 12). Therefore, if people work smarter with materials and energy, they can conserve costs. Unfortunately, the yield was below the expected level by $78,909 (see line 17 for April). Thus, the combined effect of two bonuses and one deficit nets out at $286,005 for April. One-half is distributed to the entire work force, leaving $143,002.50. The percentage of an individual's bonus is calculated by dividing total earnings for the month of those on the participating payroll into 143,002.50, which was 325 times average wage of $12.50 per hour. In this test the bonus was approximately 3 percent of earned wage and salary. In summary, if the reader scans the lines of the spreadsheet, then by adding lines 8 + 12 + 17, the total savings or loss reflects the three components of this multicost calculation.

In keeping with the objectives of the decision makers, this hybrid, multicost formula focuses attention on all aspects of this plant's technology. While it is a capital intensive process using costly materials, human performance is of great impact. Constant attention to the conservation of raw materials and utilities, along with good quality control, help to keep yields high. A three-part formula of labor, materials, and yield emphasizes the contribution each makes to total productivity. This spreadsheet analysis permits "what if" scenario testing of this formula against the contingencies this steel company may face. It also permits a better understanding of what this calculation can do.

Summary

The decision-making approach to formula development has been detailed throughout this chapter. Indeed, when one reviews Chapters 2 and 5, gainsharing failure literature often cites imprecise or poorly designed formulas as a prime contributor to the lack of success. If decision makers rely on the steps of goal specification, formula selection, and then proper assessment of the fit between the organizational characteristics and the formula, they will avoid one common pitfall of gainsharing failures.

Developing a gainsharing reward structure looks like a financial task. To some extent it is, but this chapter delineated the behavioral and organizational factors that have been shown to be important for formula development. Gainsharing is really a behavioral mechanism to change the culture of a given organization. This fact is easily seen in Chapter 4, Solving Some of the Measurement Issues. Gainsharing formula development is less a financial task than it is a behavioral design.

Strength of reinforcement, while often only an expectation, was reviewed in order to allow decision makers to honestly discuss *their beliefs about what potential rewards could or should be.*

Scope of formula is actually an underlying theme through most of this book since many different kinds of gainsharing are possible. Plans vary most on this dimension, that is, how broad does the organization wish participation and involvement to be.

Motivating harder work is distinguished from motivating smarter work in this chapter because these are two distinct ideas. They can be achieved together, but in many gainsharing applications, working smarter is the message most typically sent. Rather than send an incorrect message which may lead to demotivation, these behavioral factors require honest discussion.

Motivating nonlabor savings, as a specific issue, was discussed in order to require decision makers to explore whether nonlabor savings can be shared. Also, if they are to be shared, what mechanisms need to be in place to help those behaviors that permit nonlabor savings.

Ease of administration, so often overlooked, was reviewed so that decision makers could estimate the amount of resources required to deal with gainsharing. Here again, ease of administration may have a significant impact on the organization's ability to feed back productivity information and achieve its gainsharing fulfillment goals.

Economic flexibility is useful for a task force to discuss since it will lead to a better understanding of when and how bonuses are possible. This kind of understanding will shape more accurate expectations. In turn, accurate expectations will have greater motivational force.

Goal specification, as discussed, becomes a crucial step. When there is full understanding and agreement on the organization's goals, gainsharing formula development becomes a simpler task. This chapter reviewed those behavioral and organizational factors that must consciously fit into the organization's specified goals.

Generic formulas of gainsharing were reviewed to emphasize that there is no one gainsharing plan or one gainsharing formula. Comprehension of all the tradeoffs of each formula type will build confidence in the appropriate formula. This chapter has made clear that hybrid formulas are frequently developed to mesh the organization's goals more securely with the gainsharing reward structure.

The assessment of fairness is dealt with separately in this chapter to stress its importance. It is a primary requirement that the human resource and management believe that the gainsharing calculation is fair. This chapter discussed the most common ways to build that concept. It bears repeating that understandability and simplicity of the formula not only reinforce the concept of fairness but stimulate trust as well.

This chapter encouraged the thorough testing of competing gainsharing formulas to improve understanding. Scenario generation through spreadsheet analyses can be a task force exercise that puts "numbers" to the design decisions. The rational choice model, which is the theme of the chapter, is best elaborated when various scenarios and various gainsharing formulas are tested side by side.

Lastly, the assiduous use of the ideas reflected in the measurement chapters of this book will, in itself, be a rewarding process. No task force can pursue gainsharing formula development without developing an appreciation of the dynamics of goal specification, organizational culture, and productivity enhancement. Since formula determination has been shown to be a significant cause of failure, the diagnostic tools available and the information base about gainsharing must be acquired and used.

Notes

1. B.E. Moore and T.L. Ross, *The Scanlon Way to Improved Productivity* (New York: Wiley-Interscience, 1978).
2. Ibid.
3. B.E. Graham-Moore and R. Rodgers, "Productivity Gainsharing and Organizational Fit," unpublished manuscript, The University of Texas at Austin, 1986.
4. B.E. Moore and T.L. Ross, *The Scanlon Way to Improved Productivity*, note 1, above.
5. M. Fein, "An Alternative to Traditional Managing," in *Handbook of Industrial Engineering*, ed. Gavriel Salvendy (New York: Wiley, 1981).

Chapter 4

Solving Some of the Measurement Issues

Timothy L. Ross and Ruth Ann Ross

Although gainsharing has been around for many years, more has been written about the employee involvement, communications, and other behavioral aspects of gainsharing than the measurement aspects. In addition, misconceptions have developed over the years for a variety of reasons. For example, many writers refer to the Scanlon Plan ratio as labor cost related to sales value of production, whereas in reality Scanlon-oriented plans have used calculations ranging from standard versus actual labor time, to return on investment, and many types in between.

Although many methods can be used to evaluate calculation alternatives, essentially the issue becomes one of value system orientation along with a few practical issues. Key among these issues are:

1. Whether to aim for a narrow or a broad profit orientation,
2. Ease of attaining the financial goal or goals established,
3. Whether to reinforce long-run or short-run thinking,
4. How much financial information will be disclosed,
5. Whether the plan will have a moving or static base,
6. How much approval or support will the plan get from the corporate structure.

These and other issues are reviewed in this chapter.

Conceptual Criteria for Selecting an Approach

Before delving into some key measurement issues, some conceptual framework for measurement must be established. Such a framework is necessary even where the more packaged gainsharing approaches such as the Improshare and Rucker plans are applied.

Physical Versus Financial Performance

There are two polar types of performance—physical and financial—and all gainsharing calculations can be evaluated against these extremes.

Physical performance can be equated to a coal miner producing forty tons of coal in forty hours, or one ton per hour. This is how most employees think of productivity: widgets per hour, reports per week, people processed per day, and the like. This is an important performance or productivity concept, and some calculations are based on it.

If in the next week, the miner produces forty-four tons in forty hours, physical performance increases to 1.1 tons per hour, or a 10 percent increase. It may have been caused by mix changes, better equipment, shorter walks to the coal, and so on, over which the miner may have little control, or by working smarter or harder, less waste, or more cooperation and teamwork, over which the miners as a group may have control. Some firms may want to adjust for the different causes, whereas others may not. Yet almost everyone would agree that the miner's performance has increased, whether the increase is attributable to the miner or not.

But if between week one and week two, the selling price of coal dropped by 25 percent, has the miner's performance increased? Obviously, both yes and no. The miner's physical performance has, but his financial performance has not. Since most employees think in physical performance terms while top managers think in terms of financial performance (e.g., profits), some compromise is probably appropriate. For example, one might consider starting the calculation somewhere between the two extremes and then moving toward one extreme or the other. From our experience, it seems that many more firms move toward financial rather than toward physical performance over time.

Control Versus Reward Orientation

However, the real question is: Which side is suitable for a particular company? Since we promote a "systems" approach to gainsharing, we believe that a full range of calculations should be considered, but we still believe that it is essential to narrow the options to reduce costs, time commitment, and confusion. After exploring many alternatives, we now generally use a simple contrasting approach that we call the control/reward evaluation.

We find that in a majority of firms, most managers have a shared group of attitudes that can be described as being primarily either control-oriented or reward-oriented. These orientations require different sets of gainsharing characteristics, which are contrasted in Exhibit 4.1.

To illustrate further, a control-oriented manager would have no difficulty saying to employees: "You did a great job this month even though we did not make much profit." The reward-oriented manager would have difficulty with this. On the other hand, the reward-oriented manager could tell employees that they earned a bonus because the firm was able to raise selling prices; the control-oriented manager would have difficulty accepting this.

This control/reward comparison is extremely useful in narrowing calculation alternatives in perhaps 75 percent of all cases. The remainder need to evaluate the full range of alternatives. In some of the latter cases, an easy compromise is developed between control and reward.

Exhibit 4.1 Gainsharing Characteristics Associated With Control and Reward Orientations

CONTROL ORIENTATION	REWARD ORIENTATION
Performance productivity-based	Financial productivity-based
Prices of outputs do not influence	Prices of outputs may influence
Prices of inputs do not influence	Prices of inputs may influence
Isolation of group contributions (e.g., direct and indirect labor) is desired	Isolation of group contributions not as important
Some adjustment for volume influence	Less or no volume adjustment
Frequent adjustment for capital and other items	Infrequent adjustment of outputs and inputs
Smaller number of items affect the bonus (more variable items)	More items affect bonus (could include all costs)
Disclosure often limited	Full disclosure, including perhaps profits
More physical-based	More dollar-based
Not necessarily related to profits	More directly related to profits

Other Conceptual Criteria

In addition, once a preliminary calculation is developed, we often evaluate each calculation against a set of criteria that includes the following questions:

1. Will it be perceived as fair by participants (probably the most important criterion)?
2. Does it meet management's objectives as indicated by its orientation to control or reward? (If not, management at all levels will be less than enthusiastic about it.)
3. Can it be understood by those who make the effort?
4. Does it incorporate flexibility to changing conditions, or do constant adjustments need to be made?
5. Can it be easily administered?
6. Will it direct attention properly, e.g., not waste excluded resources?
7. Will it violate disclosure limitations?
8. Will it be useful in isolating problem areas?

These and other criteria are extremely useful in evaluating a calculation after installation.

Basic Calculations and Issues

The basic calculations can be grouped around three fundamental types:

1. physical performance (control oriented),
2. financial performance (reward oriented),
3. prospective target (future oriented).

The first two are normally established by developing a historical relationship or ratio between inputs and outputs. The third approach is discussed later in this chapter. Note that the lists below move from broader to narrower bases of calculation.

Some common inputs used in formulating the calculations include the following:

1. all costs,
2. all costs minus some noncontrollable items,
3. only controllable costs,
4. only variable costs,

5. only payroll costs including fringes,
6. only wages and salaries,
7. direct and indirect labor time,
8. only direct labor time.

Some common outputs used in formulating the calculations are:

1. sales (usually net),
2. sales plus or minus work in process and finished goods inventory change,
3. value added (sales minus outside purchases),
4. total standard costs,
5. total standard direct labor cost,
6. total standard direct labor hours earned,
7. physical outputs (thousand board feet, gallons, students taught, and so on).

Physical-oriented performance calculations would include ratios such as Input 6/Output 5 or Input 7/Output 6, above. The latter ratio basically represents how Improshare is calculated.

Financial-oriented performance calculations would include Input 1/Output 1 or Input 2/Output 2, above. The first one is essentially a form of profit sharing, with a hurdle rate, whereas the second stops somewhat short of profit.

Using the financial-based calculations, we normally analyze the past five years (three years is a minimum unless the business has totally changed or the data are not available) and the most recent year on a monthly basis to evaluate both cycles and seasonality. This helps to determine the base period percentage—that is, the base period input/output ratio—to be allowed and whether a reserve is needed to adjust for the normal ups and downs of production, such as seasonability and various spikes in activities. Simple simulations can be done by hand or computer to evaluate the effect on the bonus for, say, 10 percent increases in volume with no increases in costs.

A Calculation Example

An example at this point might help clarify the issues. Suppose that a management cannot decide whether it is control- or reward-oriented and therefore wants a middle-of-the-road calculation. This includes, say, wages, salaries, supplies, and scrap (for a manufacturing firm) as its inputs (Input 6 and part of Input 4, above), and sales plus or minus work in process and finished goods inventory change as the output (Output 2, above). Going beyond mere sales is advantageous because most firms find that employees relate more to production than to sales. Another benefit to the use of sales ± inventory change is that actual costs rather than some combination of actual and standard cost can be used. But for manufacturing firms, inventories cause problems if they fluctuate significantly, as will be discussed below.

Historically based on, for example, the most recent three years, we determine that actual wages, salaries, supplies, and scrap were 25 percent of value of production (i.e., sales ± inventories). The calculation is illustrated in Exhibit 4.2.

A brief discussion of the calculation should help explain the various issues. In Exhibit 4.2, lines 1 and 2 were taken from the actual records for the month, as was line 5 (actual costs of wages, salaries, supplies, and scrap). These would be separately monitored and disclosed. If we were to value the change in inventory (line 2) at estimated sales prices, a practice some firms find desirable for employee comprehension, then the output would be the sales value of output or production rather than the value of production (with sales at sales value and inventory at cost, as in Exhibit 4.2). This difference will vary from firm to firm. Obviously, if mix is a major problem, one can do the same procedure by each product line, adjusting the base input/output ratio (line 4) as appropriate. We call this procedure the split single ratio.

Exhibit 4.2   A Sample Calculation (Month x)

1. Sales	$ 900,000
2. Inventory change (at cost)	+ 100,000
3. Value of production	$1,000,000
4. Allowed costs (25% based on history)	$ 250,000
5. Actual costs for Month x	230,000
6. Bonus pool	$ 20,000
7. Employee share (assume 50%)	10,000
8. Less: year-end reserve (assume 25%)	(2,500)
9. Net bonus	$ 7,500
10. Participating payroll	$ 150,000
11. Net bonus % (9 divided by 10)	5%
12. Balance in the reserve	$ 2,500

The employee share of the bonus pool in Exhibit 4.2 is 50 percent (line 7), a percentage that seems to represent the trend today. The two packaged approaches, Improshare and Rucker, often pay 50 percent and 100 percent respectively of the savings. But there are numerous exceptions to these sharing formulas. The sharing decision will depend in part on past/target performance and the ease of improving upon it. Also, the broader, more financial-oriented calculations seem to share less with employees, with the exception of the Rucker Plan.

Many firms establish a reserve (line 8) to reduce the spikes or to avoid having to pay large bonuses during the easy-to-earn periods and share losses during negative periods. If the reserve is negative at the end of the year, it is normally absorbed by the firm at that time; if positive, it is distributed to employees. The reserve also helps to reinforce a long-range employee outlook. Improshare plans seldom establish a reserve because of their control orientation, but they do use a four-week moving average. The percent of the reserve depends on corporate philosophy and extent of seasonability. More conservative firms reserve more and 50 percent is common.

The net bonus percentage in Exhibit 4.2 (line 11) represents the normal method of distribution because of legal and other issues. Regardless, overtime must be considered unless there is true profit sharing. The balance in the reserve is just a running total and obviously not really a liability until the end of the year, even if some firms do accrue it for financial purposes.

Summary of Basic Calculations

Exhibit 4.3 is a broad summary of the various basic calculations, highlighting the changes that mark the evolution from performance to financial calculations.

Obviously, variations of these exist in practice. We have also had considerable success with an expansion of an allowed labor or Improshare type of calculation. Essentially, this calculation develops one pool for labor and another for items such as supplies, material quantity variance, and scrap. The pools are then aggregated to form one bonus.

While we do not cover all common calculations in detail, a careful reading and reviewing of the list of outputs and inputs and the sample calculation should give the reader a feeling for the different calculation approaches. By reviewing the inputs and out-

Exhibit 4.3   Characteristics of the Basic Calculations

CALCULATION TYPE	PERFORMANCE TYPE	COMMON OUTPUTS	COMMON INPUTS	ADVANTAGES	POSSIBLE PROBLEMS
Standard labor	Physical (control)	Standard direct labor cost Standard direct labor hours Physical output	Labor costs (direct/indirect) Labor hours (direct/indirect)	Considers some mix problems Prices do not affect or can be easily adjusted Easier to install Employees relate to Limited financial disclosures	Only limited inputs included Could result in bickering over standards Standards may have to be frozen Cost of maintaining New product difficulties Difficulty of adding other inputs, such as overtime
Single ratio.	Physical/financial (control if prices adjusted for)	Sales Sales ± inventory Total standard costs	Labor Limited other costs	Easy to understand Simple way to start Limited disclosure required Related to employee costs.	Mix may influence (different base ratio for each product line) Inflation influences Neither reward nor control Inventory may influence more
Value added	Financial (reward)	Sales minus outside purchases	Labor Some other costs	Broader More financially oriented Increases flexibility Handles some mix problems	Some items still excluded Defining an outside purchase (e.g., material, supplies) Determining what to do with capital (Is it an outside purchase?) More difficult to understand
Multicost	Financial (reward)	Sales Sales ± inventory Total standard cost	All variable costs Most costs	Shares overall success Most costs included Congruent with management's broad goals Adaptable to mix changes Increases possibilities for commitment	Not performance productivity based More difficult to educate employees More information dissemination Changing pricing strategies may influence Requires more involvement
Profit sharing/ Return on Investment	Financial (reward)	Sales	All costs	Similar to multicost	Similar to multicost, plus not a gainsharing concept unless a hurdle is established Lack of controllability of some items

puts presented above, one should be able to evaluate and choose from many alternatives. A historical analysis would give significant insight into which costs are more variable and which are more fixed.

Refining the Calculations

Much of the information that we have presented on choice of calculation is found in most gainsharing books and in Chapter 3. What follows are a number of other issues related to refining the calculations for particular situations that are not discussed adequately in the literature. Most of the decisions associated with these issues are made essentially independently of the type of calculation employed, except in obvious cases—for example, the issue of standards pertains primarily to standards-based plans such as Improshare.

Limited or Poor Past Performance (Base Ratio Movement Considerations)

If the firm is new, a moving rather than a static ratio base is often used with no period allowed to be higher than an average of the past periods. That is, performance cannot become worse. For example, the base ratio in Exhibit 4.2 could go from 25 to 24 percent but not to 26 percent. More recent periods are sometimes given extra weight. We normally have a comprehensive quarterly review to maintain equity until a stable base is determined.

If the firm is not new but has had poor past performance for whatever reason, should a bonus be paid for improvement upon an unacceptable level of performance? Some managers say no, or at least not 50 percent of any improvement. One obvious approach is to reduce the percentage going to employees to, say, a 20 to 30 percent range. Another approach is to weight good performance periods more heavily. Another is to use a moving average by:

1. adding each new period to the old,
2. adding each new period while dropping an old, or
3. weighting recent periods more heavily.

Another approach is a little more complex: It consists of increasing the percentage going to employees as improvement occurs. For example, employees may get 20 percent if improvement occurs to a certain point, 30 percent if improvement reaches the next hurdle, and so on. If industry statistics are available, they are generally acceptable for setting hurdles in firms with good trust levels.

In any case, an attempt must be maintained to develop perceived equitability between the shareholders, employees, and customers. Management does itself no justice by allowing the earning of bonuses too easily, and if such a practice decreases the firm's ability to compete, no one gains in the long run. Similarly, if management tries to limit the bonus artificially, the system will also deteriorate, to the detriment of everyone for many of the behavioral reasons covered in Chapter 3. We normally suggest an annual comprehensive review to evaluate equitability.

How to Consider Volume

Many managers do not desire to pay large bonuses just because volume increases, even if the increase really is a productivity improvement. That is, if the amount of output is doubled with the same level of input, productivity has increased. But the improvement may be due to fixed or semivariable factors. Detailed monthly simulations will help determine whether this could occur, and how great a problem it is likely to be. We often use simple regression analysis (i.e., plotting inputs against outputs) to evaluate a cost's fixed and variable portions. Several options are available to help solve this problem:

1. reduce the fixed portions of inputs in the calculation,
2. reduce the semivariable inputs included,
3. put a cap on a period's bonus,
4. pay over a longer period (e.g., bimonthly or quarterly).

In actual practice, various combinations are used.

Some novel approaches are being used, especially for semivariable costs. One is a flexing approach. If, for example, standard labor earned should increase over a norm of some level, increased quantity or costs of semivariable inputs would be allowed but not a proportional increase. That is, if standard direct labor earned should increase by 10 percent over a period's norm, 2 percent more semivariable labor would be allowed; if a 20 percent increase should occur, then 4 percent more semivariable labor would be added, and so on at each level. Although complex, this does help solve the objection to paying large bonuses just because volume increases.

If you want to include, say, all wages for philosophical reasons, fixed labor costs can be included based on a head count allowed at the beginning of the year or adjusted for approved reasons, and at an average wage. Still more complex options are used, but we do not believe they are desirable. Perhaps the more fixed costs should be excluded if management feels strongly enough about reducing the volume impact.

Two points should be made, however. First, costs or hours to be included is a separate decision from that of who participates in the bonus plan. (Everyone participates in its operation but does not necessarily share in the bonus.) These are two completely separate decisions, which many confuse. Second, reducing the volume impact on the plan is really a form of smoothing or reducing the bonus highs and lows. Frankly, we see no reason why bonuses should not be high when volume is high and vice versa but would feel uncomfortable with a 30 percent to 40 percent bonus or higher in one period and a zero bonus the next solely because of volume. Corporate staffs also seem bothered by such fluctuation possibilities, although we personally have never seen this degree of short-run volatility in plans that are installed, even if we have seen it in calculations under consideration.

Caps and Leverage Effects of Labor Costs

To correct for major spikes in performance, some managers like the idea of caps on bonus size. Improshare normally imposes an automatic weekly payment cap of *60 percent with one half returned to the company*. Others set a lower cap of 10 percent to 20 percent, with any gain in excess frequently credited to the reserve. Others dislike caps and let bonuses go up. We have heard of bonuses exceeding 100 percent for a period. Large, easy-to-earn bonuses, especially if the calculation has a large fixed component, can be a problem because of heightened expectations so we are not against caps in such situations. Also, corporate staffs of large companies whose units are installing gainsharing systems are more receptive to such plans when there are caps.

A final caution in the area of caps and volume applies to firms where labor is a small component of all costs. If wages and salaries are less than about 10 percent of total costs, a firm is practically precluded from using one of the broader calculations such as value added, multicost, or even more profit sharing based on a hurdle rate unless large bonuses are acceptable. Such bonuses result from the high leverage relationship between output and labor costs. If wages are 5 percent of sales and one saves 1 percent on other costs either because of volume or cost reduction, the contribution to the bonus is 20 percent (1 divided by 5). In fact, in almost all cases of large bonuses—that is, bonuses over about 30 percent—the calculation normally is fairly broad and labor is a small percent of costs. Watch for this possible problem by completing numerous simulations on specific periods.

Bonus Size and Bad Times

Most studies indicate that long-term bonuses average in the range of 6 to 8 percent, with smaller bonuses distributed in earlier years and often larger ones in later years. Obviously, many exceptions can be found.

With respect to bonus size and bad times, some firms' policy is that if the profits are negative, no bonuses are paid, regardless of how they are computed. This smacks to us of management trying to have its cake and eat it too. Management should live with the results of its choice of a reward- or control-oriented calculation, although some limitations may have to be imposed at the outset to get corporate approval.

Building identification with the system is extremely important to the plan's survival during difficult times. During the most recent deep recession, many firms' plans survived with little difficulty, but only because identification was developed.

Inventories and Accounting of the Bonus

As mentioned earlier, inventories pose a calculation problem because of their relationship to the standard cost system. After a certain point of production, the actual cost of inventory items is not separately determined—just the standard cost. Because of this, most firms base their calculations on production rather than sales. But to maintain a close ratio between costs and output for more financial-based productivity calculations, one should compute inventory change at sales prices rather than costs. For those firms that do not, a standard markup for changes can be developed, if appropriate. Computerization makes the whole area of inventory adjustments somewhat easier.

One reason why firms are attracted to standards-based plans such as Improshare is their somewhat easier handling of the inventory problem. But if the inventory cycle is long, "what goes in the box" at the end of the period is not entirely acceptable as the sole measurement point. The key is to do simulations of various "what ifs," carefully monitoring changes, and attempting to be fair and open about the problem.

Some managers also do not want to give any credit toward the bonus until the product is sold, since only at that time are resources available to pay the bonus. Employees normally seem to understand and accept this thinking, even though it is not related to physical performance, or at least to production.

A final note is necessary on how to account for the bonus. From a purely accounting standpoint, the bonus is a cost, and is normally accounted for as an overhead item but not charged against the plan.

Mix Changes and Capital

Narrow, standards-based calculations and broad ones such as multicost/profit seem to handle mix problems the best. Mix problems can be of several types, and each must be analyzed separately to determine their impact and the calculation change required.

1. *Substitution of capital for labor.* If capital is not included in the calculation, some adjustment is probably necessary if significant capital investments are made. Standards-based calculations are probably the easiest to adapt. For example, standards-based types of calculations such as Improshare often have a policy of adjusting the standard for 80 percent of the change so that everyone benefits somewhat from the equipment. Many other approaches are used, ranging from no adjustment to an immediate adjustment for 100 percent of the change, or in some cases, allowing the standard to remain as is until the end of a period. Combinations are also sometimes used.

2. *Outputs and inputs increasing or decreasing in price levels at different rates.* Standards-based calculations need not be adjusted at all if prices are excluded. Broad calculations adjust almost automatically. Also, reward-oriented managers, who tend to use broad calculations, are not as concerned about this issue as control managers because of their philosophy. But major pricing strategy changes can seriously affect some broad calculations, and these will

have to be evaluated before a plan is established. Calculations of intermediate breadth must be monitored and adjustments made as required. As part of the normal study and evaluation, consider such fluctuations for this and other mix issues.

3. *Changes among the physical components of a product, such as changing from one quality of material to another.* Some calculations handle these changes easily, but others do not. Each such possible change in this area should be considered and planned for. Major adjustments can be made without difficulty if sufficient details were incorporated into the base period ratios and were maintained after installation.

Issues involving mix and different margins have resulted in some novel approaches over the years, such as split multicost. This entails separate calculations for each facility, for example, or each product line, which are then aggregated. Careful monitoring is necessary, and equity must be maintained.

New Products

Some plans have a stated philosophy of allowing the same bonus potential for new as for old products. These are normally standards-based plans, such as Improshare, since broader calculations are fairly well insulated from these problems unless profit margins fluctuate considerably for new versus old products. This approach is difficult for some managers to accept because they feel their ability to produce new products may be reduced if they have to pay a large portion of past productivity increases to employees for new products.

We tend to accept this logic and feel some tightening is acceptable, provided a process review is maintained. For standards-based plans, running a comparison with a sample of old and new products can help evaluate how great a problem, if any, there will be after installation. Sometimes one or two trial runs are made before developing standards, which are then reviewed at a later date. Again, intermediate types of calculations seem to present more difficulty than very narrow- or very broad-based types when adjusting to fundamentally new products and must be more carefully monitored for equitability. If a company can capture the performance improvement by recalculating the standard of new products, this helps to keep them competitive. Since there is generally a mix of new and old products, opportunities for bonus represents a tradeoff between incentive equity and market competitiveness.

Individual Incentives and Gainsharing

Most experts claim that individual incentives are incompatible with gainsharing. This is certainly an overstatement, and successful applications of both have been made in some firms, including Lincoln Electric, Steel Case, and Textron. But the individual orientation prevalent in some individual incentive systems is certainly incompatible with the group or teamwork concept underlying gainsharing.

At any rate, the combination of individual incentives and gainsharing would probably not work in most cases because most individual incentives are not as effective as firms anticipate. In fact, we have isolated 21 reasons why firms get rid of individual incentives, the most common reasons being the impact on quality and the cost of maintenance. There are also numerous ways to eliminate individual incentives, the most common of which are some form of buyout and the red circling or guaranteeing wage levels of higher-paid employees for some period. A reduction of job classifications is often instituted along with elimination of incentives to increase the flexibility of the work force.

Management likes the idea of introducing gainsharing when individual incentives are eliminated, since in this way the inducement to increase productivity is maintained. Unions generally find individual incentives a problem and will often cooperate somewhat in their elimination unless union leaders are among those earning high bonuses. When gainsharing replaces individual incentives, the former, unlike the latter, is usually outside the union contract by mutual agreement. The union does not want management to use the argument in bargaining that large gainsharing bonuses are being earned so wage increases are not needed. Gainsharing normally includes all employees, not just union members, which is not true of individual incentives. Obviously, some education is needed on how to manage in a nonincentive environment.

Loose Or Tight Standards

Managers often say they cannot install a standards-based system because their standard cost system is poor. Although this is partially true in all cases, it is not very relevant. To start gainsharing, one merely has to determine the relationship between standard time (or costs) earned and actual time (or costs). All that tight or loose standards do is change the relationship. Exhibit 4.4 should help explain this (some readers may disagree on our definition of loose and tight standards).

In the two situations, if standard hours earned increases by 10 percent to 66,000 hours and 49,500 hours respectively while actual hours stay the same and 66,000 is multiplied by 1.5 and 49,500 by 2.0, the result is allowed hours of 99,000 in both cases. Thus, each yields the same bonus earning opportunities (i.e., 99,000 allowed minus 90,000 actual hours).

But the process of changing the standards does weigh heavily in the decision to apply a standards-based system. In such a case, two sets of standards must be maintained—one for gainsharing and another for scheduling, pricing, and so on (which is not entirely bad). Obviously, if the system is not standards based, the problems are reduced considerably, and standards are not as sensitive an issue. Firms that have major problems with trust in standards are likely not to select a standards based system and, if one has already been installed, are likely to move away from it. Accounting rather than engineered standards are also frequently used.

Percent to Employees and Percent Versus Flat Amount

The percentage of measured savings returned to employees range from around 15 percent to 100 percent depending on management, the broadness of the calculation, the base period, and corporate philosophy. This issue is perhaps more philosophical than

Exhibit 4.4 Loose and Tight Standards

Situation 1: Loose standards (one-year period)
1. Actual direct labor hours   = 50,000 hours
2. Actual indirect labor hours   = 40,000 hours
3. Standard hours earned   = 60,000 hours

$$\text{Base productivity:} \frac{50{,}000 + 40{,}000}{60{,}000} = 1.5$$

Situation 2: Tight standards (one-year period)
1. Actual direct labor hours   = 50,000 hours
2. Actual indirect labor hours   = 40,000 hours
3. Standard hours earned   = 45,000 hours

$$\text{Base productivity:} \frac{50{,}000 + 40{,}000}{45{,}000} = 2.0$$

technical. As stated earlier, 50/50 has a good ring if adjustment procedures are adequate to maintain equitability and the base period performance is adequate.

Whether to pay the bonus as a percentage of gross wages or as a flat amount per hour of work is one of the most sensitive issues of gainsharing. A percentage is probably more uniform in its motivational impact and is probably more fair because it is congruent with normal pay systems. But many employees, including some managers, feel that a flat amount per hour of work is more fair because the bonus results from a team effort.

From the point of view of federal regulations, a percentage of pay including overtime is probably the only consistently acceptable payment method. The Fair Labor Standards Act states that the computation of overtime must be based on a calculation of regular wage (that includes production *and* other bonuses plus numerous other items such as shift premium). Excepted from recomputation are profit sharing *and* bonuses based on a percentage of all wages including overtime. Profit-sharing plans apparently can pay the bonus on a flat basis to everyone. A few firms distribute the bonus on hours with overtime weighted at 1.5 or more times but no formal ruling has been made on this approach that we know of.

Quality Considerations

Most gainsharing firms place great emphasis on quality. There are often double and triple or more penalties for employee-generated quality problems such as returns. We believe that this approach is desirable. It can take the form of a direct charge as a cost against the plan, an addition to returns and allowances, or some other procedure. This approach must be especially emphasized in certain service-sector firms such as hospitals (see Chapter 13).

Targeted Performance Instead of Past Performance

In some instances, because of philosophy, nature of the situation, unique measurement problems, or short history, past performances may not be an acceptable base. For example, using past performance has limitations if one wants to add numerous performance and financial productivity measures; to tie the system into one's business plan; or to apply it to contracted performance, government, some other nonprofit organizations, some job shop situations, or some very important performance measures.

In such cases, a targeted performance approach is sometimes preferable. Calculations can be formulated through indices, contract costs, or ratios allowed and, in some situations, targeted return on investment. Such approaches are readily accepted if identification, involvement, and communications have been effectively developed before installation and are maintained thereafter. Obviously, a good level of trust in management is also necessary.

Tradeoff of Resources

People obviously focus on what is important to the bonus. Narrow calculations based, for example, on standards, may encourage a waste of resources to save on labor. Care must be exercised to help prevent this from happening by establishing a frequent review and a plan of action for dealing with a tradeoff if it should occur. The most commonly wasted resources are materials, supplies, tooling, and, in some situations, energy. Care should be taken, both before installation and during operation, to evaluate possible impacts in these areas and who or what group should be involved in evaluating the consequences and developing some plan of action.

Reserves and Frequency of Payment

As stated earlier, many firms like the idea of maintaining reserves to help protect against spikes in performance and reinforce a long-run view. Reserves range from 10 percent to 70 percent of the employee share of the bonus pool, depending often on seasonality, past history, and corporate input (which normally means higher reserves). If positive at the end of the year, it is normally paid on the same basis as the normal periodic bonus. If negative, it is normally absorbed by the company.

Although most firms calculate and pay each period separately, some make the plan pay back any negative deficit in the reserve before paying any bonus in subsequent periods. If the reserve is 25 percent of positive periods and 100 percent of negative ones, it could become negative rapidly. Consequently, some firms increase the reserve to something like 50 percent of positive periods while always paying out something for positive periods, even if a negative deficit for the previous period has not yet been fully paid back. Other options are used, but these are the most common. Obviously, some employees would prefer no reserve so as to maximize their possible return, but they are not sharing equally in the deficits which would be unfair to the shareholders. Also, it would mean that long-run attitudes were not being reinforced.

Frequency of payment ranges from weekly for some standards-based calculations to yearly for a few firms. Monthly payments may be the most common. We find little perceived difference in success between firms that pay monthly or quarterly; it really reflects whether the orientation is short run or long run.

Unique Industries

Although the techniques discussed in this chapter probably apply to many, if not all situations, some unique perceived or actual measurement problems can be found in some industries. These must be solved by using the conceptual approach discussed earlier or developing simpler sharing techniques such as lotteries, departmental prize awards, or unique measurement techniques. In just about all cases, however, some sharing formula can be developed if the firm really wants one regardless of whether management is control or reward oriented or how major a change process it desires. The key is to be convinced that something will work rather than to try to discover the "perfect" measurement system. A workable formula is generally possible, but a perfect one does not exist.

Conclusion

This chapter, along with Chapter 3, should provide significant assistance in investigating, implementing, and monitoring a gain-sharing calculation. Perceived fairness and meeting organizational objectives are probably the most important factors to long-term success. Some more complex/broader calculations require much more education than do others. The key is to conceptually decide on the calculation orientation and then reinforce it after implementation. In most situations however a calculation can be developed and maintained without major difficulties.

Chapter 5

Why Gainsharing Sometimes Fails

Timothy L. Ross

Most experts in the field of gainsharing would probably say that the success rate is not over 65 percent. (This percentage does not include firms with marginal plans, which is a common practice). No one really knows the failure rate, since most of the plans have been installed by consultants who are frequently unwilling to share their client's experience with others.

Overall, failure of gainsharing is most often linked with the managerial expectation of increased performance with little effort directed toward making it happen. This rarely occurs, and disenchantment may set in. Similarly, if employees expect significant bonuses without major behavioral changes to increase performance, they are likely to become discouraged if bonuses do not materialize. Expectations and changed behavior are the key elements of success or failure.

Overall Review

We could state very simply that firms that do not develop the variables outlined in Chapter 1 to a significant degree would probably see their plans fail. Firms install gainsharing for many good as well as poor reasons. Those whose plans fail exhibit in high probability the following characteristics to an extensive degree:

A. *Organization Variables*

1. low trust or confidence in management, low accountability, low levels of participation, and lack of direction,

2. poor communications among and within departments, and communications patterns that are primarily from the top down (i.e., "don't listen" managers),
3. inability of people to relate to the system,
4. low control over revenue and unstable employment,
5. low levels of identity with organization, its past, present, and future opportunities and problems,
6. inequitable wages when compared with other employees and area firms.

B. *Social, Cultural, and Institutional Variables*

1. poor industrial relations and confidence; poor union relations,
2. low level needs for involvement and commitment.

C. *Financial Information and Competition Variables*

1. poor internal financial information system,
2. lack of accuracy of the financial system,
3. low levels of financial understanding or ability to relate to the system,
4. lack of knowledge of, or dedication to beat, the competition,
5. unstable conditions in output or input markets; declining markets,
6. severe competitive conditions and limited commitment to change,
7. severe governmental constraints.

The more these variables are present in a firm, the greater the risk of failure. But if one analyzes them carefully, one should not be surprised to note that they are the variables commonly cited as important to the success of any organization. That is, if the company is unsuccessful or lacks improvements, in all likelihood its gainsharing plan is doomed to failure unless drastic actions are taken. Thus, to be successful as a gainsharing company, an organizational need to change or to be better than others must exist. Without these attitudes, neither the employees nor management are likely to make the changes necessary on a continuing basis and the system will likely fail. The more a firm experiences the above problems, the greater the rush to failure.

Some Evidence from the Literature

Several studies have attempted to explore correlates of gain-sharing success. For example, in order to assess the differences in managerial attitudes, Ruh, Wallace, and Frost contrasted managerial attitudes in 10 firms with active gainsharing systems with those in 8 firms that had implemented and abandoned their plans. Their general findings were as follows:

1. Managers in firms that abandoned their plans perceived the rank-and-file employees to demonstrate significantly less judgment, creativity, responsibility, dependability, pride in performance, initiative, self-confidence, and willingness to change compared with managers in firms with continuing gainsharing plans.

2. Managers in firms that abandoned plans had less favorable attitudes toward participative decision making than continuing firms' managers. The same results were found regarding the perceived impact of participation on morale and performance.[1]

Of the abandoned plan firms, the expectations of managers regarding success were negative either before or after installation. Nevertheless, the firms obviously did not sink into bankruptcy or experience other dire consequences as a result of gainsharing failure.

Although generally congruent with our predictions, the study did not validate any cause/effect variables in that the failure of the plans may have been caused by the poor attitudes or may have been the result of the plans. Obviously, such pregainsharing attitudes as these could spell failure. But variables outlined above could also have actually caused the abandonment of the plans and, as is often the case, differentiating and isolating the cause/effect variables is difficult.

White found a number of corroborative pieces of evidence in his study of 23 gainsharing firms, 12 of which had abandoned their plan at the time of the study.[2] All were manufacturing firms. Some of his major findings follow.

1. High levels of failure are associated with low levels of employee participation. That is, if participation is perceived by employees to be low, the plan is likely to be marginally effective and perhaps doomed to failure.

2. Larger size does not seem to be a major factor for failure. Obviously, larger firms must be committed to significant communications and participation.

3. Low levels of managerial confidence in participative man-

agement are strongly associated with failure or marginal success. This variable should be useful in predicting gainsharing success if the system is participation-oriented.

4. The longer the plan is in existence, the less likely that the firm will abandon it. High expectations of immediate change tend to lead to disappointments. (Some longstanding firms do of course eventually abandon the plan because of economic downturns, managerial changes at the top, and so on.)

5. When installing a plan, realistic favorable expectations are important. Consequently, organizations with poor employee attitudes should not be selected for gainsharing plans. Getting the proper people involved at the beginning is also important.

6. If a high-level executive does not take a leading role, the plan's failure probability increases.

7. Technology does not seem to be positively or negatively related to failure.

Numerous other researchers have hypothesized problem areas and possible failure from a series of cases or conjectures over the years. Although these are not definitive, they provide valuable insights into the forces that may play in an actual situation and indicate where possible problems may arise. Problem areas are not listed in order of importance but generally expand on the studies discussed above.

1. poor calculation,[3]
2. lack of bonuses or opportunities to earn them,[4]
3. poor union/management cooperation and leadership,[5]
4. lack of supervisors' commitment,[6]
5. management defensiveness,[7]
6. lack of management's commitment of time, money, or enthusiasm,[8]
7. little perceived need to change or be different,[9]
8. poor communications or information sharing,[10]
9. lack of support for continuance from the top of the organization.[11]

The evidence seems to substantiate many of our propositions. If future researchers and businessmen use the model shown in Chapter 1, we feel that most of the variables included there will provide extremely useful information in predicting both success and failure. A successful gainsharing system does not occur by chance but is carefully developed and nurtured over the years. It can survive managerial succession if support from the top is high.

Three Other Studies

In the following sections three analyses made by Ross are examined based on studies completed. The first is a general study of accountants and supervisors. The second is a record of an actual failure, where the employees voted for abandoning the plan after a year's trial period. The third situation is a comparison between a successful plan in a very trying situation and a plan of limited success. The data and identity of all are disguised for purposes of anonymity.

Study 1. Accountants and Supervisors Contrasted

In an attempt to partially validate primarily the financial aspects of our model, a group of 22 accountants (mostly controllers) and supervisors at existing gainsharing firms were requested to rank a set of 22 variables from very important (1) to very unimportant (5) to gainsharing success. These variables ranged from bonus earning opportunities (number 1) to departmental goal setting (number 22). A day was then spent discussing the implications of the findings. The overall findings are outlined in Exhibit 5.1.

Regarding areas of significant differences between the two groups, five areas in particular stand out. These are:

1. accuracy of standards (ranked 2.6 by accountants versus 1.4 by supervisors),
2. knowledge of competition (2.8 versus 1.8),
3. government constraints (3.2 versus 2.3),
4. control over sales growth (2.5 versus 1.6),
5. current pay levels (2.5 versus 1.4).

In all cases, supervisors perceived these five areas to be of more importance than did accountants. Each was discussed in detail to find the reasons for the differences and how to close the gap. The results follow.

In most cases, standards do not affect the bonus directly. If they do, then their accuracy is very important, even as perceived by accountants. If they are just tools of performance expectations, then they are less important directly to gainsharing as perceived

Exhibit 5.1   Variables Important to Gainsharing Success/Failure

	MEANS	
	ACCOUNTANTS	SUPERVISORS
1. Bonus earning opportunities	1.6	1.4
2. Understanding of the calculation	1.9	2.2
3. Accuracy of standards	2.6	1.4
4. Knowledge of competition	2.8	1.8
5. Stability of selling market	2.3	1.6
6. Trust in accounting staff	1.7	1.4
7. Market growth potential	2.4	1.6
8. Simplicity of calculation	2.7	1.8
9. Type of work force	2.4	2.0
10. Government constraints	3.2	2.3
11. Knowledge of company's (plant's) performance	1.3	1.2
12. Accuracy of production/inventory control system	2.0	1.4
13. Trust in accounting system	1.3	1.2
14. Stability of materials market	2.6	1.8
15. Success of company (profit)	1.3	1.4
16. Product pricing practices	1.9	1.6
17. Frequency of new products	2.0	1.8
18. Control over sales growth	2.5	1.6
19. Current pay levels	2.5	1.4
20. Stability of employment	1.9	1.4
21. Departmental performance feedback	1.4	1.2
22. Departmental goal setting	1.6	1.2

Scale: 1 = Very Important
2 = Important
3 = Undecided
4 = Unimportant
5 = Very Unimportant

Highly ranked by both groups included:
1. Bonus earning opportunities,
2. Trust in accounting staff,
3. Knowledge of company's (plant's) performance,
4. Trust in accounting system,
5. Success of company (profit),
6. Departmental performance feedback,
7. Departmental goal setting.
(Obviously, any actions or programs directed in these areas should contribute significantly to success or failure if the results are validated for all groups of managers.)

by the participants. Supervisors perceived accuracy of standards to be more important to success than did accountants. But everyone agreed that accurate standards are important to a successful firm for a variety of reasons. Most agreed on the undesirability of standards that are too loose. Supervisors also seemed to want to become more involved in the whole standards area, which would be a good opportunity for more involvement. No significant ideas were offered to help people to overcome the fear of changing standards.

Regarding control over sales growth, supervisors again believed that this was more important, due mainly to inefficiencies that result when production is pushed too hard to increase sales. This probably affects a supervisor's tasks more than the accountant's. Supervisors desire more stability. One participant compared uncontrolled growth to a form of cancer.

Supervisors also believed pay levels to be more important because low pay makes it difficult to retain employees. They have a strong need to maintain a stable and skilled work force.

Knowledge of competition was extensively discussed. Some points made included: (1) accountants more than supervisors realize how complex this issue is, (2) this may be more important to sales than to production, and (3) the area needs to be more heavily emphasized for all gainsharing firms of the future.

Although differences occurred regarding government constraints, both groups relegated this to a low status.

Although the differences between accountants and supervisors regarding trust of accounting staff and understanding of the calculation were not great, the participants believed that both are of about equal importance.

People can relate to broader calculations but they are frustrated by their inability to do much about them. An effort must be made to get to the lowest common denominator to increase understanding, and accountants probably do a poor job in this area.

Most participants agreed that one need not have a bonus in the short run but that expectations for a future bonus are important. (Some newer gainsharing participants disagreed, since the bonus is a common goal.) Some perceived the bonus as an add-on but some did not; goal clarity is at issue here. Others viewed the participative management aspect as the most important aspect. But how far can one go without a bonus? There was much disagreement on this point.

The question was asked, Do people really want to be involved? Movement is toward more participation even if workers resist. Many employees want more from their job than just money. But it takes much effort to get them to participate in a gainsharing system. If they do become involved, problems can result if they don't continue their involvement.

Another inquiry area focused on whether a plan could be successful if everyone knew that a bonus would not be earned without a large layoff or other drastic measures. Much disagreement existed on this point. Most belived that it would be a mistake to sell it on this basis.

The key question brought up by most was, What turns an employee or group on? This is the key to measuring success. To some it is money or bonus, but to others, it might be involvement or recognition. If employees relate strongly to bonuses, then they should understand why one is or is not being earned.

An extensive discussion took place regarding whether people should know who is and who is not earning or contributing to the bonus, a possibility to document with some calculations. This can be divisive but also can be quite constructive, depending on how used. Who really earned and contributed to a bonus is frequently difficult to establish because of the complexities of cause and effect.

Likewise, considerable differences were expressed regarding how much individual recognition should occur. Most agreed that the best recognition is the type in which the entire organization is recognized. Effort should also concentrate on both low and high performers.

All of these areas need considerable research before definitive answers can be developed.

Study 2. A Case of Failure

This is a fairly brief case of a gainsharing failure. The background is as follows:

The firm in question was a small, 60-employee manufacturing firm, involved primarily in assembly operation, located in a depressed area of a large city. The highest profit in the five years prior to the installation of the plan was less than 1 percent of sales before corporate charges and interest. The firm had made no profits during four of the five years. The work force consisted of minority workers with low skill levels; wages were approximately 50 cents above minimum wage requirements. Although the work force was unionized, the firm received no interference from the local. In fact, it succeeded in obtaining wage concessions. It was further hampered by weak financial information systems. Training and other activities were severely limited by financial conditions. Its market was declining and sales were decreasing in absolute dollars. The firm was part of a major conglomerate and was given a "last chance" to improve its performance.

A behavioral evaluation was conducted, including an employee survey. A management team effectiveness profile indicated low evaluation of fellow managers, especially of the president. A survey of employee attitudes indicated the following key summarized results. The survey was on a five-point Likert-type of scale with 5 being the highest mean and 1 the lowest.

	Mean
1. How satisfied would you say you are with your earnings?	2.36
2. How would you rate cooperation between departments?	2.40
3. How would you rate communications between departments?	2.20
4. To what extent do you have confidence and trust in your supervisor?	2.90
5. Is management willing to accept suggestions you make?	2.74
6. Is the take-home pay here as good as similar companies in the area?	2.20
7. Do you feel that the pay for your job is fair compared with the pay for other jobs in this plant?	2.10
8. The feeling of satisfactory relationships with management?	2.20
9. How much confidence and trust is there in management?	2.00
10. How much concern is there for controlling costs?	2.60

Obviously, conditions were poor for the installation of a plan on several key variables:

1. Because of very low earnings, employees would probably view the plan as a substitute for equitable wages.
2. Poor communications were apparent.
3. There was little trust in management and little reason to trust them.
4. Supervisors were poorly trained.
5. There was low concern for controlling costs.
6. Written comments indicated severe feelings of discrimination, pressure for performance, and poor equipment.

Additional problems centered on inadequate available time or money. Finally, neither employees nor managers perceived a real need to change in spite of the financial conditions. Also, they had low levels of expectations in general on eight key questions regarding such activities as costs, quality, productivity, job security, and need for involvement.

When the plan was finally presented to the employees following completion of the work of a steering committee, a confidential vote was taken for a trial period of one year. The vote was exactly 75 percent, too low a commitment for good initial success. (Note: it was requested that the president not be present or many employees would definitely vote against the plan.)

This was, of course, a high-risk situation at best as outlined earlier. However, the plant and divisional management believed that little could be lost by trying the plan even though they were cautioned against thinking it could work. Quite simply, they were told to do something—and plans had saved other firms from going under.

The results of the first and only year of operation are outlined below:

1. A major layoff in the first month of operation resulted in a one-third reduction of the work force. Three layoffs occurred the first year.
2. Bonuses were not paid until the fourth month of operation (5.1 percent). This was the largest of four bonuses, the rest consisted of 3.5 percent, 5.0 percent, and 2.2 percent of wages, or about 1.5 percent total for the year.
3. Volume continued to erode over the previous year; backlogs continued to erode.
4. Wide fluctuations in sales and inventory made it difficult to evaluate whether direct labor productivity increased, but management believed that it had somewhat.
5. No one served as coordinator, and communications dropped substantially after the first few months, including feedback on suggestions.
6. No training programs were established for supervisors or team representatives. Some existing committees did not meet on a regular basis.
7. Supervisors were on the screening (plantwide) committee and dominated the discussions.
8. Indirect employees were not laid off anywhere near proportionally to direct labor employees.
9. Employees had much difficulty relating to gainsharing with the fluctuations in volume and employment.
10. Because of volume fluctuations and pressures to improve performance, production control apparently deteriorated.

11. Because of erratic volume, trust in management had probably deteriorated.
12. Little emphasis was placed on communications, including calculation education, feedback of performance, follow-up of suggestions.
13. Inconsistent supervision was a constant throughout.
14. Misunderstandings occurred between the office and factory.
15. Bickering among management continued to expand.
16. Less than 50 percent of employees submitted suggestions, and follow-up procedures were frequently not completed.
17. Wage increases were nominal.

Considering the above problems, there is little wonder that the employees voted the plan out in December, at the conclusion of the trial period. Management made no attempt to salvage either their own or their employees' commitment to the system.

Obviously, this is a perfect example of where not to install a plan. Most of the variables in our discussion above were obviously violated. A perceived need to change does not bring it about. In this particular case there was need for change in many areas. Although the firm went through the motions of instituting a plan, management obviously missed the opportunity to make a major change.

A final note to this summary is appropriate. In spite of the problems outlined above, operating profit for the first 11 months went from a negative $57,000 to a plus $114,000. Was the plan a total failure? Perhaps it did help to save the firm from extinction although no one would certainly consider it a success.

Study 3. Contrasting Two Firms

The difficulty of measuring success or failure will now be considered by contrasting two firms, one a traditionally successful, fairly high bonus-earning firm and the other in a poor market with a very competitive and low bonus-earning situation. Most unbiased observers, however, would probably note the lower bonus gain-sharing firm as having a much more successful plan when compared with the other. Firm A is the lower bonus-earning firm and Firm B the higher, as depicted in Exhibit 5.2.

Financial and Bonus Performance. To simplify the discussion, the presentation of these two cases is in summary form and limited

Exhibit 5.2.   Comparison of Firms A and B: Recent Three-Year Period

	FIRM A	FIRM B
Change in number of employees	(365) no change	(150) 5% increase
Man-hours per unit of output	24.2% increase	N/A
Scrap	41.1% decrease	N/A
Sales change	51% increase	34% increase
Average bonus	6.1%	16.2%
Monthly average number of suggestions	29	N/A
Turnover	29.2% decrease	N/A
Wage increases (simple)	21.0%	27.3%
Profit changes (absolute)	471%	23.2%
Sales per employee	54% increase	34% increase
Average assets	11.6% increase	28.6% increase

to three recent years where both behavioral and financial information are available. What follows is some financial and bonus-related information for the three-year period. Information not available is indicated by N/A.

When reviewing Exhibit 5.2, one can see that Firm A is really doing much better in spite of the much lower bonus (6.1 percent compared to 16.2 percent). The greater amount of information that is available from Firm A reflects its greater emphasis on measurement, goal setting, and accountability in general. Even though it is in a somewhat depressed industry compared with Firm B, its growth is measurably more impressive.

Behavioral Analysis. Since most contemporary gainsharing systems emphasize employee involvement and management commitment, we believe that it is important to evaluate this process through employee surveys. Exhibit 5.3 summarizes some comparisons between Firms A and B on a few of the variables covered in a comprehensive survey.

In most areas, Firm A scores significantly higher on most questions than does Firm B—but not always, in spite of its greater commitment to communications and involvement. Undoubtedly, the type of work force has some impact on this effort as does the general wage level. Firm A also has a part-time coordinator for the plan while Firm B does not.

Since Firm A has had the plan in operation for only three years, it was decided to inquire into the operation of the plan in more depth. Considering the low level of wages, the attitudes are quite good regarding the operation of the plan. Exhibit 5.4 provides additional evidence supporting our earlier discussion.

Unfortunately, quantitative surveys often do not "collect" as

Exhibit 5.3   Two Gainsharing Firms—A Comparison of Attitudes

	PERCENT POSITIVE	
	FIRM A: SUCCESSFUL	FIRM B: MARGINAL
1. Is management willing to accept suggestions you make?	87	86
2. Does your supervisor ask your opinion when a problem comes up that involves your work?	75	66
3. How often do you offer suggestions about improving the operations of your job, work area, or department?	86	66
4. How important to you is the opportunity to participate in decisions concerning your job, work area, or department?	96	94
5. How well do you understand the Gainsharing Bonus calculation?	81	60
6. How well do you understand the Gainsharing Committee system?	80	65
7. How well do you understand the suggestion system?	86	78
8. Are suggestions processed quickly and efficiently?	40	47
9. Your committee representatives do everything they can to get suggestions from employees.	60	42
10. Your committee representatives put a lot of time and effort in their committee activies.	54	28
11. Committee representatives know what is expected of them.	78	54
12. Committee representatives keep us well-informed about the Plan (bonuses, problem areas, and so on).	63	59
13. Gainsharing encourages us to work as a team.	87	79
14. Gainsharing encourages an individual to use his/her experience and knowledge on the job.	85	83
15. Most employees don't really care what the reports show, just if we have a bonus or not.	39	27
16. Many suggestions are put into effect immediately without being written upon a suggestion form.	46	56
17. The Gainsharing Plan helps improve communications.	72	63
18. Cooperation between departments is good.	70	59
19. Communication between departments is good.	65	57

much of the general attitudes as one might like unless the number of questions is expanded greatly. On both of the surveys, written comments were also requested regarding the general operation of the plan in general. Although the comments were obviously se-

Exhibit 5.4 Satisfaction, Supervision, and Gainsharing Perceptions: Firm A

GENERAL SATISFACTION   PERCENT POSITIVE

1. All in all, how satisfied are you with your company? — 87
2. All in all, how satisfied are you with your job? — 88
3. All in all, how satisfied are you with your supervisor? — 89
4. How satisfied would you say you are with your earnings? — 46
5. How do outsiders feel about your company? — 74

ABOUT YOUR SUPERVISOR

6. To what extent do you have confidence and trust in your supervisor? — 82
7. How well does your supervisor do planning and scheduling of your work? — 78
8. How well does your supervisor handle the people side of his/her job (giving recognition, building teamwork, giving feedback, etc.)? — 75

GAINSHARING OPERATION

9. Participation has increased under the Gainsharing Plan. — 83
10. The Gainsharing Plan helps improve cooperation. — 80
11. The Gainsharing Plan helps improve communications. — 72
12. The Gainsharing Plan helps increase quality. — 81
13. Management is committed to the plan. — 81
14. Employees are committed to the plan. — 77
15. The Gainsharing Plan is good for us here at _____ . — 88
16. The Gainsharing Plan has made this a more enjoyable place to work. — 67
17. The calculation fairly reflects performance. — 71

lected, they do reflect the general differences in attitudes that exist at the two firms. Firm A's employees are much more positive in spite of a poor market situation and low wages.

Knowledge of the Calculation. As part of the survey at both firms, an attempt was made to investigate how much each of the work forces understood about the calculation since some researchers have stated that understanding is important to building trust. Firm A had 14 true, false, don't-know questions on the calculation whereas Firm B had 11. The average respondents to Firm A marked 59 percent of the questions correctly whereas 49 percent of Firm B's were recorded correctly. This area is of importance to both firms but has received more attention in Firm A.

This section evaluated and contrasted two firms. Firm A is much more committed to the Gainsharing concept than is Firm B, but the results do not always indicate the difference, perhaps because of conflicting variables such as pay, geographical area, work force characteristics, and size of bonus. Situations like this illustrate the difficulty of evaluating gainsharing plans.

Summary

Obviously, the perceptions of success and failure of a plan become very complex as the reasons for installing it are investigated. If gainsharing is installed solely as a form of contingent compensation with little effort directed toward building commitment, communications, employee involvement, or even need to improve in an already successful firm, one should not be surprised when little improvement occurs. The key is to develop management and nonmanagement commitment to the system while still maintaining reasonable expectations.

To summarize, it is important to agree on philosophy of installation, commitment required from everyone and a structure of involvement/communications which reinforce the entire system. Continuous reviews of these and other variables are extremely important to long-term plan success.

Notes

1. R.A. Ruh, R.L. Wallace, and C.F. Frost, "Management Attitudes and the Scanlon Plan," Industrial Relations, 1973, 282–288.
2. J.K. White, "The Scanlon Plan: Causes and Correlates of Success," Academy of Management Journal, June 1979, 292–312.
3. J.J. Jehring, "A Contrast Between Two Approaches to Total Systems Incentives," California Management Review, 1967, 7–14; B.E. Moore, A Plant-Wide Productivity Plan in Action: Three Years of Experience with the Scanlon Plan (Washington, D.C.: National Commission on Productivity and Work Quality, 1975); T.L. Ross and G.M. Jones, "An Approach to Increased Productivity: The Scanlon Plan," Financial Executives, February 1972, 23–29; A. Ashburn, "Devising Real Incentives for Productivity," American Machinist, June 1978, 115–30.
4. R. Helfgott, Group Wage Incentives: Experience with the Scanlon Plan, (New York: Industrial Relations Counselors, Industrial Relations Memo, 1962); Ashburn, "Devising Real Incentives," note 3, above.
5. R.W. Davenport, "Enterprise for Everyman," Fortune, January 1950, 50–58; R.B. Gray, "The Scanlon Plan—A Case Study," British Journal of Industrial Relations 9, 191–213; E. Puckett, "Productivity Achievements—A Measure of Success," in The Scanlon Plan: A Frontier in Labor Management Cooperation, ed. F.G. Lesieur (Cambridge, Mass.: Technology Press of M.I.T. and New York: Wiley, 1958); Helfgott, Group-Wage Incentives, note 4, above;

H. Thierry, "The Scanlon Plan: A Field Experimental Approach" (Symposium, 81st Annual Convention, American Psychological Association, 1973).
6. Moore, *A Plant-Wide Productivity Plan in Action: Three Years of Experience with the Scanlon Plan*, note 3, above; Helfgott, "Group Wage Incentives," note 4, above; Thierry, "The Scanlon Plan," note 5, above; Ashburn, "Devising Real Incentives," note 3, above.
7. H.R. Northrup and H.A. Young, "The Causes of Industrial Peace Revisited," *Industrial and Labor Relations Review*, October 1968, 31–47; R.J. Doyle, "A New Look at the Scanlon Plan," *Management Accounting*, September 1970, 48; F. Whyte, *Money and Motivation* (New York: Harper and Brothers, 1955).
8. Moore, *A Plant-Wide Productivity Plan in Action: Three Years of Experience with the Scanlon Plan*, note 3, above; C.F. Frost, J.H. Wakely, and R.A. Ruh, *The Scanlon Plan for Organization Development: Identity, Participation, and Equity* (East Lansing: Michigan State University Press, 1974); G.P. Shultz, "Variation in Environment and the Scanlon Plan," in *The Scanlon Plan: A Frontier in Labor Management Cooperation*, ed. F.G. Lesieur (Cambridge, Mass.: Technology Press of M.I.T. and New York: Wiley, 1958); A.J. Geare, "Productivity From Scanlon-Type Plans," *The Academy of Management Review*, July 1976, 99–108; Helfgott, "Group Wage Incentives," note 4, above.
9. Helfgott, "Group Wage Incentives," note 4, above; C.F. Frost, "The Scanlon Plan: Anyone for Free Enterprise?," *MSU Business Topics*, Winter 1978, 25–33.
10. G.S. Burtnett, "A Study of Causal Relationships Between Organizational Variables and Personal Influence Variables During the Implementation of Scanlon Plans," (Ph.D. dissertation, Michigan State University, 1973); Helfgott, "Group Wage Incentives," note 4, above; Ashburn, "Devising Real Incentives," note 3, above.
11. G.P. Schultz, "Worker Participation on Production Problems: A Discussion of Experience with the Scanlon Plan," *Personnel*, November 1951, 209–11.

Chapter 6

Making Productivity Programs Last

Paul S. Goodman and James W. Dean, Jr.

In the 1970s and 1980s we saw a proliferation of new forms of work organization projects designed to improve on productivity and quality of working life. In many ways the new forms were revolutionary because they represented fundamental changes in how work should be organized, in how organizations might be designed, and in the nature of labor-management relationships. Some examples of these new forms are discussed below.

Autonomous work groups represent one new form of work organization. Basically, these are self-governing groups organized by process, place, or product. There is a substantial shift in authority and decision making as the group takes over such responsibilities as hiring, discipline, and allocation of production tasks. Most autonomous groups encourage job switching. Pay is based on knowledge of jobs rather than actual job performance.[1]

Labor-management problem-solving groups represent another common form of change. In this type of program, a hierarchy of linked problem-solving groups is superimposed on the existing organizational structure. The groups are generally arranged following the current organizational structure, with lower-level groups dealing with problems specific to their areas, and higher-level groups dealing with problems that cut across multiple organizational units. These groups meet regularly. Products from these groups include,

This chapter is adapted from B.E. Graham-Moore and T.L. Ross, *Productivity Gainsharing*, Chapter 8, "Making Productivity Programs Last," by P.S. Goodman and J.W. Dean, Jr. (Englewood Cliffs, N.J.: Prentice-Hall, 1983).

for example, work simplification, flex-time projects, and new performance appraisal systems.

Companywide gainsharing programs represent another organizational change strategy that has proliferated over the past 20 years. These programs, which typically include organizational changes and new monetary reward systems, are designed to improve productivity.

Many other organizational changes have been introduced during this period. They all represent fundamental changes in an organization's communication, decision-making, authority, and reward systems. They also create fundamental changes in the relationships among people within the organization.

Beyond merely enumerating work organization projects, we now turn our attention to the focus of this chapter—whether these programs last. That is, after some period of initial success, do these productivity programs persist or remain institutionalized? Are they just temporary phenomena? Why do some projects decline while others do not? What factors shape whether new forms of work organization have some long-term viability?

Significance

The importance of understanding more about the concept of persistence of new programs or institutionalization of change should be apparent. If one is interested in bringing about long-term change in productivity, in quality of working life, and in labor-management relationships, then we must know more about why some change programs remain viable while others decline.

Unfortunately, there are few well-developed frameworks for understanding this problem area.[2] So it is difficult to go to the organizational literature to gain insights, in some systematic way, of why change programs do or do not decline over time. Yet there is some evidence that some of these new forms of work organization projects do not last.[3] Goodman and Dean examined the persistence of change in a heterogeneous sample of new forms of work organization projects. They selected organizations in which the change program had been successfully introduced and where some positive benefits had been identified. They interviewed participants four to five years after the project had been implemented. They wanted to know whether the change activities had persisted. Only one-third of the change programs designed to increase productivity and

quality of working life exhibited some reasonable level of persistence. Two-thirds were either nonexistent or in decline. The
program that exhibited the strongest persistence was a Scanlon
Plan.

Of course, it is difficult to ascertain any national percentages
about the number of these change programs that exhibit persistence. We will never know exactly how many of these new projects
will decline and fail. However, common sense and growing empirical findings suggest that maintaining change is a significant
problem for labor leaders, managers, and practitioners of organizational change.

Institutionalization

A Definition

Institutionalization in this chapter is examined in terms of
specific behaviors. We are assuming here that the persistence of
employee involvement-type change programs can be studied by
analyzing the persistence of specific behaviors associated with each
program. For example, job switching is a set of behaviors often
associated with autonomous work groups. To say that these and
other behaviors associated with a program are practiced over time
is to say that program is institutionalized. An institutionalized act,
then, is defined as a behavior that is performed by two or more
individuals, persists over time, and exists as part of the social reality
or culture of the organization.

When we say that a behavior, such as making productivity
suggestions by a high percentage of the work force for many years,
is "part of the organization," we mean that members of the organization know how to make productivity suggestions, like to do it,
and consider it appropriate for all its members to make suggestions.
Remember, institutionalized behavior does not depend on any one
individual; it is an organizational phenomenon.

In summary, the defining characteristics of institutionalization
of an organizational change program are performance of the change
program behaviors, persistence of these behaviors, and the incorporation of these behaviors in the daily functioning of the organization.

Degrees of Institutionalization

It should be clear from our definition of institutionalization that an act is all or nothing. Yet, an act may vary in terms of its persistence, the number of people in the organization performing the act, and the degree to which it exists as part of the organization. The problem in some of the current literature on change is the use of the words success and failure. This language clouds the crucial issue of representing and explaining degrees or levels of institutionalization. Most of the organizational cases we have reviewed cannot be described by simple labels of success or failure. Rather, we find various degrees of institutionalization.

The basic questions are: What do we mean by degrees of institutionalization? How do we measure these degrees?

We have identified five factors that constitute the degree of institutionalization.

1. *Knowledge of the behaviors.* Here we are interested merely in how many people know about these behaviors, and how much they know. Do they know how to perform these behaviors? Do they know the purposes of the behaviors? For example, making productivity suggestions is a part of many gainsharing programs. However, if only some people know that they are supposed to make suggestions, the change program is not very institutionalized. This is why knowledge of the behaviors is important.

2. *Performance.* Here we are interested in how many people perform the behaviors, and how often they perform them. This is not as simple as it sounds. First, some behaviors are supposed to occur more often than others. A labor-management committee, for example, may be expected to meet occasionally, say, once a month, while team meetings are held weekly. This does not mean that team meetings are more institutionalized than the labor-management committee because they are more frequent. Second, some behaviors are supposed to be performed by more people than others. Most employees would be involved in team meetings, but only a few would take part in a labor-management committee. The idea is not merely to count the number of persons or the frequency of the behaviors, but rather to compare numbers and frequency to the levels required by the change program. Only then can reasonable comparisons be made.

3. *Preferences for the behaviors.* Here we are interested in

how much people either like or dislike performing the behavior. In well-institutionalized change programs, most organizational members will like the critical program behaviors. In change programs on the decline, negative feelings are generally expressed toward the critical program behaviors.

4. *Normative consensus.* This aspect of institutionalization measures two levels of awareness among individuals in an organization: (1) that other people are performing the behaviors, and (2) that other people feel they should perform the behaviors. Normative consensus means the work group expects all members to support the expected program behaviors (e.g., suggestion making).

5. *Values.* The final measure of institutionalization is the extent to which people have developed values about the behaviors in the change program. Values are general ideas about how people ought to behave. For example, many change programs include behaviors consistent with the values of freedom and responsibility, as in autonomous work groups. In gainsharing, we expect to see the emergence and strengthening of values of cooperation, communication, and participation. The more people have developed these values, and the more aware they are that others have developed these values, the greater degree of institutionalization for the change program.

The five aspects above represent measures of the degree of institutionalization. But how do we combine them to get an overall measure? The answer is relatively simple, because the five aspects of institutionalization generally occur in the order we have presented above. People develop (1) knowledge about the behaviors, (2) they begin to perform them, (3) they start to develop feelings about the behaviors, (4) others come to be aware of these feelings, and (5) finally, values start to evolve concerning the behaviors. The further this sequence has progressed, the more the program has become institutionalized. Thus, in one program, people may know about the behaviors and perform them, but the other aspects of institutionalization may not be present. In another program, the behaviors may be known, performed, liked, and supported by norms and values. The latter program is obviously more institutionalized.

Summary

A change program designed to increase productivity and quality of working life is institutionalized when the behaviors required by it are performed by two or more persons over a period of time, and persist over time. We have argued that institutionalization is not an all-or-nothing question, but a matter of degree, and we have identified five aspects of institutionalization that measure the degree to which it has occurred. A program is institutionalized to the extent that it has progressed from levels of knowledge to performance, and finally to preferences, norms, and values that support the new institution.

Factors that Affect Institutionalization

Now that we have a way to represent the degree of institutionalization, we can try to explain how and why it happens. Why are some gainsharing programs more institutionalized than others? Five processes affect the degree of institutionalization. These processes are important in explaining why some programs decline, while others grow and persist over time. The processes are:

1. *Training.* This is a broad category, which includes any source which helps an employee learn about a program such as gainsharing.

2. *Commitment.* High-commitment individuals invest a lot of themselves into a gainsharing program, and they will resist attempts to change behaviors that facilitate such a program. Commitment toward a new form of work behavior is enhanced when people voluntarily select that behavior in some public context.

3. *Reward allocation.* This refers to what rewards are distributed in the program, who gives and who gets them, and when they are distributed.

4. *Diffusion.* This refers to the extension of productivity programs into new work areas. If a productivity program is introduced into Department A, and it is transferred to Department B, diffusion has occurred.

5. *Feedback and correction.* These refer to the processes by which the organization can assess the degree of institutionalization, feed back information, and take corrective action. Many organizations have no way of measuring how well their programs are doing. Therefore, they have no way of taking corrective actions. One advantage many gainsharing programs have are monthly bonus

meetings where progress of the program is reviewed and changes are initiated.

We believe that these five processes are the major factors in predicting the degree of institutionalization a program will attain. There are, however, other important factors that affect these five processes. They are the structure of the change program and its organizational characteristics. Structure of the change program means such things as the goals of the change, how general it is, the critical roles associated with the change (consultant, facilitator, and so on). Organizational characteristics are the existing arrangements in the organization prior to the change program. It is the canvas on which the program will be painted. Organizational characteristics include such things as work force skill level, labor-management relations, and existing values and norms. It should be emphasized that these factors are important only to the extent that they affect the five processes listed above. For a clear example, see Chapter 3, which assesses how organizational characteristics affect whether gain-sharing would "fit" into a particular organizational context.

Empirical Findings

This section will discuss the findings of the authors, as well as others, about the processes and other organizational factors related to institutionalization. We will consider findings about the processes, structure of the change, and organizational characteristics, to see if studies bear out what we have argued in the section above. The main results are from a study by Goodman and Dean,[4] but the findings of other authors have been included where appropriate.

Five Processes

Training

Training is providing information to organization members about new work behaviors. Training is important in three major situations: training as the program is started, retraining after the program has been in place for a while, and training of new incoming members of the organization. Most organizations do an extensive amount of initial training but are less consistent in retraining and in the training of new members.

Golembiewski and Carrigan report that retraining can lead to persistence.[5] In a program designed to change the practices of high-level managers in the sales division of a manufacturing firm, they found that a retraining exercise several months after the program was instituted strengthened the persistence of the program. Similarly, Ivancevich compared Management by Objectives programs in two large manufacturing firms.[6] One firm had a retraining exercise, while the other did not. After three years, the program in the former plant was more institutionalized. Goodman, in a study of a change project in an underground coal mine, reports that a decrease in frequency of training after the first year of the project contributed to its decline.[7] Organizations vary in their attention to training new members once a program is in place. Goodman and Dean[8] found that programs which trained new members were likely to be more institutionalized.

Commitment

Commitment refers to how much of themselves people are willing to invest in a new program. For example, a high degree of commitment toward a gainsharing program should increase the chances that behaviors would continue or be institutionalized. Commitment to a behavior is increased when people voluntarily select that behavior in some public context.[9] For example, an autonomous work-group program seemed to grow and develop when personal choices were carried out freely. Later in this program, when the organization required others to participate in the program, it began to decline. Also, it is found that programs offering more frequent commitment opportunities were more institutionalized than those with limited commitment opportunities. Ivancevich attributes the failure of a Management by Objectives program to lack of commitment by top management.[10] Walton, on the other hand, notes high levels of commitment in several successful programs of work innovation.[11] Other studies report that consistent levels of commitment throughout the organization are necessary for persistence of a change program designed to increase productivity and quality of working life.[12] Chapter 7 reviews seventeen years of experience with DeSoto's Scanlon plan, wherein commitment by top management has contributed significantly to gainsharing viability.

Reward Allocation

This is the process by which rewards are distributed to employees in connection with the change program. Three aspects of the reward allocation process are important in understanding institutionalization: (1) the types of rewards that are available, (2) the links between behaviors and rewards, and (3) problems of inequity in the distribution of the rewards. The types of rewards related to work are generally categorized by psychologists as extrinsic or intrinsic. Extrinsic rewards, such as pay and promotion, are given by someone else. Intrinsic rewards, such as feelings of responsibility and accomplishment, come from within the individual. Many organizational change programs have been based on the assumption that intrinsic rewards are sufficient for institutionalization. However, Goodman and Walton have questioned this assumption.[13] Programs that combine both extrinsic and intrinsic rewards have attained the highest degree of institutionalization,[14] while programs with intrinsic rewards alone have been less institutionalized. Of the programs evaluated, gainsharing made available both types of rewards.

The second aspect of reward allocation concerns the link between the behaviors required by the change program and the rewards. It is important that rewards be linked to the actual performance of the behaviors, as opposed to mere participation in the program. We have found that there is a higher degree of institutionalization in programs where the link between performance and rewards is strong. This is consistent with statements by Vroom and Lawler concerning reward allocation.[15] Reward allocation links are found to be psychologically strong in gainsharing studies.

A final aspect of reward allocation is the potential for problems of inequity. Inequity problems occur when employees feel they are not being fairly compensated for the work they are doing. Results of studies have shown that new programs often become complicated by these problems. For example, Locke, Sirota and Wolfson report on a job-enrichment program in a government agency that did not become institutionalized.[16] The major reason was that workers were not compensated financially for the new skills they had learned. It is important to note that they had never been promised more money, but the fact that they were accomplishing more for the same pay was perceived as inequitable. Goodman reports similar problems developed among autonomous work groups in a coal mine.[17] Part of the program involved job switching, whereby each new member would eventually learn all the jobs in the crew. The problem evolved because the entire crew was to be paid eventually at the same (higher) rate of pay originally earned only by certain crew members. Since it had taken years for some of the workers to attain this rate, they felt it inequitable that the other crew members should come up so easily. This contributed to the decline in the change program. There are no reported problems with inequity and gainsharing. Its reward allocation structure complements the overall organization reward system. Obviously, if the overall system is unfair, gainsharing will reinforce those areas of inequity.

Diffusion

Diffusion refers to the spread of the change from one part of an organization to another. Diffusion is significant because the more the change program becomes diffused, the stronger the level of institutionalization. As long as the program is restricted to one part of the organization, people may not feel compelled to take it seriously, or they may object to it. But as diffusion occurs, people in other parts of the organization will begin to consider whether they should participate. As the program spreads, there also are chances for counterattacks on its validity.

The importance of diffusion for institutionalization has been noted by Goodman in the coal mine study mentioned above.[18] In this case, when the intervention failed to diffuse beyond the original target group, it was perceived as inappropriate and failed to become institutionalized. Similar findings have been reported in a study of work teams in several plants of a large manufacturing company.[19] When the innovations continued to be limited to a few parts of the organization, they were seen as inappropriate to the company as a whole and failed to become institutionalized. However, the researchers in this study caution against diffusion that is too rapid, without the supports of widespread understanding, acceptance, and resources that are needed for such an effort. Without these requisites, the program will collapse under its own weight. In general, then, a moderate course must be found between no diffusion and diffusion that is too ambitious for the resources supporting it. When applied to gainsharing however, diffusion is slightly different, since gainsharing is organizationwide by definition, and the entire organization is affected at the same time. Nevertheless, in multiplant organizations, diffusion of gainsharing across similar plants is important to ensure long-run viability of these programs.

Feedback and Correction

Feedback and correction are the processes by which an organization finds out how well the program is doing and takes steps to correct problems that have emerged. One of the common findings was that what actually occurred in change programs was often different from what was intended.[20] The organizations had seldom established any formal way of detecting whether the intended change was in place. Only in the most institutionalized programs in our study did mechanisms exist for feedback and correction. Walton says that lack of feedback and correction mechanisms is a major cause of the failure to institutionalize.[21] In another study, feedback mechanisms were in place, so that information about the program was available.[22] However, no one did anything about the problems that were detected. Perhaps the information was not available to those who had the power to do something. Or perhaps the information was available to them, but they had other reasons for their inaction. In any case, both sensing and correction mechanisms are important in attaining a high degree of institutionalization.

Structure of the Change

Now that we have discussed the findings about the processes, we can discuss some of the factors that affect the processes. First, we will discuss the structure of the change, which refers to the unique aspects of the change program. Specifically, we will talk about the goals of the programs, the formal mechanisms associated with the programs, the level of intervention in the programs, how consultants were used, and sponsorship for the programs.

Goals

One way to characterize goals is by whether they are specific and limited or general and diffuse. In our study,[23] we found that programs designed to improve productivity or quality of working life with specific goals became more institutionalized than those with diffuse goals.

Another way to characterize goals is by whether they are common or complementary. Common goals are those desired by both parties to the change (for example, improving safety). Complementary goals aim to give each party something it wants, but the parties want different things (for example, productivity for management and bonuses for employees). In *Assessing Organizational Change*, Goodman indicates that common goals can contribute better to institutionalization.[24]

Formal Mechanisms

Most change programs have some new organizational form and procedures associated with them. These include, for example, the self-governing decisions made by autonomous work groups and by gainsharing production and screening committees. Here we are interested in how formal these arrangements are. For example, are meetings scheduled in advance? Are procedures written down? In general, we have found that programs with more formal mechanisms and procedures attain higher levels of institutionalization. For example, well-institutionalized gainsharing organizations operate with a "Memo of Understanding," which describes the goals, policies, procedures, and structure of gainsharing.

Level of Intervention

Here we are interested in whether the productivity program was introduced in a part of the organization, or in the whole organization. In our study, programs that were introduced throughout the organizational unit became more institutionalized than programs limited to a part of the organization. One of the problems with smaller-scale intervention is that people from other parts of the organization sometimes attempt to sabotage the program. This was true in four of the organizations that we studied, none of whose programs were very institutionalized.[25]

Consultants

Many organizations that undertake a change program employ a consultant to help them. Some organizations use consultants for considerably longer periods than others. We found that firms that rely on consultants for a long time are less able to develop their own capacity for managing the program. Consequently, after the consultant leaves, they are less able to institutionalize the program.

The greater the dependence on the consultant, the less successful the program.

Sponsorship

Another factor that appears to affect the degree of institutionalization is the presence of a sponsor. The sponsor is an organizational member in a position of power who initiates the program, makes sure that resources are devoted to it, and defends it against attacks from others in the organization. If the sponsor leaves the organization, often no one steps in to perform these necessary functions, thus making it harder for institutionalization to occur.

The withdrawal of sponsorship can arise from common organizational practices. For example, Crockett reports a major organizational intervention in the State Department, in which substantial changes were observed to persist for years.[26] However, when the initiator of the project, a political appointee, left office, the organization reverted to its traditional form. The new administrator was not sympathetic to the values and the structure of the change program. As support and legitimacy of the program decreased, the degree of institutionalization declined. Similar effects are reported by Walton[27] and Levine.[28] In some cases, the sponsor left temporarily;[29] in other cases, the sponsors focused attention on other organizational matters.[30] In all cases, however, the persistence of the new structures declined.

The key factor is not so much the success of sponsors, but whether the replacement provides the same level of sponsorship. In some gainsharing programs we have observed, the programs exhibit institutionalization although there was natural turnover at high plant levels. In these cases, sponsorship from the new manager was still in place.

Organizational Characteristics

Organizational characteristics are those aspects of the organization that exist prior to the change program and have an effect on the degree of institutionalization a program can attain. These characteristics are important to the extent that they affect the five processes we have discussed—training, commitment, reward allocation, diffusion, and feedback/correction. Chapters 3 and 4 focus on those organizational characteristics known to affect gainsharing success and failure.

Congruence with Organizational Values and Structure

Whatever the nature of the change program, one important factor for institutionalization is the degree of congruence or incongruence between the change program and existing organizational characteristics in general, the more congruence, the greater the likelihood of institutionalization. Various organizational characteristics may be important in understanding congruence. In all cases studied by the authors, congruence between the change program and management philosophy led to higher degrees of institutionalization.

Several other authors have come to similar conclusions about congruence and institutionalization. Fadem suggests that when there is a great degree of incongruence between the change program and corporate policies, the project is less likely to be institutionalized.[31] Seashore and Bowers explain the level of institutionalization in terms of the congruence between the organizational change and the values and motives of the individual participant.[32] They found that a higher level of institutionalization resulted when the changes were more congruent with the values and motives of the employees. Mohrman, et al., studied organizational change in a school system.[33] They found that change programs were more likely to become institutionalized when the intervention structure was congruent with the existing authority system. Walton has shown that in some change programs, there is a gap between the behaviors required by the change and the skills possessed by the employees.[34] The greater the gap (or the more incongruence), the lower the expected degree of institutionalization.

Levine describes a set of innovations attempted at a state university.[35] Some of the innovations were more congruent with organizational norms and values than others. Over time, those innovations that were congruent were more likely to persist than those that were incongruent. Similar conclusions were drawn by Warwick and Crockett about a major organizational change undertaken in the State Department.[36] The new structure favored the taking of initiative by lower level officials, although this was incongruent with the reward system. Not surprisingly, the change did not last. Finally, Miller shows that a change program must be congruent with cultural norms and values, as well as with those

peculiar to the organization.[37] An organizational innovation in several weaving mills in India was hampered because it did not provide
for the workers' need for recognition by superiors, which is strong
in the Indian culture. Chapter 7 shows how a gainsharing change
program, which was congruent with an organization's culture,
achieved long lasting changes in cooperation and participation as
measured by suggestion making.

In summary, we have shown that programs can decline as a
result of incongruence with existing organizational or cultural norms
and values, the organizational authority system, or individual skills
and motives. Of course, if those are already in conflict with one
another, it will be difficult for programs to be congruent.

Stability of the Environment

From the evidence reported so far, it should be clear that
institutionalizing a change program in an organization is a difficult
task, even in the best situations. In some situations the added
instability of the environment only makes things worse. In our
study, there were only two cases of instability in the environment.[38]
In these cases there was a major decline in demand for the organization's products, which led to curtailments in the work force.
This, in turn, changed the composition of many of the groups that
were an integral part of the change program. These groups became
less effective, lowering the degree of institutionalization. Similar
results were observed in another study as an economic recession
led to layoffs and bumping.[39] Environment instabilities such as
these represent a major obstacle to institutionalization.

Union

The union can play a major role in determining the degree of
institutionalization. If there are high levels of labor-management
conflict in the collective-bargaining area, we expect this to spill
over to the productivity programs and negatively affect their viability. If the relationships at the plant or site level are cooperative,
the productivity plans will exhibit longer-term viability. In other
studies there is evidence that the quality of the relationship between the local district and the international has a critical impact
on the viability of any productivity program.[40]

How Do You Make Productivity Programs Last?

The above discussion identifies a set of factors that can contribute to the persistence of productivity and similar types of labor-management programs. It is important for the reader to remember that these factors to promote institutionalization, which are reintroduced below, are based on empirical findings, not on just the opinions of the authors.

What should we do to make productivity programs last?

1. *Selecting Organizations.* Some organizations simply should not get involved in productivity-type change programs. A careful diagnosis is needed to be sure an organization is ready or not. The more that labor and management can acknowledge that some of their organizational units should not get involved, the more realistic their working relationship will be, and the more likely that a change program, when initiated, will last. Some of the reasons for not getting involved include:

   a. Unstable economic environment. Organizations experiencing economic instability and high fluctuations in their labor force will be hard put to mount a successful long-run productivity program.
   b. Instability in leadership environment. If there is likely to be turnover in key labor or management sponsors of the change program, it is best to delay the start of a program or abandon it.
   c. Mistrust between employees and management or union and management. If there are some basic problems in the relationships between employees and employers or union and management, a productivity program change effort should not be introduced. These problems need to be solved before a program such as gainsharing is considered.

2. *Plan for Institutionalization in the Beginning.* In most of the labor-management change programs we have reviewed, attention has been devoted largely to starting up a program. Little attention has been given to maintaining the program. A program has greater chances of success if mechanisms for maintaining it are considered in the early planning stages. That is, maintenance needs to be designed into the front end of a program.

3. *The Fit Problems.* There needs to be a good fit (or congru-

ence) between the organization's values, philosophy, and structure and the nature of the change program. When the proposed change program (e.g., autonomous work groups or gainsharing) is in conflict with the organization's value system (e.g., high authoritarian), it simply will not last. How does 'a low-trust, high-authoritarian hierarchical system move toward a more participative system? The answer has to be in a carefully designed evolutionary change program that will occur over an extended time period.[41]

4. *Characteristics of Changes.* While no one program is suited to all organizations, the following characteristics should ensure a long-run effort.

   a. Specific statement of goals, written out and approved by labor and management.
   b. Specific procedures to implement labor and management program activities. These activities are complex processes. Failure to clarify them can lead to trouble. Where feasible, there should be some formalization of issues such as who should be in the labor-management committee, when it should meet, how members should rotate, what are the boundaries of the committee's work. Formalization increases long-run viability of the change program.
   c. Total system intervention. Change programs that can be introduced into the total organizational unit, rather than in part, will last longer, but only if sufficient organizational resources are allocated to them.

5. *Training Over Time.* Most productivity programs advocate training to start up a program. We advocate periodic retraining over time to reaffirm program change principles. Special training programs for new organizational members are necessary to ensure long-run viability.

6. *Commitment.* High commitment will facilitate the persistence of most labor-management change programs. High commitment comes from (1) voluntary participation in program activities, and (2) opportunities for recommitment over time. Productivity programs that offer continuous opportunities for recommitment exhibit higher levels of persistence.

7. *Effective Reward Systems.* The design of organizational rewards systems can substantially determine the longevity of a productivity program. An effective reward system should:

    a. Include both extrinsic (e.g., pay) and intrinsic (e.g., more autonomy) rewards.

    b. Link rewards to specific behaviors required by the productivity program (e.g., assuming greater decision-making responsibilities).

    c. Introduce a mechanism for revising the reward system. It is unlikely rewards will maintain their attractiveness over time. A successful program will need some procedure, approved by labor and management, to revise rewards over time.

    d. Minimize problems of inequity over compensation issues.

    8. *Diffusion.* As the productivity program is introduced in one unit (e.g., a department), it must be quickly spread to include all organizational units at one location. Isolated productivity programs will have trouble in persisting.

    9. *Feedback and Correction.* One major characteristic of many productivity program failures we have studied was the lack of mechanisms by which the organization could judge how well programs were functioning. But they were either not being performed or not being performed well. A direct and accurate feedback mechanism for measuring performance of program activities is necessary if the change program is to adjust, grow, and remain viable.

Conclusion

    Many productivity and employee involvement programs, although initially successful, do not persist over time. We now know some of the critical processes that affect long-run viability or failure of these programs. The set of action plans presented here ensure the long-run viability of productivity programs, in general, and specifically for gainsharing.

Notes

1. P.S. Goodman, *Assessing Organizational Change: The Rushton Quality of Work Experiment* (New York: Wiley-Interscience, 1979).

2. P.S. Goodman and J.W. Dean, Jr., "Creating Long-Term Organizational Change," in *Change in Organizations*, ed. P.S. Goodman (San Francisco: Jossey-Bass, 1982); R.E. Walton, "Establishing and Maintaining High Com-

mitment Work Systems," in *The Organizational Life Cycle*, ed. J.R. Kimberly and R.H. Miles (San Francisco: Jossey-Bass, 1980).

3. P.H. Mirvis and D.N. Berg, eds., *Failures in Organization Development and Change* (New York: Wiley-Interscience, 1977); Goodman and Dean, "Creating Long-Term Organizational Change," note 2, above.

4. Ibid.

5. R.I. Golembiewski and S.B. Carrigan, "The Persistence of Laboratory-In--duced Changes in Organizational Styles." *Administrative Science Quarterly*, 15, 1970, 330–340.

6. J.M. Ivancevich, "Changes in Performance in a Management by Objectives Program," *Administrative Science Quarterly*, 19, 1974, 563–574.

7. Goodman, *Assessing Organizational Change*, note 1, above.

8. Goodman and Dean, "Creating Long-Term Organizational Change," note 2, above.

9. Ibid.

10. J.M. Ivancevich, "A Longitudinal Assessment of Management by Objectives," *Administrative Science Quarterly*, 17, 1972, 126–138.

11. Walton, "Establishing and Maintaining High Commitment Work Systems," note 2, above.

12. Goodman, *Assessing Organizational Change*, note 1, above.

13. Goodman and Dean, "Creating Long-Term Organizational Change," note 2, above; Walton, "Establishing and Maintaining High Commitment Work Systems," note 2, above.

14. Goodman and Dean, "Creating Long-Term Organizational Change," note 1, above.

15. V.H. Vroom, *Work and Motivation* (New York: Wiley, 1964); E.E. Lawler, *Pay and Organizational Effectiveness* (New York: McGraw-Hill, 1971).

16. E.A. Locke, D. Sirota and A.D. Wolfson, "An Experimental Case Study of the Successes and Failures of Job Enrichment in a Government Agency," *Journal of Applied Psychology*, 61 1976, 701–711.

17. Goodman, *Assessing Organizational Change*, note 1, above.

18. Ibid.

19. E. Trist and C. O'Dwyer, "The Limits of Laissez-Faire as a Socio-Technical Change Strategy," in *The Innovative Organization*, eds. R. Zager and M.P. Rosow (New York: Pergamon Press, 1982).

20. Goodman and Dean, "Creating Long-Term Organizational Change," note 2, above.

21. Walton, "Establishing High Commitment Work Systems," note 2, above.

22. P.S. Goodman, personal correspondence; R.E. Walton, "Teaching an Old Dog Food New Tricks," *The Wharton Magazine*, Winter 1979, 38–47.

23. Goodman and Dean, "Creating Long-Term Organizational Change," note 2, above.

24. Goodman, *Assessing Organizational Change*, note 1, above.

25. Goodman and Dean, "Creating Long-Term Organizational Change," note 2, above.

26. W. Crockett, "Introducing Change to a Government Agency," in *Failures in Organizational Development: Cases and Essays for Learning*, ed. P. Mirvis and D. Berg (New York: Wiley-Interscience, 1977).

27. Walton, "Teaching an Old Dog Food New Tricks," note 22, above.
28. A. Levine, *Why Innovation Fails* (Albany: State University of New York Press, 1980).
29. L.L. Frank and J.R. Hackman, "A Failure of Job Enrichment: The Case of the Change That Wasn't," *Journal of Applied Behavioral Science*, 11, no. 4, 1975, 413–436.
30. R.E. Walton, "The Diffusion of New York Structures: Explaining Why Success Didn't Take," *Organizational Dynamics*, Winter 1975, 3–21.
31. J. Fadem, "Fitting Computer-Aided Technology to Workplace Requirements: An Example" (paper presented at the 13th Annual Meeting and Technical Conference of the Numerical Control Society, Cincinnati, March 1976).
32. S.E. Seashore and D.G. Bowers, "Durability of Organizational Change," in *Organization Development: Theory, Practice, and Research*, eds. W.L. French, C.H. Bell, Jr., and R.A. Zawicki (Dallas: Business Publications, 1978).
33. S.A. Mohrman, et al., "A Survey Feedback and Problem Solving Intervention in a School District: "We'll Take the Survey But You Can Keep the Feedback," in *Failures in Organizational Development: Cases and Essays for Learning*, ed. P. Mirvis and D. Berg (New York: Wiley-Interscience, 1977).
34. Walton, "Establishing High Commitment Work Systems," note 2, above.
35. Levine, *Why Innovation Fails*, note 28, above.
36. D.P. Warwick, *A Theory of Public Bureaucracy* (Cambridge, Mass.: Harvard University Press, 1975); Crockett, "Introducing Change," note 26, above.
37. E.J. Miller, "Socio-Technical Systems in Weaving, 1953–1970: A Follow-up Study," *Human Relations*, 28, no. 4, 1975, 349–386.
38. Goodman and Dean, "Creating Long-Term Organizational Change," note 2, above.
39. Paul S. Goodman, personal correspondence.
40. Goodman, *Assessing Organizational Change*, note 1, above.
41. Goodman and Dean, "Creating Long-Term Organizational Change," note 2, above.

Part Two

Cases and Applications

Chapter 7

Seventeen Years of Experience With the Scanlon Plan: DeSoto Revisited

Brian Graham-Moore

In the summer of 1988, I contacted Tom Lester, general manager of DeSoto, Inc., of Garland, Texas, to ask his permission to videotape their monthly screening committee meeting. He agreed to allow my University of Texas at Austin video crew to spend the day, if necessary, capturing a typical problem-solving meeting. The videotape we made was of 20 or so managers, staff, and hourly workers doing what they have been doing since 1971—processing productivity suggestions. Granted, 17 years had changed some of us a little more than we'd like to admit, but how had those years changed DeSoto's Scanlon plan? That visit let me take stock of a gainsharing plan that had matured or "institutionalized," as Goodman and Dean point out in Chapter 6. This chapter will review the history of the Scanlon plan at this one location.

Let's begin at the very beginning, in 1970, when I presented a lecture on incentives to an evening class of M.B.A. students at the University of Chicago. Afterwards, a student asked me if I was interested in Scanlon plans. That student was Richard Anderson, general manager of Chemical Coatings Division, DeSoto, Inc. On his invitation I was present when Fred Lesieur explained how the Scanlon plan would increase productivity for DeSoto. At the end of the meeting, I was asked for my opinion. Not only was I convinced that this form of gainsharing was potentially useful, but I also offered to evaluate how and why the plan was to be learned so that other DeSoto manufacturing units could benefit from the first installation. That same day, I first met Tom Lester, the plant manager, who, it turned out, had wanted a Scanlon plan even before corporate management. It was soon decided that DeSoto Southwest in Garland, Texas, would be the first attempt at gain-sharing. A close colleague, Paul S. Goodman (now at Carnegie-Mellon University) joined the research project. We were to have a free hand to design a complete evaluation study to focus on what is learned, who learns, and whether learning the principles of gainsharing influences productivity.

DeSoto, unlike some firms that are drawn to gainsharing, is a high quality corporation. DeSoto management is loyal to cor-porate goals and is considered to be of top caliber in their industry. Historically, DeSoto employment practices are excellent, with a commitment to full employment. Its compensation and fringe ben-efits are among the best in the paint industry. In 1970, 65 percent of DeSoto's product was sold as private label to Sears. Given this drive for continued excellence, it was not surprising that manage-ment was drawn to the Scanlon plan.

Our original study indicated remarkable changes in attitudes and increased productivity during the trial year of 1971.[1] Some of these findings are reported later in the chapter. In 1972, I left Chicago for The University of Texas at Austin. At Tom Lester's invitation I continued to monitor the Garland site. During the years of 1972–1974, I also studied DeSoto plants at Chicago Heights, Illinois; Greensboro, North Carolina; and Columbus, Ohio. All have patterned successful Scanlon plans after the Garland plant. In the ensuing years, I have visited and communicated frequently with the management and work force at the Garland plant. This case study is one of the few longitudinal studies of a gainsharing Scanlon plan. It has only been possible because of the cooperation and kind assistance of the personnel of DeSoto, Inc., Garland, Texas. To them, I extend my most grateful thanks.

Key Aspects of DeSoto's Plan

Presence of Three Basic Elements

Before proceeding with a discussion of DeSoto's experience with the Scanlon plan, a clear description of their plan is necessary. DeSoto's Scanlon plan is a companywide productivity improvement plan. It consists of three basic elements: a philosophy of cooperation, an involvement system designed to increase efficiency and reduce costs, and a formula that permits a bonus to be paid based on increases in productivity.

DeSoto's Philosophy

Employer-employee cooperation is essential. Teamwork is promoted in the belief that both worker and manager have valuable information to share. This sharing of knowledge provides the worker with the means to collaborate and cooperate with management. Management leads, but the workers actively participate.

DeSoto's Involvement System

A new committee structure was established in the organization and thus became a new mechanism for communication. This structure facilitates the communication, evaluation, and disposition of suggestions. Two kinds of committees were organized. A production committee was formed in each department or working unit and consisted of carefully selected chairmen and then elected members. The screening committee consisted of management and selected members from the production committees. The functions and authority of both committees is covered in greater detail later in this chapter.[2]

DeSoto's Formula

Since DeSoto management opted for a traditional Scanlon plan (see Chapter 3 for other choices), a baseline measurement of productivity was developed. This baseline or base ratio was determined between (1) total labor costs, including factory and salary payroll, vacations, and holidays, and (2) sales value of production, including adjustments for such items as inventory fluctuations and price variations. The formula relates total human resource costs to the sales value of production.

$$\text{Base ratio} = \frac{\text{Total human resource costs}}{\substack{\text{Value of sales including inventory changes} \\ \text{(finished and work-in-process inventories)}}}$$

This relationship between the human resource cost and the production value is the normal ratio of labor to output, or the base ratio. Any increase in the denominator (sales value of production) relative to the numerator (total human resource costs) represents an increase in labor productivity. When such an increase occurs, a bonus is distributed to everyone on the participating payroll. Therefore, with the entire organization focusing its attention on this relationship between human resource investment and productivity, the formula encourages employees to learn more productivity-linked behaviors in order to do better than the base ratio.

The philosophy of cooperation, the involvement system, and the formula make up what is generally known as the Scanlon plan at DeSoto. These three elements mutually reinforce each other in definitive ways as we shall see. DeSoto's experience with the plan shows how a well-managed firm can successfully increase its productivity goals.

Productivity Outcomes at DeSoto

Over the course of seventeen years, DeSoto has seen many changes in its ways of doing business. For example, in 1970, 65 percent of their output went to Sears. In 1988, they produced almost as much industrial trade and non-Sears private label as they did Sears business. In 1973, the first OPEC crisis hit all manufacturers using petrochemical raw materials with a 400 percent increase in raw material cost. Without an adjustment to the Scanlon ratio for equity, that increase in cost would have created huge Scanlon bonuses without any commensurate increase in labor productivity. Then, in 1976, DeSoto increased capacity with a huge capital investment which nearly doubled the ability to produce. In this expansion, the work force increased by approximately 25 percent. Recent acquisitions have resulted in further work force expansion of an additional 13 percent. Thus, in 1988, the company, with a 38 percent increase in total work force, could produce twice what they could produce in 1970. These kinds of changes can wreck a Scanlon bonus calculation if left unadjusted. Nevertheless, DeSoto management was able to pay bonuses. Exhibit 7.1 represents the annual average bonus percent of pay from 1971 to 1988. Annual average bonuses for this seventeen year period range from 2.5 percent to over 22 percent with the overall annual average of 9.6 percent. To understand this, take the sum of your own annual pay for the past seventeen years and multiply it by 9.6 percent! Though this somewhat underestimates the actual payout, *all* DeSoto em-

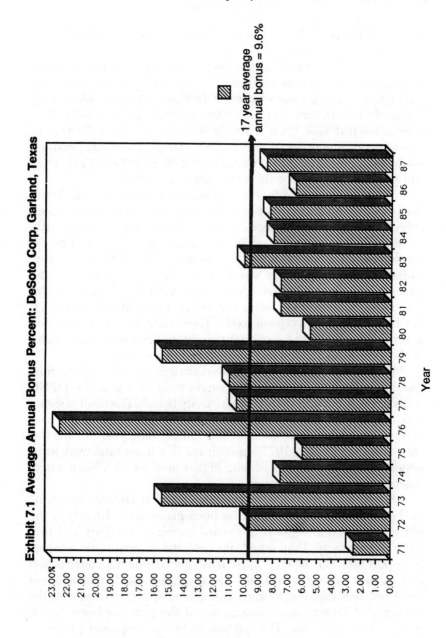

Exhibit 7.1 Average Annual Bonus Percent: DeSoto Corp, Garland, Texas

ployees at Garland, Texas, (except Tom Lester) received this bonus on top of competitive wages and salaries.

Care must be exercised in the interpretation of any measure of productivity, such as Exhibit 7.1, since output per work-hour can be influenced by many factors. Obviously, the gainsharing plan is one of these factors. Even after seventeen years, it is difficult to determine just how great a role gainsharing plays at DeSoto in increasing productivity. However, the intangible benefits provided solely by gainsharing are more than enough to justify its existence and provide a reason for its continuation at DeSoto.

While the overall history of the bonus program is good, DeSoto's single Scanlon ratio was subject to a series of modifications which reflect management's concern to make the formula measure true increases in productivity while retaining equity for all. For example, with the single ratio they soon saw that the labor value added of produced goods was higher than those bought on the outside and merely passed through packaging and distribution. Therefore, they use two ratios separately (the split ratio discussed in Chapter 3) for each type of goods. These ratios are then combined in order to value total labor productivity. Given the characteristics of their business, this split ratio is more precise.

Exhibit 7.2 shows how DeSoto management was able to adjust the denominator of the Scanlon single ratio to reflect the OPEC crisis in 1973 and still show a productivity bonus. The exhibit shows productivity as measured by gallons of paint and the bonus as a percentage of pay. Employment level in the base year of 1970 was 160. Scanning 1971 to 1977, one can see that more total work force appears positively associated with higher productivity, but not necessarily with higher bonuses.

Specific formula changes have occurred at DeSoto, and trust in the fairness of management has been maintained. Clearly, if the objective of the formula is to reward cooperative efforts and true labor productivity, then equity for both the company and workers is important. The worker must trust management's construction and calculation of the formula. On the other hand, management must not feel that the formula is a giveaway. Indeed, one of the concerns of DeSoto management about the plan has been the efficacy of the formula. This proves to be an empirical problem, answerable only when the accounting data are assembled.

Exhibit 7.1 shows that DeSoto's best bonus ever was approximately 23 percent of annual pay in 1976, but beginning in 1977,

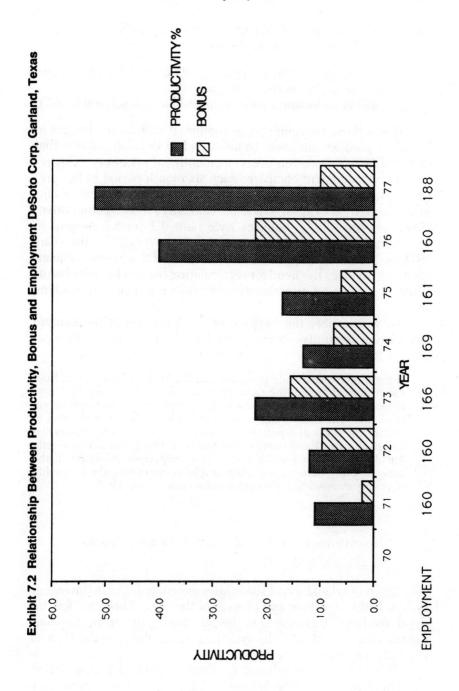

Exhibit 7.2 Relationship Between Productivity, Bonus and Employment DeSoto Corp, Garland, Texas

the effects of doubling plant capacity and the significant increases to the payroll have caused the following outcomes:

1. Bonuses are lower, yet productivity is good (there are more people on the participating payroll).
2. 1970 is no longer a good historical base (it was until 1977).

When those outcomes were combined with large changes in DeSoto's product mix, management had to develop policies that would allow recalculation every six months, if necessary. This review by management compares each six month period to the previous six; this in turn is compared with the previous year. Gains in productivity are captured and the company remains competitive. However, since 1977, bonuses have ranged from 5.5 percent to 15.5 percent and average 8.8 percent. The average for the years 1971 to 1976 is 10.6 percent. Thus, by careful adjustment management balances the need for recalculating the productivity bonus while not reducing opportunities to achieve a bonus by working smarter.

To summarize, the purpose of the formula and its accurate formulation is equity—a fair share for all. As stated by Frost *et al.*:

> If the employees decide favorably and the formula is arrived at from the historical accounting facts, then the ratio is set at the most representative position consistent with current market and production demands. The ratio is subject to continuous study and evaluation to ensure the optimal equity for everyone. If the ratio jeopardizes the company's fiscal and competitive position, the deficiency in equity for all is recognized and the ratio is appropriately modified. If the ratio severely disadvantages the employee investors, the inequality is clearly defined and the appropriate change is made.[3]

Involvement System as Structure and Process

Often overlooked and sometimes overstated, the involvement system is the structure and process of the plan. There are few in-depth studies of this system in the gainsharing literature. Explaining the characteristics of the system, as exemplified at the DeSoto plant, is the objective of this section.

The plan was introduced by Fred Lesieur, a highly skilled consultant in the specific field of Scanlon plans. The introductory process at DeSoto included the three steps basic to any Scanlon plan introduction:

1. Presentation of the three components of the plan, i.e., the philosophy, the involvement system, and the formula;
2. Election (companywide) to determine if the plan will be instituted for a trial year;
3. Installation of the productivity formula and the involvement system, assuming a positive vote.

These steps appear simple, but it is important to understand that each one is a detailed process requiring careful execution. DeSoto management spent a great deal of time discussing exactly how these steps would be achieved.

After the presentation and the vote were completed, the next step was to staff the production and screening committees. A description of the production and screening committees, their governing procedures, and guidelines for handling suggestions was distributed to the employees to help them understand the plan. Management then considered the number of production committees needed and decided on eight (one for each department in 1971). Each committee would consist of three to five committee members per department depending on the size of the department and the number of night shift workers. This number would ensure balanced representation among departments, shifts, and job levels. A provision was made for changing the numbers at a later time if the circumstances warranted. Currently there are ten production committees.

DeSoto management feels that representation is essential to the success of the plan for two reasons: First, it guarantees good representation of ideas. By involving all functional units of the company, the system gets input that reflects the viewpoints of all employees. Second, good representation aids in the process of peer review. Critical evaluation of all suggestions on many different levels is made possible through adequate work force representation.

The purpose of the committee is to use workers' ideas to improve the performance of their jobs. The production committee consists of the departmental supervisor and at least two employee representatives. Suggestions for improved operations are presented to this production committee as they occur. At least once a month the production committee reviews the suggestions that have been submitted. Suggestions not affecting other departments and not exceeding a specified dollar amount ($200) (in 1971) are put into effect at the departmental level by the production committee. Also, any suggestion rejected at the production committee level always receives another hearing by the screening committee once a month.

The screening committee is made up of management and hourly representatives from the production committees. Its three main activities are to (1) review and evaluate suggestions, (2) announce the bonus (or deficit), and (3) discuss the business reasons for the bonus or deficit.

The purpose of reviewing and evaluating suggestions is to process all relevant information and to guarantee that collective points of view intersect at the point of decision. The ultimate decision, however, is the plant manager's.

After seventeen years, Tom Lester, DeSoto's plant manager, knows that immediate feedback is necessary for the plan to be effective. The announcement of the bonus or deficit provides some of this feedback. Controller Jim Barker's Scanlon report is made at a meeting attended by a representative from each department or functional area. After the meeting, the representatives announce the bonus or deficit in their respective work areas.

The third principal activity of the screening committee, discussing the reasons for the bonus or deficit, includes a discussion of how the bonus or deficit affects the company and its objectives in terms of production costs. This activity is illustrated by the following portion taken from a DeSoto screening committee meeting.

> *Tom Lester:* Our orders normally fall off in June when we add summer workers to cover vacations. Naturally, personnel costs will go up while sales are expected to decline below our normal base ratio. Folks ought to know we expect deficits no matter how much harder and smarter they work.
> *Production Committee Member:* Maybe we could get by with fewer summer workers since our productivity is higher than theirs?
> *Personnel Manager:* It's worth a try, Tom. We might get by with one half the number we normally hire—if everyone understands that this will reduce expected deficits.
> *Tom Lester:* Well, could we talk this up on the floor to see how people feel?

Within a mature Scanlon company, the discussion of why a firm can or cannot achieve its goals surfaces within the screening committee meetings. As a result of these discussions, the screening committee becomes a task-oriented classroom for combining individual and corporate goals to achieve success. DeSoto has developed specific procedures for handling suggestions. Explanation of these procedures should provide the reader with an overview of the involvement system, and more important, how the production and screening committees make this system work.

Although concrete procedures for handling suggestions are described below, it is the *process* of handling them that ensures the involvement system. In other words, one should always keep in mind that these procedures are by no means absolute. The important thing is that DeSoto managers make every effort to deal with people face to face in all aspects of the suggestion-making process. By doing so, lines of communication are developed and expanded at all job levels. The involvement system gives an employee not only the opportunity to exchange ideas with his peers but, more important, to exchange ideas with his supervisors. In this respect the Scanlon plan offers the advantage of increased communication that leads to increased employee participation in the overall attainment of company objectives. The procedures that follow should not become a bureaucratic device that interferes with or takes the place of open communication.

1. Someone with a suggestion should submit it in writing to a departmental representative.
2. The supervisor or departmental representative should discuss the suggestion with the person making it, and with others who may be affected, and take appropriate action as soon as possible.
3. Meeting at least once a month, both committees should review the status of previously discussed suggestions, should expedite delayed suggestions, and should discuss new suggestions.
4. Suggestions involving more than the specified dollar amount (more than $200 in 1971 at DeSoto) should be referred to the screening committee.
5. The production committee should assign the responsibility for following through on delayed suggestions to one of its members.
6. The production committee should keep records of its activities. These records should include all suggestions submitted and their status—action proposed, action taken, and so on.
7. By a certain day of the month, the production committee

should submit all suggestions received during that month to the screening committee.

8. All suggestions and actions taken by the production committee should be reported to the screening committee monthly.

The production committee can take one of five actions on the suggestions it receives:

1. Reject suggestion with carefully stated reasons.
2. Accept suggestion and use it.
3. Accept suggestion and place it under investigation. (A suggestion is normally investigated when there is insufficient information to make a decision or when it is necessary to ascertain if net savings will offset the cost of implementing the suggestion).
4. Accept suggestion by recommending it to the screening committee (This is generally done with a suggestion that a production committee feels should be placed into effect but which costs over the specified dollar amount).
5. Refer suggestion to a screening committee if production committee members cannot agree on its acceptability.

In summary, the involvement system is a new committee structure superimposed on the organization to facilitate communication, evaluation, and disposition of suggestions. As mentioned, two kinds of committees are established—production and screening. Obviously, the involvement system is an integral part of the Scanlon plan. The production committee and screening committee coupled with employee participation and cooperation help determine the success of the plan. For this reason, it is important that all employees have a basic understanding of this system and how it operates.

Personnel Manager Bob Highland developed these guidelines for production committee members. As they are elected to their positions, they meet with Highland to review and discuss these responsibilities:

As the Production Committee Representative you will have certain responsibilities in coordinating the Scanlon activities for your department. Since you were elected as the representative for your department by your fellow employees, it will be necessary for you to spend some time in soliciting suggestions, following through on suggestions, giving clear and accurate reports to your group as to the status of their suggestions, and also doing your homework for the Screening Meeting. Remember your fellow employees are counting on you!

1. *How much money can we spend to implement a suggestion?*

Production Committees are authorized to spend up to $200; Department Heads up to $400; and the Plant Manager is authorized on expenditures up to $500. Any expenditure of more than $500 would require capital expenditure and needs to be budgeted.

2. *When should our Production Committee Meeting be held?* This meeting can be held any time prior to the Screening Committee Meetings. It probably would be helpful if you held the meeting two or three days before the Screening Meeting so you can do some last-minute checking. You may also wish to hold more than one meeting in a month, if suggestion activity warrants it.

3. *Where should our meeting be held?* The meeting can be held anywhere at any time. The most important thing is that we meet!

4. *How soon should a suggestion be put "in use"?* If a suggestion is made and has merit, don't wait for a Production Meeting or a Screening Meeting to implement. If the cost is within your expenditure guidelines, get it working.

5. *What should be covered at our meeting?* It is most important to review the status of all active suggestions. Be prepared for the Screening Meeting with quotes, maintenance schedules, and the present status of the suggestion. The key is to act and keep the suggestion moving.

6. *If a suggestion needs to be investigated, what should we do?* On suggestions requiring an investigation, assign an investigation team, and list these employees so their names are typed on the minutes. It is very important that all investigation team members be notified and asked to investigate a suggestion and gather all pertinent facts concerning the suggestion. If members of other departments are concerned, be sure to notify the appropriate people.

7. *What should I report at the Screening Meeting?* At the Screening Committee Meeting, it is not necessary to read the entire suggestion, but only to refer to the suggestion and report on the disposition. It is most important to have as much information about a suggestion as possible in case it will be discussed. If you need to refer a suggestion for additional approval for expenditures, do so at this meeting. Remember your committee can spend $200, and department heads may approve $400 in expenditures.

8. *What should I report to my department after a Screening Committee meeting?* At the Employee Information Meeting give the bonus disposition and the status of the reserve account. Also review the status of all suggestions, and be sure the individual who made the suggestion has an explanation of the disposition. This includes giving the reason for a rejection in the event the suggestion is not approved, or the status of the suggestion at the present time. This is most important to the suggestion maker since there is no suggestion as important as the one he or she made.

Results of Suggestion-Making Process

After seventeen years, would the results of the suggestion-making process still be favorable? Would ideas dry up? Would everyone get tired of the Scanlon plan? When we set up to videotape in July of 1988, I wasn't sure that the screening committee meeting would still show a sincere dialogue between blue collar and white collar workers, managers, and R & D people. Since the process of group problem solving involves the entire organization in new ways regardless of the prevailing organizational culture, can it sustain itself over time? One way to answer these questions is to look at the results of the involvement system across seventeen years.

Exhibit 7.3 graphs total suggestions made by year. They range from a low of 120 to a high of 360. Remember that the employment level in 1970 was 160 and, in 1988, it is 219. Nevertheless, the ratio of suggestions to employees has never fallen below .6 suggestions per employee. The highest is 1.6 suggestions per employee. Rejection rates of suggestions since 1981 range from 37 percent to 11 percent or roughly *63 to 88 percent of all suggestions were accepted*. It is revealing to do an in-depth analysis of suggestions by their content. These analyses allow numerous inferences to be made and provide even greater insight into the plan and its overall effect on the organization. A management committee (consisting of the plant manager, the controller, and the personnel manager) was established at the DeSoto plant for the purpose of evaluating suggestions. The participation of the technical director of the plant was also especially helpful. The results of these analyses are depicted in Exhibits 7.4 and 7.5.

Exhibit 7.4 indicates that all suggestions of the trial year (1971) fall into one of four categories. Suggestions spanning multiple categories were tallied in their primary category. The first category is irritants, i.e., suggestions that improve working conditions, but not necessarily the quality or quantity of the product being manufactured. Other categories represented in Exhibit 7.4 are (1) quantity, suggestions that increase the number of units manufactured; (2) quality, suggestions that increase the product value so that it will obtain a higher price or draw fewer complaints; and (3) cost reduction, suggestions that increase the use of waste-reducing methods, the conservation of raw materials, and the conservative use of resources allocated for overhead costs. McKersie states that most workers focus on cost reduction suggestions.[4]

During the first three months of 1971 91 suggestions were made, and these involved the majority of the work force. By the end of the trial year, 82 percent of the work force at DeSoto had made at least one suggestion. These facts clearly indicate that the installation of this type of system does increase communication

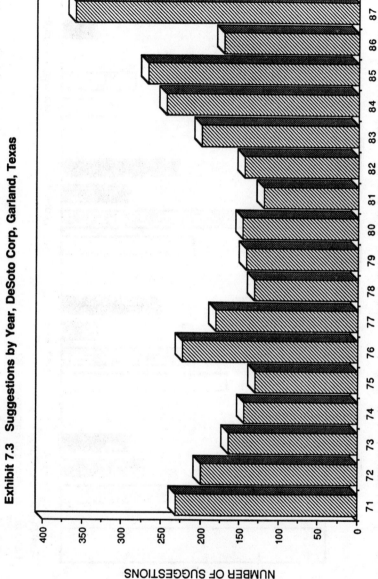

Exhibit 7.3   Suggestions by Year, DeSoto Corp, Garland, Texas

Exhibit 7.4   Type of Suggestion and Degree of Participation Over Time, DeSoto Corp., Garland, Texas

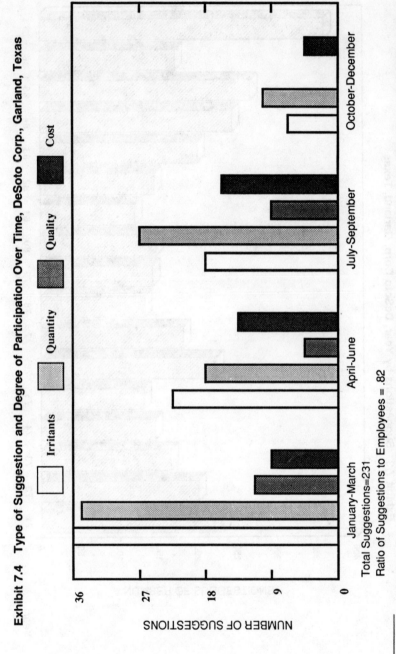

Total Suggestions=231
Ratio of Suggestions to Employees = .82

Adapted from: B.E. Moore, *A Plant-Wide Productivity Plan in Action: Three Years of Experience with the Scanlon Plan* (Washington, D.C.: The National Commission on Productivity and Work Quality, 1975) 14.

within an organization as measured by their suggestion making. The involvement and participation of all employees within the organization is a result of refining, processing, deciding, and feeding back the disposition of all suggestions. In other words, the involvement and participation of all employees is a result of open communication.

Also, Exhibit 7.4 indicates that in the first three months of operation under the plan, irritations with the working conditions at DeSoto dominated the suggestions made by the employees. This situation is to be expected for two reasons: (1) suggestion making is a new activity, and common sources of ideas come from the irritants (the factors that produce dissatisfaction among workers); and (2) time is required for the consultant, management, and the committee system to determine which suggestions influence the bonus. Because production committees can implement some suggestions immediately, they are required to look at costs. It is at this time that employees, at all levels, become aware of the true effect of a given suggestion, and, as a result, priorities are established. This learning process helps reduce the flow of suggestions, since only suggestions which improve productivity are sought.

If suggestions are not implemented, employees may stop making them. A factor that seems to influence the rate of suggestion making is the ability of the organization to put good suggestions to work. When business conditions are not expanding, management may be reluctant to make a capital investment on worthy suggestions. Failure to implement a suggestion implies to the employee who offered it that future suggestions have little probability of being accepted.

Exhibit 7.5 provides an extended look at suggestion-making activity over a nine-year period at DeSoto. The irritants category in Exhibit 7.4 is changed to nonproductivity-related (NP) suggestions. The only reason for this change is that careful analysis of the suggestions indicates that most NP suggestions are related to safety rather than irritations with the work environment. Almost all NP suggestions are accepted into the system by DeSoto, as this is their philosophy. NP suggestions, however, are then referred to the safety committee. Those remaining NP suggestions that could be classified as irritants are dealt with outside of the involvement system.

Exhibit 7.5 shows that more quantity suggestions are made than any other type in all years (1972–1979) continuing the trend from the trial year (1971). The ratio of employee participation suggestion making to number of employees ranges from .53 to .91 over the eight-year time span. A careful review of DeSoto's sug-

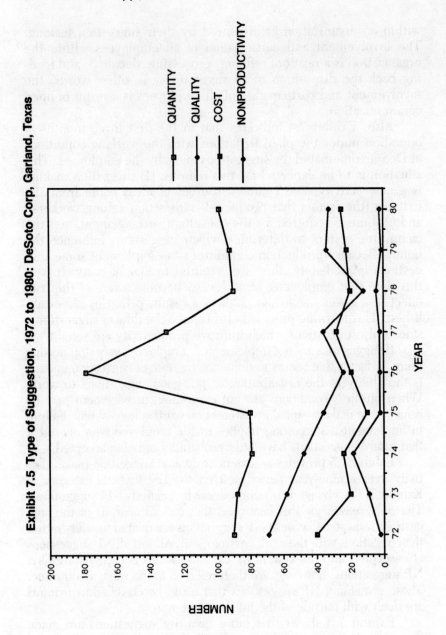

Exhibit 7.5 Type of Suggestion, 1972 to 1980: DeSoto Corp, Garland, Texas

gestion history has shown that periods of favorable economic activity, good markets, and other positive external environmental factors vary along with the type of suggestions made. That is, increased productivity focuses worker attention on how to increase quantity, improve quality, and reduce costs. During slack periods there may be high rates of suggestion making, but productivity-related suggestions are more difficult to implement. Examples of the different types of suggestions made at different economic time periods are provided below.

> *Slack Period:* "Have a bonus of $3.00 or $4.00 a week if you are not late or absent from work.
> *Disposition:* Rejected. It is the employee's responsibility to work every day and arrive on time.
> *Busy Period:* "Tanks D-61, 62, and 70; install 2" valve on bottom of tanks for draining off materials. Understand this was approved first year of Scanlon, but never completed.
> *Disposition:* Accepted. S. will see that this done over a period of time.

Slack-period suggestions in mature plan organizations such as DeSoto signify search behavior on the part of well-motivated employees. However, DeSoto management believes it is often unrealistic to expect useful suggestions during this time. In order to foster problem-solving behavior, problems must exist that require immediate, implementable solutions. The suggestions made during busy periods exemplify the immediacy of this type of problem solving. In slack periods, for example, it does not matter as much how quickly the tanks are turned around. However, when the rate of production picks up, the productivity-minded worker sees that a larger valve would increase quantity by speeding up drain time. Obviously, outside forces of demand fuel problem-solving processes within the company.

Major developments within the organization are a second reason for significant changes in the suggestion mix. These developments include such things as an addition of a new department or work area, technological changes in production, and turnover in management or supervisory-level postions. Exhibit 7.5 represents this situation very clearly. Looking at the 1976 data, a significant increase in quantity suggestions occurred. This increase can be attributed to the addition of a new latex department within the DeSoto plant. This period also coincides with DeSoto's highest bonus. Again this shows how the three components of gainsharing (philosophy of cooperation, involvement, and bonus) mutually reinforce each other.

When the structure of the involvement system is considered, the amount of time spent on committee meetings is a constant source of discussion. The screening committee at DeSoto spends one to two hours per month on prescribed duties. Production committees meet officially at least once a month for a period ranging from ten minutes to one hour. Meetings are scheduled at slow periods, yet breaks, lunch periods, and even car pools also provide opportunities for the discussion of suggestions. Also, many suggestions are group authored and represent the culmination of much "pilot-testing" behavior.

DeSoto management raised the question to me, "How do group suggestion systems compare with individual suggestion systems?" We both discovered that group suggestion systems, such as those used in the Scanlon plan, are difficult to cost out. There is no cost measurement, per se, employed in gainsharing. On the other hand, most individual suggestions use the formula of 10 percent to 20 percent of the estimated annual cost savings of a suggestion as a bonus payout to individuals. Using this formula, firms can actually generate a dollar amount of estimated savings.

A multivariate analysis of 200 U.S. firms with individual suggestion systems revealed the following. Regardless of the type of industry, type of suggestion system administration, or some 70 other variables, the principal finding was that one strong norm appeared to govern the payouts for individual suggestions. This norm reflects the remarkable consistency of award payouts by size of award, type of suggestion, administration, and relative frequency of awards across all industries studied.[5] This lack of variability of suggestion award payouts combined with low ratio of suggestions to employees that never exceeded .35 suggestions per employee. This makes the group suggestion system stand out in marked contrast to the individual suggestion system. The Scanlon plan promoted cooperation, participation, and the sharing of information by both worker and management, as clearly indicated by Exhibits 7.4 and 7.5. Group suggestion systems tend to foster higher quality suggestions since the acceptance rate of productivity-related suggestions is greater than under individual suggestion systems.

Challenge to Management

DeSoto also discovered that dealing with the Scanlon plan over time provides management with both its greatest problem and its greatest challenge. The trial year is filled with much to learn, much excitement about this new organizational development, and much optimism about the bonus. However, time and familiarity diminish these factors significantly. The ability to handle this situation as it occurs is a true sign of a successful firm. Successful firms such as DeSoto manage to rekindle the enthusiasm from that first year through a genuine interest in organizational development. Another factor that can help the firm keep the plan fresh is the natural relation of the bonus to the firm's ability to meet its markets effectively. No bonus accrues automatically. The bonus exists only if all employees zealously pursue the goals of increasing quantity, improving quality, and reducing costs.

As seen in Exhibits 7.4 and 7.5, the number of suggestions can decline. At least two factors cause this situation. First, irritations in the work environment are taken care of as suggestion-making behavior related to productivity is learned. Second, the potential for continued suggestion making declines. However, look at Exhibit 7.2. Over the seventeen year period 1987 is the best!

Four Key Roles

At DeSoto, four key roles emerge in support of the Scanlon plan: (1) plant manager; (2) controller; (3) personnel manager; (4) departmental supervisor. Each of these roles has different duties, pressures, and opportunities that shape the quality of plan involvement and maintain this quality over time.

The most important role in the promotion and maintenance of the plan is that of the plant manager or chief executive officer. After seventeen years of experience with Scanlon, DeSoto Plant Manager Tom Lester has clearly demonstrated his expertise in performing the duties necessary to sustain the initial enthusiasm and vitality surrounding the plan. He has been a catalyst for successful and realistic goal setting and an ardent proponent of quality communication. Based on interviews with his workers, Tom Lester is viewed as a fair person and, thus, he exemplifies a truly successful Scanlon plant manager.

Another important role in promoting and maintaining the plan over time is that of the company controller. His role cannot be minimized. Jim Barker has more than adequately handled the ever-increasing responsibilities required of him under the plan. He is available to the production committee meetings and reviews their ideas. By doing this, he constantly reminds workers of areas in which high costs occur, situations that could be remedied by increased suggestion making. In this sense, Jim Barker is often viewed as the key to problem solving in the involvement system.

Another major role in the maintenance of the plan is the company personnel manager. His overall goal consists of communicating what Scanlon is and what it is not to all levels of personnel. Bob Highland, personnel manager, has successfully achieved this goal. He provides orientation to all new personnel regarding the plan and notes plan activity that could be useful for future training and promotion decisions. More important, Bob Highland often serves as a reinforcer of the policy that affects the other roles previously discussed. In other words, not only does he provide training and discussion regarding DeSoto's current situation, but he also provides planning toward DeSoto's future with their gainsharing program.

DeSoto departmental supervisors occupy the fourth key role in maintaining successful operation of the plan over time. Besides the fact that they influence many important decisions in terms of the acceptance or rejection of suggestions, departmental supervisors provide the essential link between management and workers. This link is necessary for the quality communication advocated by the Scanlon philosophy. In this regard, the departmental supervisors play an indispensable role in the overall operation of the plan.

Use of Task Forces

It takes more than these key people to successfully maintain or "feed" the program over time. DeSoto has developed task forces to stimulate the suggestion-making process. The task forces are formed at the departmental level and are given specific assignments. The information obtained from these assignments is then used for determining areas needing improvements, and this information is later referred to the appropriate department.

Feeding the system requires managers and workers to share their concerns, thoughts, and information on which production areas require attention. DeSoto obviously possesses such people, and it is these people who have made the entire plan successful for seventeen years.

Intangible Benefits of the Plan at DeSoto

Observations of Management Personnel

As mentioned earlier, the plan provides the organization with both tangible and intangible benefits. Following 17 years of experience and observations, DeSoto management from five Scanlon plants were asked to cite the intangible benefits stemming from the incorporation of the Scanlon philosophy into their specific organizations. The following observations surfaced—

1. The plan provides the employees with the assurance that they will receive some degree of recognition by peers, by supervisors, and more importantly, by management. This provision is accomplished by the documentation and evaluation process required for all suggestions.
2. The plan increases the communication among all employees within the organization through their participation in the involvement system.
3. Increased representation and variety of ideas are provided by the plan since management receives suggestions from employees at all levels.
4. Many suggestions result in savings to management in terms of time, training, and development. Examples of these are as follows:

    a. Scanlon helps develop employees at all levels. This is done by encouraging workers to participate actively in the involvement system and thus become better acquainted with the entire production process.
    b. The plan identifies employees with the potential to serve as supervisors or managers. The production committees and screening committee provide a forum for the emergence and observation of leadership abilities.
    c. The plan educates employees regarding the need to justify capital budget requests. The mutual sharing of information and constant feedback on suggestions between management and workers educates the workers as to management's reasons for accepting or rejecting suggestions.
    d. Where suggestions result in the addition of a capital item, the employees have a greater interest in getting

the unit operating faster or overcoming start-up difficulties. Since the plan emphasizes productivity improvement, the workers want the production process to
run as smoothly as possible.

e. Workers become better acquainted with the entire production process through increased communication with
all employees. This flow of information can provide a
fresh approach to improving plant safety and house-
keeping.

f. Scanlon helps workers understand the rationale for holding the total plant labor force to a minimum. Here again,
this is the result of open communication between management and workers.

g. The plan provides a means of uniting two or more departments in a common project. The involvement system and increased communication make this situation
possible.

h. The plan is an important addition to the benefit package
of the firm and provides the firm with a competitive
advantage in the recruitment of new employees.

While tangible benefits are important in the assessment of the
plan and its effect on the organization, the intangible benefits cannot and should not be ignored. They also influence productivity in
a more subtle, yet very important, way. These intangible benefits
lend further support to the fact that the plan provides the organization and its workers with many advantages, thus making it a
superior productivity improvement program.

Social-Psychological Outcomes of the Plan

Consequences for Employees

There are many kinds of consequences resulting from gainsharing. These consequences affect not only the organization as a
whole, but each individual employee as well. These social-psycho-
logical outcomes merit discussion in the fact that they add a more
human quality to our discussion of Scanlon at DeSoto. Also, by
looking at employees' attitudes regarding the plan and its effect on
the organization and on themselves, ideas for improvement and
revitalization of the system are provided.

These outcomes were studied intensively in 1971, 1972, 1980, and 1984. The attitudinal data were collected at different intervals during that time. The first took place during an 11-month period dating from October 1971 to August 1972. Seven years elapsed between the first survey and the data collected in July 1980. In 1971, there were 145 employees contacted. Of them, 142 (98 percent) agreed to participate in the survey. This group included managerial, clerical, and blue-collar personnel. The sales force was not included, as it lay outside the scope of the plan.

Later in 1971—after the plan was introduced, but before a bonus was announced—each worker who had agreed to participate was contacted again. Three months had elapsed. During this time, 6 individuals declined to participate and 17 were unavailable because of separation, illness, vacation, or military leave. This left 119 remaining in the survey group.

Very late in 1971, measures assessed the amount of learning that had occurred based on communication and experience with the plan. Uniform questions with standard rating scales were carefully administered in face-to-face interviews. Comparisons of all three surveys use each individual's scores as his or her own control. In other words, any increase or decrease in knowledge of the plan or change in personal attitude toward the plan is measured by subtracting each person's score from his previous score on the same variable. In 1980, measurements were intended to evaluate workers' knowledge and attitudes regarding the plan over an extended period of time (eight years). Although this group was considerably smaller (18 people) than the last measurement group, 16 of these individuals had participated in the three previous measurements. These attitudinal data were collected through informal group and single interviews occurring over a two-day period.

In 1984, a replication study was undertaken by Amy M. McDowell. Using a stratified random sample, she presented all the questions from the original study of 1971–1972 to 65 of the 208 employees (31 percent).[6]

Chronological Evaluation

The social and psychological outcomes of gainsharing at DeSoto are best evaluated chronologically—across these three studies. These three sets of data provide useful information in determining the short-term, as well as long-term, effects of learning the gainsharing philosophy at DeSoto.

In 1971, the entire DeSoto population reflected high levels of general satisfaction with the plan. For example, over 90 percent of the employees expressed satisfaction with their employer "compared to most they know of." The hourly group, which is the main population for suggestion making, revealed that 77 percent of the DeSoto employees surveyed were satisfied with job security and 74 percent were satisfied with their pay.

Employee Satisfaction

It is interesting to note that many plan studies reveal initially low levels of employee satisfaction (including outright dissension— see Shultz, 1951).[7] This relatively low level of satisfaction elsewhere could be a reflection of skepticism on the part of the employee. Since the employee has had no prior experience with the plan, naturally he or she is skeptical about the possible benefits that can be obtained from it.

However, late in 1971, a significant increase in the satisfaction scores of the hourly group occurs at DeSoto. It should also be mentioned that interest in the job was found to be higher at this time, as was the feeling of accomplishment. These data also revealed an increase in scores in opportunity for being informed and an increase in scores in participation.

Cooperation, Participation, and Teamwork

The literature of gainsharing (Chapter 2) states that a major social and psychological outcome of the plan is the change in cooperation, participation, and communication—in other words, the results unrelated to the bonus. Also, many experts have cited that the plan produces and enhances coordination and teamwork.[8]

These findings from previous research were substantiated at DeSoto in 1972. Exhibit 7.6 reflects the net attitudinal change among both managerial and hourly workers across these two time periods.[9] DeSoto managers were optimistic that participation might increase (approximately 90 percent). Later, all the company managers surveyed (100 percent) were certain that participation had increased.

The study showed that 79 percent of the managers believed communication might improve. After eight months with the plan, 93 percent of the DeSoto managers felt communication had improved.

In the area of cooperation, the managers were less hopeful.

Exhibit 7.6   Short-Term Outcomes of the Plan Between 1971 and 1972 DeSoto Corp., Garland, Texas (Percentage)

PERCEIVED OUTCOME	MANAGERS	HOURLY
1. Participation		
Percentage "might increase" at Time 2	90	44
Percentage "had changed" at Time 3	100	82
Net change	(+10)	(+38)
2. Communication		
Percentage "might improve" at Time 2	79	65
Percentage "had improved" at Time 3	93	72
Net Change	(+14)	(+7)
3. Cooperation		
Percentage "would be better" at Time 2	74	53
Percentage "better now" at Time 3	77	71
Net Change	(+3)	(+18)

Managers = 28
Hourly   = 66
  Total   94

Source: Brian Graham-Moore, *Sharing the Gains of Productivity* (Scarsdale, New York: Work in America, 1982).

Roughly 74 percent of the managers believed cooperation would improve under the plan. Later, this percentage remained about the same, indicating that 77 percent of the managers felt cooperation had improved.

Overall, the hourly workers were more conservative in their estimates regarding increases in participation, communication, and cooperation. Early in 1971, only 44 percent of the hourly workers surveyed at DeSoto thought participation would increase. After eight months of experience with the plan, 82 percent perceived that participation had definitely improved.

Of DeSoto's hourly workers, 65 percent believed that communication (both within departments and between departments) would improve with the plan. This perception increased only slightly at a later time. At that time, 72 percent of the hourly workers thought that communication had improved.

Slightly more than half (53 percent) of the hourly workers believed that cooperation would be better under the plan. And 71 percent of the workers perceived a definite increase in cooperation.

Contrasting these two groups (managers and hourly workers) is essential for understanding the true impact of the plan on all employees. As is clearly evidenced by the change in attitudinal data, DeSoto managers had more positive perceptions of the plan and its effect on participation, communication, and cooperation than did the hourly workers. This perceptual difference between the two groups of employees could possibly be the result of increased familiarity and understanding of the plan on the part of DeSoto managers. Also, it was explained to the managers how important it was for them to be supportive of the plan in order for it to be successful, which could have caused the higher perceptions on the part of the managers. It should be remembered, however, that although the hourly workers were more conservative in their opinions about these factors, their net attitudinal change was in a positive direction and usually greater than that of managers.

Long-term Results

Until now, our discussion has focused on the initial short-term effects of the plan at DeSoto, i.e., the first year. While the net changes spanning the first year experience are impressive, most new programs do well in the first year. At the end of that first year the ultimate question was—could these nonbonus outcomes keep improving?

Looking at survey data collected in 1980 is instructional (please see Exhibit 7.7). Again, we will divide our analysis into two groups—managers and hourly workers. In terms of participation, 100 per-

Exhibit 7.7   Perceived Outcomes of Gainsharing in 1980 DeSoto, Corp., Garland, Texas (Percentage)

PERCEIVED OUTCOME	MANAGERS	HOURLY
1. Participation increased since 1972?	100	63
2. Communication increased since 1972?	89	88
3. Cooperation increased since 1972?	89	88

Managers   = 6
Blue collar = 12
    Total   = 18

cent of DeSoto managers surveyed believed participation had increased within the first year of the plan's inception.

In the area of communication, 89 percent of DeSoto's managers felt that communication had improved over the years. This percentage represented an insignificant change.

Regarding cooperation, once again 89 percent of DeSoto's managers surveyed believed cooperation had improved. This is a significant perceptual change (+12 percent) from 1971.

DeSoto's hourly workers were also questioned to determine their attitudes concerning changes in participation, communication, and cooperation over the eight-year period. With respect to participation, 63 percent of the hourly workers observed an increase in participation levels. This represents a 19 percent decline from the 1971–1972 data collection.

Of the hourly workers surveyed at DeSoto, 88 percent believed communication had improved since 1971. This percentage represents a 16 percent increase over the time span between 1971–1972 and 1980.

Regarding cooperation, 88 percent of the hourly workers perceived an improvement in cooperation by 1980. This is a 17 percent increase on this outcome. An important point to remember is that the hourly workers exhibited initially low levels of optimism regarding the chance for improvements in participation, communication, and cooperation. These significant increases in perceived improvements in communication and cooperation appear to be the result of the hourly workers' learning over time.

In 1984, the replication study by McDowell sampled 31 percent of the entire work force. When results are compared to 1971, 1972, and 1980, mean scores on the perception of interdepartmental cooperation and communication showed a decline. Mean scores of the perceptions of acceptance of suggestions, supervisory openness to ideas, and overall job satisfaction were uniformly high. That is, no drop-off occurred when compared to previous surveys. Sharing know-how perceptions, however, showed the most serious decline in mean scores in 1984. For example, when employees were asked to rate their perceptions of decision makers' awareness of lower-level problems and sharing of practial know-how, the mean scores for all employees were lower. When these lower scores were compared to the very high scores given to the importance of participation ratings, a clear indication was provided to Tom Lester that something was wrong.

His puzzlement was compounded by the fact that 1984 broke

all previous DeSoto records for suggestion making—244 suggestions were made. Yet, when he focused on the perceptions of lower-
level employees on cooperation, communication, and know-how
sharing, he knew something was amiss. Using the survey data as
a diagnostic tool, he investigated and discovered that the rate of
implementation of accepted suggestions was low. He reinstituted
a policy to get accepted suggestions implemented at the department level if at all possible, that is, not wait for maintenance to
deal with implementation. This policy eased the burden that the
maintenance department was experiencing. Supervisory training
also seemed indicated as a result of the growth in business and
employment. After all, many new people had been absorbed and
their impact on the organizational culture was significant. These
actions taken by Tom Lester and DeSoto management late in 1984
were timely. The rate of suggestion making for 1985 was greater
than the previous high of 1984 and the rate of implementation was
normal (around 70 percent).

Factors Influencing Success

Overall, the social and psychological outcomes of the plan at
DeSoto can be classified as positive. However, these positive outcomes are not assured by the plan. In other words, the success of
the plan is determined by many factors—some under the control
of DeSoto management and some not. Those factors that helped
determine the success of the plan were as follows: (1) a clear understanding of the plan and how it works by all employees; (2) a
supportive and optimistic attitude by all personnel in critical roles
in the organization (managers and first-line supervisors); and (3) an
overall organizational climate of acceptance and trust.

Clear Understanding

The first factor, clear understanding, was felt to be under
management's control. The presentation of the plan is crucial to
its successful operation. Therefore, DeSoto management paid close
attention to the methodology used to introduce and familiarize the
work force with the plan since it realized the effects would be felt
for years to come. An example of this can be seen in Bob Highland's
orientation program for Scanlon participants.

Supportive Personnel

The second factor, supportive personnel, was partially under management's control but was also dependent on the type of personality found in the organization's key roles. While all personnel in critical roles may appear supportive and optimistic, it is still possible for these key people to seriously undermine the plan. If these key people are unsure of their own abilities, autocratic in their interpersonal relationships, or threatened by change, their shallow support and optimism will soon be detected. Then, the plan may appear manipulative and spurious. Therefore, it is imperative that all management be genuinely supportive of the plan in order to ensure its success. DeSoto had only minor problems in this regard. Team building among managers and supervisors is viewed as an appropriate training technique to instill the Scanlon philosophy.

Trust

The third and final factor, trust, is also partially under the control of management but is also influenced by the personalities found in the work force. Management can and should counsel and reassure workers, which will help to promote and foster a climate of both acceptance and trust. However, management is not the sole influence on the organizational climate. The success and, in a sense, the foundation of gainsharing rests on the work force. These people should be individuals who fit the following employee selection profile—

1. high on interpersonal trust measures;
2. reinforced and motivated by group beliefs rather than individual beliefs;
3. motivated by extrinsic factors rather than intrinsic factors, i.e., pay for productivity.

It is not mandatory that all workers fit this profile, but a majority of the DeSoto work force does. If this is not the case, the goals of increasing participation, communication, and cooperation will be difficult to achieve.

In summary, an in-depth analysis supports several conclusions. Looking at the data on both a short- and long-term basis, it is clear that managers and subordinates view the plan differently. Possible reasons for this were discussed. These perceptual differences appear to be reasonably stable over time. Overall, after 17 years of experience with the plan, levels of trust and satisfaction are high. Perceived levels of participation, communication, and cooperation are good. There appears to be no reason why all these outcomes will not continue at DeSoto.

Conclusions

Productivity at DeSoto appears to be enhanced by the plan. The bonus formula, which measures labor productivity, shows an average payroll bonus of 9.6 percent over 17 years. When output of 1970 is compared to current levels, it has increased by as much as 78 percent, as measured by gallons of paint.

Development and maintenance of the bonus formula over time raises special problems in fostering an atmosphere of equity and mutual trust. Forced to change the formula because of external demand, pricing factors, and increased capacity, DeSoto management made their reasons clear. Some workers may not understand this change and, even if they do, they may see the plan as manipulative. The decision to use a simple rather than comprehensive bonus formula depends on many factors. DeSoto chose a simple formula so as to reinforce worker understanding. The rationale for this choice is discussed in Chapter 3.

The analysis of the involvement system at DeSoto reveals that irritants with the working environment are a common source of suggestions in the early stages of the plan. However, as learning occurs, productivity-related suggestions dominate—especially those that focus on quantity. Productivity also affects suggestion-making behavior. Slack-period suggestions reflect ideas not related to productivity. Feeding the system with accounting and technical information is especially helpful in overcoming this problem.

Costs associated with operating the plan, such as time spent in meetings, appear to be outweighed by the benefits, both tangible and intangible. Indeed, the benefits of gainsharing appear to be the reason it has remained viable through the years at DeSoto. Numerous studies have indicated that the quality of the national labor force is constantly improving. As this occurs, the industrial culture becomes more conducive to the sharing of information in order to improve productivity.

Recommendations of Management

Finally, the installation and maintenance of gainsharing required DeSoto management to consider a number of key issues. Based on the available information and the result of management's evaluation, the following recommendations were made. It is important to note that these recommendations are not unique to DeSoto. Therefore, they might be applied to any firm contemplating using the plan.

1. Key people in management and working ranks should possess a thorough understanding of the formula and filter this knowledge to others in the organization. These people should be identified and exposed to the mechanics of the formula early on in the formulation and installation process. Good distribution and circulation of these individuals enhance employee acceptance and trust in the plan.

2. Complaints or dissatisfiers in the work environment have been shown to be the most common suggestion type received at the initial stages. Managers should anticipate these nonproductive suggestions in such a way as to (a) instruct production committees that these suggestions will have no effect on the bonus, and (b) deal with the substance of the nonproductive suggestion by encouraging union leadership to handle them. If no union exists, then management must still deal with the nonproductive suggestions on a basis perceived to be outside the plan. Some of the nonproductive suggestions may be processed as suggestions, i.e., accepted and implemented. These suggestions should be reviewed at a later time as nonproductivity-related suggestions and be processed (in terms of policy) outside of the plan.

3. Another suggestion-related issue is the decline in the number of suggestions over time. All organizational leaders should actively seek out opportunities to "feed the system" and direct idea generation efforts toward new areas. One role in the organization keenly suited for this task is the controller or chief cost accountant. By participating in production committee meetings, he or she can indicate high-cost services or operations, inform the committee of redundancies in services or operations, or point out cyclical

costs with the objective of smoothing the production process.

4. Front-line supervisors may feel threatened by new types of participation and high rates of suggestions from their departments (including grievances). Managers and consultants must work with the supervisors by counseling and reassuring them. There may be some turnover at this level of supervision, but the suggestion system can help solve this problem by identifying promotable individuals.

5. Relevant cost information should be provided so that everyone can perceive a definite and causal link between behaviors and rewards. Committee meetings can and should be utilized to transmit this information.

6. Since individuals differ in the ability to communicate information, it is often necessary to individualize communication regarding the plan. That is, the communication must be tailored to the ability of the employee to receive the information. Again, the committee system can facilitate this end.

7. Finally, the plan is frequently presented as a structure or formula that will produce greater cooperation and productivity. This emphasis ignores the process of participation. Basic human values and attitudes about work, coworkers, the organization, and our economic system are at stake. Therefore, DeSoto management believes that there is no substitute for organizational policies built on trust and mutual dependence. The process of participation can be enhanced by supportive training in interpersonal skills for all organization members. This type of training helps smooth the process of group interaction so basic to the plan's success.

DeSoto (Garland) has had its Scanlon plan 17 years at this writing. The ensuing years have brought many changes to the people of DeSoto. However, the plan is still alive and vital to the interests of all concerned. It has accomplished the original goals of Tom Lester, while introducing many new objectives worthy of pursuit. Solely for its value as a communication system, DeSoto management would keep the plan. As a way of life at the workplace, however, it appears that the entire work force wishes to keep the plan.

Notes

1. B.E. Moore, *A Plant-Wide Productivity Plan in Action: Three Years of Experience with the Scanlon Plan* (Washington, D.C.: National Commission on Productivity and Work Quality, 1975).
2. B.E. Moore and T.L. Ross, *The Scanlon Way to Improved Productivity* (New York: Wiley-Interscience, 1978).
3. C.F. Frost, J.H. Wakely, and R.A. Ruh, *The Scanlon Plan for Organization Development: Identity, Participation, Equity* (East Lansing: Michigan State University Press, 1974).
4. R.B. McKersie, "Wage Payment Methods of the Future," *British Journal of Industrial Relations*, June 1963, 191–212.
5. J. Short and B.E. Moore, "Preliminary Findings of a Multivariate Analysis of Suggestion Systems Impact on Productivity" (working paper, Graduate School of Business, The University of Texas at Austin, 1975).
6. A.M. McDowell, "A Study of Employees Attitudes Toward the Scanlon Plan and Its Effect on the Involvement System at DeSoto, Inc., Garland, Texas" (unpublished research paper, Grand Canyon College, Phoenix, Arizona, 1984).
7. G.P. Shultz, "Worker Participation on Production Problems," *Personnel*, November 1951, 209–211.
8. Frost et al., *The Scanlon Plan for Organization Development*, note 3, above; F. G. Lesieur, ed., *The Scanlon Plan—A Frontier in Labor-Management Cooperation* (Cambridge: Technology Press of M.I.T. and New York: Wiley, 1958); R. B. McKersie, "Wage Payment Methods of the Future," *British Journal of Industrial Relations*, June 1963, 191–212; J. N. Scanlon, "Talk on Union Management Relations" (Proceedings on Conference Productivity, Industrial Relations Center, University of Wisconsin, 1949) 10–18.
9. B. Graham-Moore, *Sharing the Gains of Productivity* (Scarsdale, N.Y.: Work in America, 1982).

Chapter 8

Gainsharing and the Government Sector

James E. Jarrett

Introduction

Gainsharing should be of extraordinary appeal to elected governmental officials since it promises to instill capitalism into the bureaucracies and supports the thoroughly American value of rewarding those who produce more. The fundamentals of gainsharing can be understood relatively quickly by employees and can be easily explained to citizens. Most important, gainsharing would appear to be a better course of action than raising taxes or reducing constituent services.

Gainsharing should appeal to appointed senior government officials and to classified employees as well. Criticism of government performance has only recently become muted after more than ten years of harsh judgments. Government services are expanding at a far slower rate than in the period after World War II, and, as a result, advancement opportunities for governmental employees have been dramatically reduced. Compensation for public employees, with some exceptions of course, has failed to keep up with increases in salaries in the private sector, and this trend has continued for more than a decade.

In each case, gainsharing offers a possible solution. It is a

Marion Jarrett and Elizabeth Black provided assistance with this research.

method for improving performance, enables services to expand without budget expansion, and provides additional remuneration.

This chapter will review gainsharing in local, state, and federal agencies. It will provide a chronology of past experiments and will profile more recent and current examples. Some of the unique features and environments of government gainsharing projects will be cited. Analysis of the characteristics and factors associated with successes and failures leads to conjecture about gainsharing's potential in coming years. Since approximately one of every six American workers is a government employee, its value to employees, to taxpayers, and to recipients of government services could be significant.

Early Group Incentive Experiences

Review of Twelve Programs

Group incentives for government employees are not widespread. However, there have been a surprising number of actual cases since 1970. A review by Saggese in 1980 identified 12 gainsharing programs in state and local governments during the previous decade.[1] The jurisdictions involved were the following:

Nassau County, New York
New York City
Rockville, Maryland
Lake Charles, Louisiana
Detroit, Michigan
Flint, Michigan
Orange, California
State of North Carolina
State of Wisconsin
State of New York
State of Washington
State of Connecticut

The projects in Lake Charles, Detroit, and Flint covered only sanitation workers. The Orange, California, effort involved the Police Department, and the states of Washington and Connecticut operated projects in only one department, the Department of Printing and the Department of Motor Vehicles, respectively.

Results from this group of programs generally were negative. According to Saggese,

> Only 12 programs at the state or local level seem to have gone beyond the level of discussion. Three were total failures; the others were at least somewhat successful. Yet, most of those programs that produced gains initially were not able to sustain them for more than a few years, and only two programs are still effectively operating.

Detroit

This program in the sanitation department illustrates the use of productivity bargaining to gain acceptance of a shared savings program.[2] City officials offered to share with employees cost savings generated by the introduction of larger garbage trucks. Started in the summer of 1973, the program initially proved to be successful, generating average bonuses ranging from 5 to 6 percent of an average employee's salary and reasonable cost savings for the city. Bonuses were paid quarterly. The formula relied not on actual savings, but on an estimate of potential savings and proved to be too complex for employees to understand. Quality was supposed to be maintained through a cleanliness monitoring system and by a component in the formula. After several years, savings deteriorated, and the program was dropped from the contract in 1980.

Flint

As in Detroit, this shared savings plan involved the sanitation department. It was started in 1973 along with productivity bargaining, a task system, and a form of work standards. The shared savings formula emphasized overtime reduction along with paid work-hours per ton factor, route completion factor, and so forth.[3] The bonus earned was divided 50–50 between sanitation employees (including supervisors) and the city. Results initially were impressive. Overtime dropped from 6,700 hours in fiscal 1973 to 2,200 hours in fiscal 1974. Bonuses for individual employees were reasonable, averaging $261 per year in 1974 and $458 in 1975. Later, problems arose with vehicle maintenance, and, due to resentment by sanitation employees, the supervisors were removed from the original plan.[4]

An altered form of the plan is still operating. According to city officials, the 47 sanitation employees are awarded a bonus of $0.24 per hour, which is reduced by any chargeable overtime.

State of Washington Printing Plant

Implemented in July 1974, this shared savings incentive program was designed to reduce spoilage and improve efficiency. The formula was based on the ratio of hours sold/hours bought, where the numerator is the idealized time a job would require (and determines the price the customer pays) and the denominator is the actual hours required to complete the job. Data acquired by Saggesse, suggests the program was successful; production levels went up from 77.3 percent to 82.8 percent and savings totaled approximately $170,000 the first year and $176,000 the second year.[5] Calculations of results were performed quarterly. Inexplicably, management's share of the bonus pool was 71 percent in 1975 and about 90 percent in 1976. As a result, the average employee bonus dropped from $1,993 to $661. There was no indication of a formal employee involvement component. While the plant management considered the program successful, the program was halted by the legislature in 1976. State legislators did not find the premise of paying bonuses to state employees acceptable.

Connecticut Department of Motor Vehicles

This late 1970s demonstration project was conducted in one branch office with 46 state employees. Its size belies its importance, however. This was the first specific project of a statewide labor-management committee examining possible improvements in productivity and employee job satisfaction.[6] While the actual demonstration period was for one year only, April 1979 to April 1980, considerable effort over more than two years was expended by state and federal officials.[7] The program was intended to improve output, not reduce aggregate expenditures. A base level of productivity for seventeen discrete transactions of the branch office was calculated for the base year.

Improvements during the one-year demonstration period were designed to yield a quarterly bonus for each employee. The amount of the bonus was calculated by taking the midpoint of each employee's salary scale and multiplying the rate by ½ the percentage of productivity improvement. Annual bonuses turned out to be relatively small—about $154 per employee. Overall quality of work declined, there was the need for more supervision, and the project proved difficult to administer. So while productivity improvement and increased labor-management cooperation occurred, analysts determined the model would prove difficult to transfer to other sites. After one year, the project was dismantled.

Summary of Early Experiences

As a group, these early experiences contained few promising results. Many of the programs were never implemented. Those which were had mixed results. Worse yet, even some of the outwardly successful efforts, such as Connecticut and Washington, did not survive very long.

Some of the programs seem to have had fundamental design flaws. Some, especially those established through adversarial collective bargaining probably fared no worse or better than most other elements of the agreements during those years. Causes of the other failures seemed idiosyncratic.

One Important Model: State of North Carolina

While many efforts were faltering and others never beginning, the state of North Carolina started a demonstration project on small group incentives. Begun in 1978, the plan was voluntary and provided annual bonuses to groups that achieved cost reductions. If members of a group successfully achieved a productivity increase, employees shared equally (in absolute dollars) up to 25 percent of the demonstrated cost savings. The remaining 75 percent of the savings were retained by the state government, sometimes within the department and other times returned to the treasury.

North Carolina's approach was innovative for a variety of reasons. It was a larger effort than previous state government attempts; it included a variety of different types of work units in multiple locations; and it was strictly voluntary. Perhaps the most important feature was the creation of a statewide structure so that growth could be accommodated later, if necessary.[8]

The concept, then loosely called a modified Scanlon plan, appeared radical but sound. Many managers shied away from the plan because they feared that savings, once achieved, would be deleted from their budgets in subsequent years. In other work units, fear of speed-ups existed. Some units were essentially disqualified because they lacked adequate output measures or acceptable cost accounting procedures.

Eventually three work groups started the program in fiscal

year 1978–1979, with one later withdrawing because of employee fears that cost reductions would hurt patient care. The two remaining units were from the State Department of Transportation. Both groups earned small bonuses, approximately 2 percent of annual base salary, at the end of the test period.

In retrospect, the bonuses were not nearly as important to the program over the longer term as were some other decisions made during the first-year test period. Inflation, a factor which had not been addressed in the statute, was disrupting the basic premise of the program—that is, that expenditures could be reduced from earlier base periods due to productivity enhancements. The policy committee determined that part of the ongoing inflation would be an allowable exclusion because it was outside the control of the groups. Other important changes permitted bonuses to be paid from funds other than those of the participating unit (for example, from funds elsewhere in that unit's department), and allowed incentive pay for situations in which a unit's costs were constant but services had increased.

After the test period was extended, additional work units were brought into the program. The program still was minuscule, however, with fewer than 1,000 employees in all of the working units. (Preference was given to line-of-sight units, that is, work groups not generally larger than can be seen.) Subsequently, other defects of the legislation were tackled. Policies were adopted regarding nonrecurring expenditures, interpretation of cost, and service level. These were important policies, which have been features of legislation in other states' programs and enabling legislation. (These are briefly outlined in Exhibit 8.1.)

With many significant decisions made during the second year, the North Carolina program began expanding more rapidly. Participation in the third and fourth years increased—by 1982, almost 2,000 of North Carolina's approximately 57,000 state workers were in participating units. Savings grew as well. In the 1984–1985 period, total gross annual savings were about $3.6 million. Incentive pay was about $900,000, and awards ranged from nothing in 11 of the 62 participating units to more than $1,100 per employee in two units. The average employee's bonus was $331.[9]

By the end of 1985, cumulative net savings approached $7 million. Poised for great expansion in terms of additional units and participating employees, the program was then abolished by the North Carolina Legislature in 1985. The principal reason cited was the poor situation of the state budget. No one disputes the success

Exhibit 8.1   North Carolina's Policies

1. Nonrecurring expenditures—requires that cost of operation be real and not the result of nonrecurring expenditures that were single-outlay or one-time expenditures in the preceding fiscal year. Requires a unit to depreciate nonrecurring expenditures of $500 or more over the life of the purchased equipment. Also stipulates conditions for nonrecurring contractual services.

2. Interpretation of cost—requires that participating units operate "at less cost than the immediately preceding year" or "at no greater cost than the immediately preceding fiscal year." *Cost is interpreted to be "cost per unit of work,"* not only *reduced expenditures.*

3. Level of service—specifies that the level of services during the fiscal year must be maintained or improved and that the participating work group provide an acceptable definition and measurement of level of services both for the base period and for the participating period.

Source: Original documents from North Carolina Department of Administration as reported in Jarrett, 1981.

of the program. Nevertheless, a strong political effort was never made to resurrect the program. The new executive administration took no interest in reviving a bonus program for state employees, a progran which had been started and cultivated by a previous administration.

Successors

Unanswered Questions

Even before its premature termination, there were many important unanswered questions about the long-term viability of North Carolina's gainsharing experiment. These questions included the following:

- Was the incentive formula properly designed in terms of the sharing? Were the awards sufficiently large to motivate? Would the formula need to be changed later for units that participated many years?
- How would the individual-oriented employee suggestion program and gainsharing interact over time?
- How could gainsharing be expanded into different types of service delivery units, for instance, patient care institutions?
- Would the program work as well with larger work units? Would employees worry more about loafers?

- Were any measurement standards being compromised? Were service levels truly not being diminished?
- How could these results be achieved in the virtual absence of a formal employee involvement program?
- Would the program ever make significant impact in terms of cost savings as long as the program remained voluntary and cost reductions were not explicitly returned to the fund from which they had originated?

Despite these lingering doubts, the auspicious early results proved sufficiently promising to others. In rapid succession, identical or similar programs were adopted by the states of New Hampshire, California, and Washington. In a number of other states such as Ohio, Massachusetts, and Minnesota, bills were introduced and hearings were held.

Impetus for the New Hampshire and California programs arose from legislative officials rather than executive departments, which, unfortunately, resulted in the demise of each program. In New Hampshire, executive officials had not requested the program and did not implement it. Effective July 1985, the statute was repealed, having never been tested in four years. In California, the shared savings program became effective January 1, 1983. From the outset, there were problems, both with the design and with implementation. No meaningful changes were ever made in the program, however. Legislative leaders and staff still endorsed the concept, but the statute was automatically repealed January 1, 1985, never having been truly tested.[10]

State of Washington

Created in 1982, the state of Washington's Teamwork Incentive Program (TIP) continues its expansion. Patterned on North Carolina's program, Washington's has proved equally successful. The parallels are numerous.

Washington's program started slowly with only two work groups in fiscal year 1984. Savings totaled a mere $130,000. Four work groups were added in the Department of Transportation in the following year. Savings were similar: $145,000. By 1986, nine units, mostly in the Transportation Department, were involved, and savings were $557,000.[11] In 1987, participating units included two from the Department of Revenue, three from the Department of Labor and Standards, and seven from the Department of Transportation. The number declined to eight units in fiscal year 1988 as a special focus developed. Multiple units from the Department of Corrections and from community colleges concentrated primarily on reducing energy consumption, and in the current fiscal year, 1989, the savings are beginning to accumulate appreciably.

Washington's program is unique in several respects. First, groups can enter the program at any time, not only at the beginning of the government's fiscal year. This feature enables units to participate according to their timetable and also eases the application process for the oversight staff and board. Second, in some ways Washington's program should not be acceptable politically, but it is. Employees in Washington receive 25 percent of documented savings, but the annual *TIP awards are not limited*. Awards have ranged from $89 to $6,273 per employee. Ten employees involved in photogrammetry and mapping analysis received these large awards in fiscal 1986. During the next year, no awards were given to these employees because their workload, highly variable due to contracting, declined significantly.

Third, none of the cost savings are returned automatically to taxpayers. The majority of savings (73 percent since 2 percent are used for operational costs of the program) remains in the agency and is placed in an unallotted status, which allows for reprogramming by agency officials, not legislators. Funds are returned to the original fund source only if they are unused at the end of the two-year state appropriation cycle.

Another equally interesting aspect of Washington's gainsharing program is that it coexists with a successful employee suggestion award program. Although some advocates of gainsharing in private firms believe the two are inherently incompatible, this may be less of a problem in public organizations. Given the voluntary aspect of the program in Washington, as in North Carolina, perhaps the two can indeed be complementary.

Washington's success to date suggests that North Carolina's experience was not a fluke. It does not suggest, however, that there is unlimited potential for group incentives. The program is still quite limited in scope and size. Some expansion to different departments has materialized but the units are still more production-oriented than many other groups within state government agencies. Nevertheless, with careful nurturing by capable staff and executive leaders, TIP's experience should prove encouraging to government officials elsewhere. The Appendix at the end of this chapter shows the application procedures and the TIP gainsharing formula.

Other Examples

State of Texas

In September 1986, Texas passed legislation creating a group incentive demonstration program similar to the ones used in Washington and North Carolina. The key differences from the two other state examples are as follows: (1) the formula distributes 25 percent of savings to employees, 25 percent to the respective department for further productivity enhancing projects, and 50 percent to the originating fund; (2) savings, in the absence of clarifying policy, would be determined as the difference between appropriations and actual expenditures. Due to a legal issue regarding composition of the policy-making commission and due to insufficient staff support, the program had not been implemented as of August 1989. However, both issues had been resolved, and implementation was expected to begin in late 1989.

City of Loveland, Colorado

One interesting municipal gainsharing program can be found in Loveland, Colorado. Begun in 1982, the program covers all of the approximately 400 city employees. Three tests must be met before employees may receive funds. First, city revenues must exceed actual expenses. Second, expenses must be less than or equal to the prior year's expenses *on a per capita basis*. Third, there must be acceptable satisfaction with city services as determined by a citizen satisfaction survey performed in May/June of each year (see Exhibit 8.2).

Loveland's program supports two elements of the city's mission statement: cost-effectiveness and high quality client service.[12] Each year since its inception, a bonus has been distributed:

1987	$206
1986	310
1985	250
1984	353
1983	308
1982	100

Ongoing reinforcement is provided by monthly monitoring of the status of net income, and placing statements in work stations

Exhibit 8.2   Gainsharing Pool

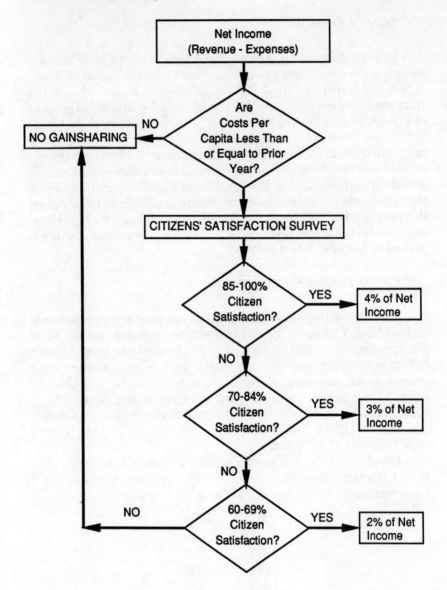

throughout the city. Bonuses are distributed the week before Christmas. There is no formal employee involvement program; nor is there an employee suggestion system. Some citizen reaction against the program has surfaced, but it has not been vehement.

Federal Projects

Similarity to Other Programs

Federal demonstration projects in the late 1970s and early 1980s seem to have been similar to projects in state and local governments. Many of the state and local government programs just described were limited to relatively small numbers of government employees. Many, also, lacked traditional employee involvement dimensions. Results were mixed at best. Initial federal projects appear to have fared just as poorly.

According to a General Accounting Office report released in September 1986, most early projects at Department of Defense installations were terminated within two years, if they ever were started.[13] Of 13 group projects examined, only three were ongoing: (1) A 36-person data transcription project at the Redstone Arsenal in Huntsville, Alabama; (2) A 90-person maintenance project at Newark (OH) Air Force Station; and (3) A 230-person warehousing project at the Defense Logistics Distribution Center in Tracey, California.

This latter project is one of several projects which mark a new phase in federal gainsharing work. These projects at several major federal installations are large-scale and more parallel to private sector gainsharing models.

Tracey, California

The first phase of the Tracey gainsharing project, begun in 1985, ended in September 1987. Reported results were encouraging. As reported by the U.S. Office of Personnel Management, the depot, which receives, stores, and issues supplies which are common to all military services, achieved about $576,000 in productivity gains over an 18-month period.[14] The 190 participating employees received half of that amount in bonuses, which were paid quarterly. Bonuses averaged about $1 per employee per hour. Quality did not deteriorate.

One major goal set for the depot was to reduce costs by 10 percent each year over a three-year period. During the 18-month test period this goal was surpassed—14 percent fewer employees were needed. Reductions were achieved by attrition and reassignment. As a consequence of the test period, the project was set for expansion to an additional 600 employees at the depot.

Pearl Harbor

The first Navy group incentive project was at the Pearl Harbor Naval Shipyard.[15] About 500 of the yard's 5,000 employees were involved in this project from July 1983 to December 1985. Machine Shop 31, in which the project was situated, performed light and heavy machine work, hydraulic repairs, and equipment testing. Work in the shop was highly interdependent, and the work could only be performed by teams. Work measures or incentives for individuals were meaningless.

Performance was determined by the Allowed Labor/Improshare formula explained in Chapter 3. It is based on engineering work standards, divided by actual hours. This performance factor then was reduced slightly because of the shop's historically low performance—otherwise, officials thought the standard would have been viewed as unattainable by employees. No employee involvement system was developed. The bonus distribution was divided, 50–50 between the government and employees. Despite a reduced workload for the shop during the project period, results were encouraging. Employee awards were as high as $2,488 during the first 18 months. Initial net savings during the period exceeded $600,000. (No detectable changes emerged in job satisfaction.) The plan was being readied for expansion to the entire shipyard when a new commander was installed who stopped all efforts on the program.

Charleston, South Carolina

There is one entire shipyard currently operating under a gainsharing plan. Moreover, the Charleston Naval Shipyard is perhaps the largest single gainsharing project ever undertaken by a government in this country. About 8,300 shipyard employees are involved following the yard's successful competitive bid for the overhauling of two ships. When the overhauling process is completed, bonuses will be distributed. As this paper was being compiled, Navy officials indicated that bonuses would be paid. The amounts, however, could not be calculated until the ships were at sea and all warranty work had been processed.

McClellan Air Force Base

Charleston's experience may be unique because of its function. More relevant to other governmental jurisdictions is a project at McClellan Air Force Base in Sacramento, California. About 2,000 federal employees are involved in this major, five-year (1987–1992) demonstration project on compensation and classification. In terms of compensation, this may be one of the most pure gainsharing projects ever attempted in government.[16] There are in excess of 80 work teams established, each having between three and ten employees, whose purpose is to discuss anything related to improvements in the accomplishment of mission outputs.

Baseline measures were computed for federal fiscal year 1987 (October 1986–October 1987). Progress is being measured against the budgeted baseline with an "expected cost minus actual cost" formula, which is adjusted for inflation, technology, and workload changes. Progress will be computed quarterly with measurement data being collected by three groups, the Comptroller's Office, the Office of Personnel Management, and the Rand Corporation.

As this chapter was being compiled, the experiment was proceeding as planned. Because of reduced workloads, however, the first two quarterly periods did not produce productivity improvements, or bonuses. A method for handling the reduced workload had been devised but had not been implemented early enough to make a difference.[17] McClellan is a major project. Their experiences should be monitored by anyone seriously interested in gainsharing within government. The project should be monitored also because of its employee appraisal process— during the five-year period no individual performance appraisals will be conducted. This decision, which will reinforce employees' orientation toward group performance, is highly unusual in the public sector.

Cherry Point

The first Defense Department installationwide gainsharing program began at Cherry Point Naval Aviation Depot, North Carolina. The aviation depot is one of six operated by the Navy and is the only one managed by Marines. Spread over 114 acres with more than 1.5 million square feet of buildings, Cherry Point has 3,000 employees and an annual budget of about $300 million. It is a maintenance facility for engines and aviation components.

On the surface, there is nothing unusual about Cherry Point. The gainsharing effort is based on a three-part formula (a 50–50 sharing of benefits with employees) of costs, timeliness of work, and quality.[18] And yet, there is a difference. A participative management approach has been adopted throughout the Depot. The normal authoritarian, whip-and-work-harder incentive method has been dismantled surprisingly easily, except for pockets of resistance at the midmanager level.

The first two quarterly awards to employees have been $265 and $349. Gainsharing is clearly an integral component at Cherry Point. Officials believe in it but they use other productivity enhancement methods as well. The depot's productivity coordinator said they (1) rely on Edward Demings' 14 principles of management; (2) focus on teamwork, rather than traditional competitive behavior, at the managerial level; (3) have created customer-vendor relations programs both externally and among departments internally within the Depot; and (4) provide extensive training and utilization of statistical process control methods.[19]

Cherry Point was designated as a federal Quality Improvement Prototype in June 1988. In addition, Cherry Point received the American Institute of Industrial Engineers award for excellence in productivity improvement.

As this chapter was being prepared, the federal government situation was developing rapidly. Many other federal gainsharing projects were being processed for implementation. The U.S. Navy alone anticipated 10 active projects in the federal 1988–1989 fiscal year.[20] The U.S. Army, which has had a successful, albeit contentious, two-year Allowed Labor/Improshare project at the Army Materiel Command in Arlington, Virginia, was also planning numerous projects.[21] The federal government's plans for gainsharing, unless they are disrupted, will soon overwhelm all that has already happened in the public sector so far.

If gainsharing were as extensively pursued in the domestic departments of the federal government as it has been in the Department of Defense, the lessons would be even more pertinent for America's 17 million government employees.

Some General Observations

From the variety of programs described in the previous sections, it is apparent that group incentive plans in the public sector are diverse. Most projects, with the exception of recent federal government actions, do not fit neatly into traditional gainsharing categories typical of the private sector as described in this book.

Governmental projects tend to be Allowed Labor/Improshare in their formula construction, but the policies of bonus distribution seem to be consistently less generous to employees. This leads to relatively small awards which rarely exceed more than 10 percent of base salary and often are as low as 2 percent (see Chapter 2 for comparison). Awards have tended, also, to be paid less frequently than in private firms, even though this difference is narrowing. Employee involvement in government also seems much less common, again with notable examples to the contrary.

With the fewer number of public sector projects, it is difficult to argue persuasively which conditions and independent variables would predict successes or failures. Until there are more cases available for analysis, a theory of governmental gainsharing would be premature. One possible hypothesis, that formal employee involvement plans must be present, can be rejected now. Formal mechanisms, for whatever reasons, do not seem as important to governments as to private firms. Based on a review of the governmental projects, no correlation can be found between the success or failure of a program and the presence of an employee involvement plan.

More Barriers for Governments

There are many reasons why gainsharing projects have not succeeded. Many reasons would apply similarly to private and public organizations. Some important and added barriers seem unique to governments.

- Legal barriers to public sector incentives still exist, but the bigger problem is the mistaken perception of many officials that incentives cannot be used.
- More commonly, incentives are viewed as inappropriate, even if legal. This view has another more negative corollary. Public employees are viewed by taxpayers as already more

than adequately compensated, given the amount and type of work produced.

- Another corollary is that where incentives are deemed appropriate in the public sector, they are considered more appropriate for individual employees than for groups of employees. This may partially be due to the backgrounds of many elected officials, backgrounds not based on running businesses or motivating employees in larger organizations.
- Elected officials sometimes have ideological, antigovernment biases. A private sector parallel to this situation is infrequent—a CEO or Board whose members would rather destroy the organization than improve it. Operationally, actions are antiemployee and designed to keep the organization as small as possible.
- Other elected officials, while not antigovernment, simply do not view government management as a high priority in comparison to the unmet service needs of citizens.
- Appointed officials and agency heads, not only elected officials, often restrict progress. They rarely embrace new budgetary and operational initiatives suggested by elected officials. To them, promises that cost savings won't jeopardize future departmental requests pose credibility problems.
- Existing budgetary practices can be a major barrier as well. If existing practices permit agencies to retain most or all of any savings, departments are unlikely to volunteer for a program which turns back funds for use by other governmental bodies.
- Compensation practices also can reduce participation. When employee and managerial salaries are capped, or at their maximum limit, bonuses may not be payable.
- The tendency toward overregulation in the public sector reduces the willingness to try innovative methods such as gainsharing. Fear of negative citizen reaction toward employee pay is rarely a consideration for private managers.
- Regulations pertaining to spending practices can be a problem for governments. For instance, when funds are provided by another level of government, there normally are provisions and conditions which place limitations on their use. Local governments using state funds and state governments using federal funds have already encountered limitations to sharing any savings as bonuses.

- Measurement of white collar outputs are thought to be more difficult to make. Generally there is a higher proportion of pure service activities in governments. Measurement of government service outputs, while improving, is still imprecise in many cases. The perception by legislators and legislative staff that this kind of measurement is poor and would not be adequate to determine true productivity increases will be a continual problem for advocates of governmental gainsharing (see Chapter 7 for the discussion on service industries and measurement problems).

Conclusion

Given these problems unique to the public sector, and those gainsharing pitfalls common to both private and public organizations, it is hard to be optimistic about the future of gainsharing in government. In some ways it is remarkable that so many gainsharing projects have been started and have succeeded. After all, most governmental agencies in this country have suffered financial setbacks in the past fifteen years. Government management and productivity programs have never garnered more than minimal financial support, nor have they piqued the interest of elected officials. And recently, any interest in management has been concentrated on more highly visible approaches such as outside contracting.

While the overall situation may be unfavorable, encouraging signs can be found. As the concept is communicated to governmental officials, both elected and appointed, the reception is nearly uniformly positive. Legislators, in particular, seem enthralled by the simplicity and common sense of gainsharing. The fact that there are few initial costs and that there is a reasonable prospect for reducing expenditures adds to gainsharing's appeal.

The number of governmental sites potentially available for gainsharing is another positive sign. Large segments within government, such as education, have yet to have a gainsharing project. Large institutions in state governments and in the federal domestic agencies remain untouched. Thousands of fire and police agencies are potential candidate sites as well.

Prospects for gainsharing will be aided also by the need for governments to address some of the same near- and longer-term organizational problems facing many private corporations. As the work force bulge moves up in age, motivating government workers will become an ever greater problem. Widespread dissatisfaction with current merit increase and performance appraisal methods also may lead to more opportunities for gainsharing demonstration projects. New reward structures in the public sector may be designed around the ideas found in Chapter 3.

It is unlikely that gainsharing in government will ever be a widespread phenomenon, possibly for some of the reasons reviewed in Chapter 1. Its expansion will be limited until government services and the quality of outputs by white collar government employees can be measured consistently and confidently. Based on past experience, the majority of gainsharing projects in government do not have a realistic chance of survival. Moreover, gainsharing in government will always be more fragile than in private firms. Nevertheless, some gainsharing programs have worked, and under proper conditions the concept has been proved valid for governments.

Notes

1. M. Saggese, "Shared Savings Programs in the Public Sector" (manuscript, New York City Office of Municipal Labor Relations), September 30, 1980.
2. L. Bell, *Incentives for Local Government Employees* (Washington, D.C.: International City Management Association, Management Information Service, Vol. 6, No. 6, June 1974).
3. J. Greiner et al., *Monetary Incentives and Work Standards in Five Cities* (Washington, D.C.: The Urban Institute, April 1977), 47–53.
4. M. Saggese, "Shared Savings," note 1, above, 9–11.
5. Ibid., 18–19.
6. Institute of Public Performance, "Possible Application of the Scanlon Plan in State Service" (Albany, N.Y.: Manuscript, New York State Governor's Office of Employee Relations/CSEA Joint Labor Management Committee on the Work Environment & Productivity, Appendix 6).
7. Press Release of Connecticut Department of Motor Vehicles, April 1979, Wethersfield, Conn.; Interdepartmental Message to the Commissioner of Motor Vehicles Division from Frederick McGrath, dated February 22, 1980; and M. Saggese, note 1, above, 20.
8. J. Jarrett, *Improving Productivity Through Monetary Incentives: North Carolina's Bonus Experiment* (Lexington, Ky.: The Council of State Governments, March 1981), 2.
9. Internal memorandum from Grace Rohrer of the North Carolina Department of Administration, January 9, 1986, 17.
10. State of California, *The Shared Savings Program: How Is It Working?* (Sacramento: Assembly Office of Research, May 1984).
11. State of Washington, "Description of Teamwork Incentive Program" (Olympia, Wash.: Secretary of State's Office, Washington Productivity Board, no date).

12. J. Winters, "Productivity Improvements in Loveland, Colorado," in *Management Science and Policy Analysis Journal–Letter* (Washington, D.C.: American Society for Public Administration, Section on Management Science and Policy Analysis, Vol. 2, No. 3, Winter 1985), 11–15.
13. U.S. General Accounting Office, *Gainsharing: DOD Efforts Highlight an Effective Tool for Enhancing Federal Productivity* (Washington, D.C.: General Government Division, GAO/GGD-86-143BR), 15.
14. U.S. Office of Personnel Management, "DLA Gainsharing Program," in *Incentive Awards Notes*, September–October 1987, 1–2.
15. T. Rainey, "Gainsharing in Government" (Master's thesis, Graduate Center for Public Policy and Administration, California State University, Long Beach, Cal., June 1987), 22–26.
16. Ibid., Appendix D-5.
17. Conversation with McClellan official on August 26, 1988.
18. Cherry Point Naval Aviation Depot, "Productivity Based Incentive Award Plan, Revision 1," (Cherry Point, N.C., September 1987).
19. "Cherry Point Depot," *Government Productivity News*, Vol. 2, No. 3, July 1988, 3.
20. Conversation with Bob Sniffin, Naval Personnel Research and Development Center, Arlington, Va., July 26, 1988.
21. T. Rainey, "Gainsharing in Government," note 15, above, Appendix C.

Appendix

Washington State Productivity Board

INCENTIVE PAY PROGRAM APPLICATION FORM

Please complete all pages of this application in order to be considered for participation in the Incentive Pay Program. The Productivity Board will decide which work units will participate in the Incentive Pay Program during the upcoming fiscal year from information supplied in this form. Additional pages may be attached. Please reference the appropriate section or area covered by any additional pages.

Information about work unit: Complete the following:

Work Unit (common name)   Budget Code Agency #   Program #

Subprogram organizational index   Agency

Unit Location/Address   Unit Supervisor   Address/Mail Stop

Phone/SCAN   Chief Fiscal Officer   Agency Head

APPROVAL SIGNATURES

Unit Supervisor   Chief Fiscal Officer   Agency Head

General Information: Give brief overview of unit operations.

What is done?

Where does the work originate?

How is work load assigned? By whom?

How is work measured?

Eligibility Criteria: Check **as many** areas as applicable.

Does this unit have an **identifiable** budget?   yes   no

Do financial accounting records show receipts and
expenditures solely attributed to this work unit?   yes   no

Does this unit have quantifiable work measures?   yes   no

Program Measures: Please give concise but complete answers.

List the specific tasks this work unit does.

Approximately what percentage of the total work done by this unit is
reflected in the tasks listed above?

What measurement standards are applied to these tasks? When and
how were these measurements developed?

How are service level and quality measured? How long have these
measurements been used?

Are current level and quality acceptable? Explain.

Who determines what is an acceptable level of service and quality?

Budget Information

Agency Number   Program Number   Subprogram/Org. Index

Can factors used to calculate unit costs be identified in the
subprogram/organizational index? Check one.

     All ___   Most ___   Some ___   None ___

Are accounts payable current? If not, please explain.

If this work unit maintains an inventory of supplies, what is the current
inventory as expressed in volume, weight, dollars or other appropriate
measure?

Inflation Information

What are the cost factors for which inflation is calculated? (labor, materials, overhead, equipment, etc.)

How will inflation rate be calculated? Choose one.

General Cost Index ———
Actual Inflation Rate ———
Office of Financial Management Inflation Factors ———

Who is responsible for calculating inflation costs? Give title.

If actual inflation rate is calculated, list all cost factors and source of information.

Records Management

How are records of man hours, material costs, and task accomplishments maintained? Attach copies of standard forms, reports, or records used. Please explain who completes the information and how each form is used.

How is unit cost calculated? List items used to calculate costs and source of data. (Costs per unit of labor, materials, equipment, overhead, etc.)

Where are employee records kept? By whom?

How many FTEs in this unit directly contribute in a measured way to the work accomplished? What percent of total employees of *this* work unit does this represent?

What is the current backlog of work? Express in tasks, hours, etc. If this is not a normal backlog, please explain.

Is any of this unit's work contracted out? If so, please explain method used to account for the work and its cost.

Who is responsible for record keeping for this work unit? (Title)

TO FIGURE TOTAL SAVINGS

Total savings are calculated by comparing base year data with participation year data after adjustments are made for inflation and/or unique expenditures.

(1) Calculate Unit Cost for each year.

Divide total expenditures by total workload.

		FY 1983	*FY 1984*
Expenditures	$	$711,037.00	$713,142.00
Workload	#	1,088	1,122
CPU		$653.53	$635.60

(2) Determine unit cost differential to identify unit cost savings average.

Subtract CPU FY 1983 − FY 1984

$653.53
−635.60

Difference $17.93 = average unit cost savings

(3) Determine total cost savings.

Multiply participation year workload by average unit cost savings.

1122
× $17.93

$20,117.46 = total cost savings

TO DISBURSE SAVINGS

(4) Total cost savings: $20,117.46

−25% For Incentive Award Payment, Paid to Employees

−2% For Productivity Board, Deposited Into Department of Personnel Savings Fund

−73% For Agency Use, Used to Pay Employer Share of OASI, With Remainder Placed Into Unallotted Status

Employee Awards	*Productivity Board*	*Agency*
$20,117.46	$20,117.46	$20,117.46
× .25	× .02	× .73
$ 5,029.36	$ 402.35	$14,685.75

$5,029.36 Awards
402.35 Productivity Board
14,685.75 Agency

TO FIGURE AWARDS

(5)   To figure employee incentive awards, divide total award amount by total number of employees.

Award Total (25%) $

Total # Shares   #
(15 Employees)

$5,029.36 = $335.29 (This amount represents one full share.)

Prorated shares are calculated by multiplying the full share by the percentage of the year worked by an employee.

12@	1 share	(worked 12 months)	4,023.48
1@	.83	(worked 10 months)	278.29
1@	.66	(worked 8 months)	221.29
2@	.50	(worked part-time)	335.29
1@	.33	(worked 4 months)	110.65
Distributed			$4,969.00
(undistributed)			(60.36)
15 Shares			5,029.36

TO PAY AWARDS

(6)   The Productivity Board will authorize all awards as based upon the gross total amount. Agency accounts officers will be responsible for determining appropriate deductions and issuing a voucher-check-warrant for the net award to individual employees.

Gross Award Amount
− Deductions
Net Award Payment

In accordance with RCW 41.60, funds to pay incentive awards are drawn from the benefiting agency's budget.

Because the award is considered income, federal taxes and social security must be withheld from the employee's share. Award amounts may not be used in computing retirement allowances.

Agencies may pay the employer portion of OASI by deducting the amount from agency savings.

Example:

	Individual Award		Agency Deductions
	$392.31	Savings	$14,685.75
Employee OASI	26.28	OASI	352.05
	$366.03		$14,333.70
W/H	60.00		
Net Award	$306.03		

Chapter 9

Gainsharing and Unions: Current Trends

Timothy L. Ross and Ruth Ann Ross

In order to fully understand the relationship of all parties within a gainsharing framework, the role of unions, one important institution, needs careful attention. Should unions like gainsharing? Should they learn more about the company, get more involved, get complaints resolved, perhaps make more money, and ensure long term job security through gainsharing? Or should they attempt to preserve the status quo and oppose the institution of gainsharing plans? Walter Ruether of the United Auto Workers was famous for his goal of increasing the pie and then sharing the benefits with members through profit sharing. Theoretically, the employee involvement component of many gainsharing plans should appeal to many union leaders because it emphasizes workplace democracy.

But, in reality, unions have generally been less than enthusiastic supporters of gainsharing. Unions have offered active support for these plans primarily in situations in which wage concessions are sought and gainsharing is part of an integrative package. That is, the unions are forced to accept no increases or actual decreases in a contract with the possibility of making up some of the difference through gainsharing. Broadly speaking, contracts negotiated by the steel and automotive industries are examples of this approach. Union leaders frequently support implementation of gainsharing and then subsequently decrease their active involvement.

Why do industries encounter opposition or less than enthusiastic support and what can be done to overcome it? This chapter will discuss research dealing with these questions. We will outline the concerns of high-ranking union officials about gainsharing plans. We will discuss what aspects of the plans they find objectionable and what they find attractive. Finally, we will recommend how to address the union's concerns in a manner that is straightforward and ultimately in the best interest of the company, the employees, the union itself, and most important, the United States as a competitor in international trade.

General Union Positions

In their study on worker participation and American unions, Kochan, Katz, and Mower described four stands taken by national unions on employee participation processes in general.[1]

1. *General opposition.* The general opposition to such plans is clearly stated by national union leaders. Local unions are discouraged, but not prevented, from participating. Several unions take this stand.

2. *Decentralized neutrality.* National leaders do not take a stand either for or against such systems and leave the decision to the local unions. They do not provide significant staff support to locals that do get involved, but may offer guidelines on how to respond when employers discuss gainsharing plans. Probably the majority of unions are in this category.

3. *Decentralized policy with some national union support.* National union officials other than the president advocate such systems. These officials support and advise interested locals. At this time, the United Steel Workers and the United Auto Workers appear to best represent this position.

4. *Support from the president.* The union president goes on record as advocating such systems. Staff support is available to assist and train local officers, and movement is made toward integrating worker participation with collective bargaining and other union activities. Few unions fit this mold, with the Communication Workers of America perhaps coming closest.

It is significant that most unions take a position of decentralized neutrality. Supporting a new form of labor-management cooperation can involve risks for high-ranking union officials; their predisposition to delay or to avoid taking a stand is understandable. The idea of contingent or variable compensation in which gainsharing is the only or primary way for union members to increase their economic standing has obviously made this a much more complex issue for unions. Previously, gainsharing was always above negotiated wages and was not discussed as part of a contract. Many consultants in the field still strongly support such a total separation.

The recent increase in the number of gainsharing plans being implemented has provided considerable information as to how the plans will influence the unions involved. A survey of unions sought to identify the specific aspects of gainsharing that unions will favor, as well as those that unions will likely oppose. We also sought information on their current position on gainsharing.

The Survey

The respondent could evaluate, using a four-point scale, the importance of nine reasons why unions may favor gainsharing systems and nine reasons why unions may oppose such systems. Additional items could be added, if necessary. Other items obtained information about the respondent and assessed the respondent's familiarity with various gainsharing plans. The survey was kept as simple as possible in hopes of increasing the response rate.

Responses were obtained from 17 of the larger American trade unions out of 50 surveyed, including the UAW; the United Rubber Workers; the International Ladies Garment Workers Union; the United Brotherhood of Carpenters and Joiners of America; the International Union of Tool, Die, and Mold Makers; the International Brotherhood of Boilermakers; the International Association of Machinists; the Teamsters; and the International Union of Bricklayers and Allied Craftsmen, as well as other smaller unions. In most cases, the director of research and education for the union or a research staff member completed the survey. First and second requests were sent to numerous other unions, but even an inducement of a book on gainsharing could not generate a response.

Why Unions Would Oppose

For each item, the percentage of respondents indicating that the reason was "important" or "very important" was determined. Results are tabulated in Exhibit 9.1. Let us examine the five most important reasons for opposition.

Exhibit 9.1 Reasons Why Unions May Oppose Gainsharing (Percentage Marking "Important" or "Very Important")

	PERCENTAGE
1. Management may try to substitute it for wages	94
2. Management cannot be trusted	88
3. Peer pressure to perform may increase	77
4. Bonus calculations are not understood or trusted	76
5. Union influence is undermined	66
6. Increased productivity may reduce need for jobs	64
7. Grievances may go unprocessed	64
8. Gainsharing is incompatible with union goals	57
9. Employees really do not want more involvement	20

1. *Management may try to substitute it for wages.* A basic traditional principle of gainsharing is that the gainsharing bonus should serve as an extra incentive for improving productivity, separate from the basic compensation package. It is generally recommended that the gainsharing plan be kept out of collective bargaining negotiations on pay. As the survey responses reveal, most unions are not interested in replacing any part of their members' paycheck with a bonus that can vary in amount. Gainsharing is generally used openly for this reason only when it is part of a concessionary package. Most gainsharing firms increasingly offer wages that are competitive for the geographic area.

Frankly, union officers are partially correct if current trends continue. Unfortunately, in most situations economics will probably win and these current trends of contingent compensation based on gainsharing will continue, especially in companies where union wages are considerably higher than those prevailing in the area.

2. *Management cannot be trusted.* Much of the writing on union and management cooperative efforts expresses the concern by the union that it is not being dealt with in good faith. Unions fear that management will violate the spirit of cooperation by laying off employees after productivity gains are made, will manipulate the bonus calculation to suit its needs, or will attempt to change the rules of the plan at some later date. If management adopts such actions, the plan is likely to be short-lived. Normally, before the plan is installed, specific ground rules are established to decrease such possibilities.

3. *Peer pressure to perform may increase.* In a typical gainsharing firm, all jobs are "on standard" in the sense that perform-

ance during the base period must be exceeded to earn bonus. This means that anyone who performs inadequately hurts everyone's chance of earning a bonus. Some unions fear that workers will complain when others are not doing their jobs properly, creating divisiveness in the work force and placing unfair pressure on employees too old to perform at top levels. It has been our experience, however, that the pressure exerted to correct substandard performance is focused not so much on fellow workers as on management.

4. *Bonus calculations are not understood or trusted.* In addition to a concern that the company will juggle the figures, some unions hold that gainsharing bonus calculations are inadequate measures of employee performance. According to an International Association of Machinists' research report:

> The relationship between a worker's productivity and the bonus . . . is very remote. Not only that, but many factors beyond the worker's control, including production processes, demand, management efficiency, and quality of materials, help determine the extent of savings. Total sales, for instance, may be affected by seasonal demand for the product or by the marketing skills of the firm. Since most low to middle income families budget their income to the hilt, it is difficult to make adjustment for unexpected declines in income.[2]

One way to minimize lack of trust in the bonus calculations is to have them tied to the factory's or company's financial reports so that the same figures are used for bonus calculations as are used for tax and corporate report purposes. These figures can be attested to by the public auditors. The marketing skills of the firm can be sharpened by including the sales and marketing force in the gainsharing plan, as many firms have done. Some firms do make the plan open to audit by the union.

5. *Union influence is undermined.* In one scenario, the union could lose power if the workers come to see the employee involvement system (for example, the teams that review employee ideas) as a more effective way to handle issues that are normally channeled through the union's grievance procedure. Management gets credit for bettering the workers' condition, and the union is increasingly bypassed. Research, however, has shown that involvement in such plans typically does not cause members to evaluate their unions more negatively.[3] In most installations, a strong attempt is made to preserve the union contract provisions.

6. *Additional reasons for opposition.* Although not included as an item on this survey, one of the major obstacles to gainsharing may be the view that such worker involvement plans are used as tools against the organized labor movement. Two laid-off UAW members noted: "Quality of Work Life (QWL) programs are quickly becoming the single most important management technique being used to thwart unionization. In addition to greater productivity, nonunion firms see QWL as being decisive in keeping unions out."[4]

Labor leaders see managerial opposition to union organizing efforts in America as a major force limiting cooperative efforts and experimentation in the workplace. Unions will not embrace such plans openly until they feel that their right to represent workers is accepted. We know of no unions that were decertified after gainsharing was installed.

Many union officials also say that they are turned off by some forms of employee involvement. For example, many unions supported quality circles only to have management withdraw its support at a later date, which then resulted in failure of the program.

Why Unions May Support Gainsharing

The findings reviewed in the preceding section represent only one side of the story. Most unions are either neutral toward or "mildly" in favor of gainsharing plans. They can see a number of positive attributes in such systems. Exhibit 9.2 describes the relative importance of nine reasons why unions may favor gainsharing. Let us discuss briefly the first five reasons.

1. *Increased recognition.* A gainsharing plan can provide many opportunities for employees to receive special recognition for their

**Exhibit 9.2 Reasons Why Unions May Favor Gainsharing
(Percentage Marking "Important" or "Very Important")**

	PERCENTAGE
1. Increased recognition	95
2. Better job security	94
3. Increased involvement in job activities	94
4. More money	94
5. Increased feeling of achievement of contributing to the organization	86
6. Increased influence of union	70
7. Greater contribution to nation's productivity	69
8. Compatibility with union goals	64
9. Fewer grievances	47

contributions to company performance. Through being elected to or selected for team positions, seeing their ideas implemented, and other means, the workers find that their extra efforts are noticed and appreciated, not only by management but also by coworkers.

2. *Better job security.* Although some fear that improved productivity will result in the need for fewer employees, other unions have taken the position that a successful plan means a successful company and therefore greater job security. Raymond Majerus, deceased secretary-treasurer of the UAW, stated:

> Thus it's vital that the basic job security needs of workers are addressed when these programs are designed. We've tried to do this in a number of situations—without success I should add—by proposing that profit sharing and productivity sharing bonuses be distributed in the form of increased paid time off the job rather than cash. In this way, productivity gains can be used to increase employment and enhance job security rather than reduce it.[5]

Most national union officials probably accept the contention that productivity is important for long-run job security. Unfortunately, local leaders often fear that productivity increases will reduce job security in the short-run, and therefore they may resist such plans.

3. *Increased involvement in job activities.* Although a popular line of thought holds that unions are clinging tenaciously to outdated beliefs that workers really are interested only in getting more pay and better benefits, the survey results suggest otherwise. Respondents seem to recognize that many of the employees they represent want more control over the way they do their jobs. A gainsharing plan may be effective in helping to achieve this goal.

4. *More money.* One advantage offered by a gainsharing plan that is not found with most other QWL or employee involvement systems is the potential of earning a financial bonus. A bulletin published by the United Brotherhood of Carpenters and Joiners of America (UBC) had this comment about quality circles, a system which normally does not pay a bonus:

> We recommend that if a Quality Circle Program is accepted, it be combined with some form of Gainsharing plan for employees. The savings resulting from the Quality Circles must be shared with employees for two reasons. First, it is only fair that savings achieved as a result of employees suggestions and participation in the Circles directly benefit employees. Otherwise the program becomes a means of manipulating workers for the benefit of the company. Second,

employees rapidly lose interest if there is no incentive involved for them.[6]

The article went on to recommend the use of a Scanlon Plan and noted that this type of plan has been used successfully in UBC locals. A company may find it easier to begin with a Scanlon plan or some other "pure" gainsharing plan than to superimpose a gainsharing incentive system on a quality circles structure, even if the latter is fairly common.

5. *Increased feeling of achievement of contributing to the organization.* This certainly doesn't suggest that the era of adversarial relationships between labor and management is over, but it does imply that unions are aware that many of their members want to have an impact on the success of their companies. A gainsharing plan, if designed with the union's concerns in mind, can be one vehicle to help meet these needs. Informal discussions with a number of local union members confirm this finding.

What's in It for Unions?

Up to now we have discussed ways in which a plan can benefit individual employees. But an equally important issue is the extent to which the union as a third party can profit from its role as a joint partner in developing and supporting the system.

First, only the most productive and competitive firms will grow and hire more employees as dues-paying members. Japanese and European companies are in many cases producing better quality products at lower costs. Unionized American firms, which have been adversely affected by these pressures, can be strengthened by gainsharing. Most Japanese firms also have bonus plans.

Second, the union benefits by association with a plan desired by the rank and file. Charles Hecksher, research economist for the Communication Workers' union, observed:

> In such cases, for unions to oppose QWL is simply a suicidal strategy. It puts us in the position of opposing something which the workers see as good. It may, if anything, be worse to do what many unions have done, which is to sit on the sidelines and play a "watchdog" role. That approach lets management get all the credit for improvements resulting from QWL while the union is seen as negative, weak, and irrelevant to a process which directly benefits workers in their daily lives.[7]

By being actively involved in the gainsharing plan, the union can also raise its visibility among the 80 percent of the membership that is less active in union affairs. These members should come to see the union as a more powerful force in issues that directly influence their work life. In this way their solidarity and identification with the union are enhanced.

Often, the union's effectiveness in negotiations and grievance-handling is hampered because of a lack of detailed information regarding company finances, decision-making processes, and plans for the future. The improved communications developed under a gainsharing plan should provide the union with better knowledge. In addition to allowing the union to better serve its members, this new sharing of information is also helpful in developing trust in management and in helping the union to see business conditions as they truly are.

Firms with gainsharing systems are likely to take a longer view of employment than many other firms. That is, they have some ability to reduce wage costs (by reducing bonuses) and, thus, decrease the need for disruptive layoffs during seasonal or cyclical business downturns. Surely such policies satisfy the union's long-term interests at both the local and international levels.

Gainsharing also promotes extra pay when performance makes it available, but the firm is not saddled with a permanent higher wage level during times of economic downturns. The adjustment process is automatic; the union does not have to negotiate difficult wage concessions.

Finally, a union that has actively supported a successful gain-sharing plan probably will find itself in a better bargaining position during negotiations. If the plan has in fact resulted in greater productivity, less scrap, and higher quality, and if these improvements can be tied to the union's participation, then the union will likely be better supported in its own demands.

How to Get Cooperation

Rather than recommending outright rejection of gainsharing plans, some national unions are finding it more advantageous to take an active part in the plan, provided that certain conditions are met. These conditions include assurances that the union's power will not be threatened, that the union members will not be hurt by the plan, and that management is being honest in stating reasons for implementation.

Job Security

Often, the union's greatest concern will be that streamlined operations and other productivity improvements could result in layoffs—doing the same work with fewer people. The union is likely to demand some assurance that this will not happen.

To maintain employee job security, management will have to see that the cost savings generated under the plan are not wasted. Part of the money saved should be invested in the marketing and sales organization so that sales volume keeps pace with production. Ideally, gainsharing plans should be installed in sites where there is a potential for an expanding market.

Although a successful plan should result in more jobs in the long run, it is essential that management and the work force be flexible and imaginative in finding ways to maintain employment levels in the short run. While waiting for sales volume to develop, a firm may find it possible to reassign production workers to maintenance or some similar function. One manufacturer of industrial electrical products sent some of its production workers out with salesmen to help demonstrate products during times when they were not needed in the plant. Another problem arises when, during times of rapid growth, some companies hire new workers for temporary bulges in production. During such volatile periods, it may be best if at all possible to subcontract some work, thus affirming the company's commitment to retain the employees it takes on.

Involvement of Participants

All involvement should be voluntary. This condition is easily met because a gainsharing plan is by its nature voluntary. Employees support the plan because they see it as being in their best interest.

Union representatives should be involved in all phases of the plan development, implementation, and evaluation. This will satisfy the union's need to see to it that there are no hidden tricks up management's sleeve. More important, it should ensure the plan's success. Research has shown that systems in which the union has served as a visible and joint partner are most likely to result in improvements in the workers' views of their jobs and of their union's performance.[8]

Keeping Plan Out of Union Contract

There should be some assurance that the plan will not affect the collective bargaining agreement. Keeping the plan out of the labor agreement will avoid complications and generally make life easier for management as well as the union. Most plans have a memo of understanding, which specifically states what items will continue to be decided by management and which items are part of the union contract. Tying into wage negotiations obviously makes this separation difficult. Bonus payments have always been in the gray area of labor contracts and will likely continue to be so.

Most unions will not accept scapegoating of the workers as a major cause of poor productivity. Support of the plan eventually should lead to changing those rules that obstruct the employees' attempts to work more efficiently. To earn a bonus under gain-sharing, employees should not have to work harder or longer, but smarter and more consistently.

Sharing of Information

Finally, some unions will expect management to open its books. Management must be willing to be more open and continue to share with the union relevant information about the organization's business. This will be especially important when presenting monthly or quarterly bonus results. Sharing information on the company's performance and walking union representatives through the calculation will be basic to building and maintaining cooperation. Successful firms are normally the most willing to share this information.

Winning Union's Support

In many instances, the items discussed thus far will constitute necessary but not sufficient conditions for gaining the cooperation of the union as a joint partner in the plan. Responsibility still falls on management to convince the union that such a system is in its own best interest and, more important, in the best interest of the employees. Management must take the initiative in most situations. Additional steps will have to be taken to create an environment that will generate enthusiasm and make the plan a success, but ups and downs with regard to support should be expected. These steps will vary depending on the company and union, but a few general idealistic recommendations can be made.

1. *Pick the right facility.* If a company's long-range goal is to establish plans in several locations, it is important that things go well in the initial site. There are a number of variables to consider when making this selection, but a central one should, of course, be a good relationship between management and the union.

2. *Be frank in discussing the costs and the payoffs.* No union will risk a workplace experiment until it fully understands its advantages—financial and otherwise—for the workers. At the same time, the plan will ultimately be harmed if the potential benefits are exaggerated. Even if the plan is successful, the union's expectations could be raised to a level that cannot be satisfied. All parties involved must understand that large amounts of effort and support are required to make the plan work, and that much time may pass before they see financial rewards.

3. *Visit other gainsharing companies.* Key union representatives should be taken to firms—both union and nonunion—with active plans. (Nonunion installations are probably somewhat more common.) They should tour the facility and, if this is allowed, talk to anyone in the plant. It may be possible to arrange a meeting with the local president, who can tell what gainsharing has meant to the union. Most important, they should talk to the gainsharing plan coordinator, if available, who holds a key position in nearly all successful gainsharing plans. Obviously, some care must be exercised in site selection.

4. *Be responsive to the union's inputs.* The union will be looking for evidence that its concerns are being taken seriously. In this regard, nothing is more effective than timely feedback. Raymond Majerus of the UAW observed:

> Management has to do more than simply listen to the union and its workers; it has to understand what is being said, react quickly to suggestions/proposals, and implement changes when they are warranted. In a worker's eyes, quick feedback and follow-through are perhaps the most telling yardsticks of management's commitment to an incentive program.[9]

5. *Seriously consider formation of a labor/management steering committee.* This group can be selected by both management

and the union and can develop broad ground rules and a plan outline. When properly used, such a group is extremely effective in opening lines of communication and laying the groundwork for a plan that both sides can live with. This group can be permanent to maintain integrity of the system.

6. *Don't use gainsharing against the union.* Gainsharing could be used to exert negative pressures on the union in such instances as undermining provisions in the contract or pushing for decertification.

Conclusions

Are we on the brink of a new era of union-management cooperation? Probably not, although gainsharing plans offer much promise for improvements in this area. In general, management will continue to pursue its goals of creating a profit, providing a reasonable return for shareholders, and improving employee relations. Unions will continue to strive for higher wages, benefits, and job security, and will still work for better conditions and for workers' rights.

The desires of employees, however, remain to be considered. Items of concern for this group include interest in expanding their roles, acquiring more control over their jobs, having a more direct impact on the company's performance, and sharing in the benefits. A study dealing with a large sample of workers found that four out of five wanted substantial say over the way the work is done and the quality of the work produced. Even more surprising is the list of things which fewer respondents indicated that they wanted to influence: when the work day begins and ends, who should be fired or hired, pay scales or wages, how complaints or grievances are handled, and who gets promoted.[10]

Such findings would indicate that employees are at least as concerned about how they do their jobs as they are about traditional bread-and-butter issues.

The trend toward contingent compensation further complicates this process, but the trend is not likely to change. However, it is unlikely that U.S. firms will endorse the system as actively as has Japan, where up to 41 million employees are on bonus plans which average around 25 percent of their pay.

Employee needs will not be easily ignored, either by the

company or the union. The key is to develop systems that serve the needs of all parties, systems that currently are being devised by the country's more progressive firms and labor organizations. Such cases demonstrate that cooperative efforts can work when the different sides communicate openly, show an honest regard for the other side's concerns, and are cognizant that the goals of employees, management, and unions are essentially the same.

Because of its emphasis on establishing common goals, gainsharing has played an increasingly important role in this effort. That trend will accelerate as more firms and unions become familiar with the concepts that form gainsharing. The attitudes of union officers regarding gainsharing are not likely to change, however—some will support the idea, some will oppose it, and others will not know what position to take.

Notes

1. T.A. Kochan, H.C. Katz, and N.R. Mower, "Worker Participation and American Unions: Threat or Opportunity?" (Cambridge, Mass.: Sloan School of Management working paper No. 1526-84, Massachusetts Institute of Technology, 1984), 24–25.
2. "Profit Sharing and Group Incentive Plans," IAM Research Report, Vol. 7, No. 2, International Association of Machinists and Aerospace Workers, Spring 1979, 3.
3. T. Kochan, "Worker Participation," note 1, above, 15–20.
4. M. Parker and D. Hansen, "Using Quality of Work Life Programs to Thwart Unions," *Workplace Democracy*, Winter 1984, 8.
5. R. Majerus, Secretary-Treasurer, UAW, "Incentive Plans: Why They Work and Why They Don't," address to the Conference on the Economics of Incentive, Cooperation and Risk Sharing, New York, N.Y., March 29, 1984, 5.
6. "Quality Circles: How Should Unions Respond?" *UBC Organizing—Industrial Bulletin*, United Brotherhood of Carpenters and Joiners of America, January 1983, 4.
7. C. Heckscher, "A Union Response to QWL Programs," *Workplace Democracy*, Winter 1984, 9.
8. T. Kochan, "Worker Participation," note 1, above, 21.
9. R. Majerus, "Incentive Plans," note 5, above, 7.
10. T. Kochan, "Worker Participation," note 1, above, 8–9.

Chapter 10

Using Gainsharing for a Union Survival Strategy

Timothy L. Ross and Ruth Ann Ross

In the fall of 1984, Tech Form Industries (TFI) was in serious trouble. The company had experienced several years of inadequate financial performance, had just been sold to a private investor in a leveraged buyout, and had a deteriorating individual incentive system. The incentive system, in particular, needed revision since its failure to emphasize quality was threatening the survival of the company. In fact, all plant personnel were paid on some incentive basis, which often was contradictory in emphasis.

Because of its low quality ratings from major car manufacturers, its primary customers, TFI's future was in doubt because major long term contracts were being lost to competitors. As a partial solution, TFI turned to gainsharing as one system to help solve its performance problems. This case study traces the steps that were used in this survival situation. The steps would have been impossible without the active support of the United Steelworkers' officials and a dedicated top management leadership.

Background Information

Tech Form has generally served as an automotive supplier, primarily providing various tubular exhaust pipe systems to original equipment automotive companies. It has been owned by a variety of organizations and is located in Shelby, Ohio. For the past eight years or so, sales and profits were generally unstable, moving in unison with the overall automotive market but on a declining trend. Because of the limited returns, investment was also restricted. These limitations compounded the problems since needed systems and equipment were not added to help move the company towards an increasingly quality conscious environment. The plant employed around 400 people.

Coupled with these problems, in late 1984 the company was sold to a private investor through a leveraged buyout. Thus, the work force that was known for its ability to work with difficult stainless steel exhaust applications, confronted another problem.

In late 1984 TFI faced the following issues:

1. Being sold to a new investor created uncertainty.
2. Self financing became extremely important because of already heavy debt.
3. Early negotiations with the United Steel Workers' Local 4357 failed and new negotiations were starting in early 1985.
4. Poor quality primarily caused by a poor individual incentive system resulted in the loss of customer contracts.
5. The company's financial performance was only marginal.
6. The company badly needed new equipment and various other systems.

Options Considered by TFI

One option could have been the hard-nosed approach used by some companies. That approach often includes major job reclassifications, wage and benefit reductions, job combinations and so on. This option was not elected by the management of TFI, headed by Arch Hood, the president, and Bob Pickering, the general manager. They instead decided to adopt a major change in relationship with the union based on jointly building trust and cooperation, finding new solutions to old problems, and developing a new approach to union contract determination. The union enthusiastically endorsed this change under the leadership of Dan Martin at the Steelworker's International level and Billy Collins, Roger Markwell, and Ken Takos at the local level.

The task would not be easy, however, as a survey of top management in December 1984 indicated. Selected examples of questions used in the survey are listed below. In the scale used for scoring, a score of one (1) was the most negative and five (5) the most positive.

		Average Response
1.	Employees cooperate with each other well.	3.0
2.	Communications between supervisors and their subordinates are good.	2.3
3.	There is good teamwork in developing goals.	2.9
4.	Employees here trust management.	2.1
5.	Resistance to change to a more involvement and productivity oriented system will be limited.	2.4
6.	Our employees understand the problems faced by our company.	2.4

Only 43 percent of the managers responded that "some success or better" in improving labor productivity and customer service (a major problem) would result if gainsharing were installed. They evaluated their current organizational style as being fairly paternalistic, a situation which is not conducive to a successful gainsharing system.

Nevertheless, the commitment to change by top management was apparent as indicated by the following six survey questions (1 = most negative; 5 = most positive).

		Average Response
1.	Employees should be involved in things that affect them.	3.9
2.	Employees are valuable resources, in need of better utilization.	4.7
3.	If gainsharing were installed, employees would probably practice more self control.	4.0
4.	There is a need to change to a system which encourages employee involvement at all levels.	4.3
5.	All employees accept the need to stress quality more.	4.4
6.	You personally support the need to change.	4.3

The need to change was apparent as reflected in the high scores given by management to these particular questions.

A later survey given to all employees also suggested significant problems (again 1 = most negative and 5 = most positive). Some key problem areas indicated by the scores on selected questions are noted below.

	Overall Employee Average
1. Communications between departments are clear, open, and effective.	1.8
2. Top management communicates well with employees.	2.0
3. Departments seem to cooperate with each other well.	2.3
4. Departments act as if they are working against each other.	2.1
5. Employees here trust management.	1.8
6. Management usually makes good on its promises to employees.	2.2
7. There aren't many reasons for complaints here.	1.9
8. People get by with poor performance.	1.8
9. The better you work, the more you are rewarded.	2.0

In addition to the low responses to these key questions, negative written comments were made regarding working conditions, the state of equipment, management capabilities, and the quality of communication.

The survey of 360 employees clearly indicated that numerous problems existed. However, the need to change was also clearly recognized by the respondents as indicated by the scores on the following questions.

	Overall Employee Average
1. There are many ways this company could improve if employees were asked for ideas.	4.6
2. Many employees would enjoy the chance to help the company run better.	4.2
3. You would like to help the company become more successful.	4.4
4. Productivity could be increased greatly.	4.1
5. It is important that this company have good productivity.	4.3
6. Increasing productivity would increase long term job security.	4.2
7. It bothers you when you are making products of low quality.	4.4
8. Product quality should be increased.	4.6

To summarize, most Tech Form employees, both management and nonmanagement, believed that conditions were not ideal for implementing a gainsharing system based on principles of trust and cooperation. However, they generally believed in the need to change. Obviously with only 28 percent of employees believing that a gainsharing plan would be successful, conditions were far from ideal for developing and implementing gainsharing within Tech Form Industries.

A Key Problem—The Incentive System

One of the key problems of TFI in early 1985 was its existing incentive/bonus systems. For the direct labor employees, incentive premiums ranged from over 33 percent over base rates in 1977 to 18 percent in 1983. The average for the past nine quarters was about 22 percent. For salaried employees, the incentive bonuses ranged from 40 percent in 1977 to zero in 1980 and 1981. In 1984, the average was about 17 percent. This erratic incentive history created major problems since adjusting wages is fraught with difficulties and bound to cause resentments.

Some of the general problems with the existing direct labor incentive system were as follows:

1. Some rates were inequitable to both the employees and company.
2. Much time was spent on rate adjustments/grievances.
3. Limits on production were developed by many employees.
4. Quality was a major problem with up to 40 percent of product in some departments necessitating rework, resulting in the company losing major contracts; this was perhaps the greatest problem of the company.
5. A great deal of friction existed between employees/departments.
6. More automation (desperately needed) reduced the applicability of individual incentives.
7. The various systems used encouraged many job classifications.

These are a few of the major problems related to the direct labor incentive systems used in TFI. Less documented were the problems with the salaried incentive system. It was decided, largely as a result of these problems, that the incentive systems for both direct labor and salaried exempt employees should be eliminated.

The Incentive Systems—What Happened?

A simple explanation of the TFI approach to eliminating the incentive systems is that both systems were bought out based on average performance. That is, both groups were paid (bought out or average wage increased) on an average of the group's performance. For general purposes, half of the people received increases for their job classifications and half received decreases. Job classifications were narrowed somewhat to increase flexibility.

The union portion of this approach was negotiated and resulted in opposition among those who received reductions in wages. Another option would have been a more complex red circling (higher pay for some people for some period of time) which was rejected since such an approach would have perpetuated the problem of high incentive rates. Needless to say, some high incentive/lower post incentive employees either reduced their performance, bid out of jobs, or retired. Management and the union officials agreed to undertake such an approach no matter how difficult it would be.

United Steelworkers' Role in Beginning the Gainsharing Installation

Frankly, the individual incentives program would not have been eliminated, nor would the gainsharing systems have been installed, without the union's support. Encouragement and assistance were provided by officers ranging from the subregional director, Dan Martin, to plant union officials, especially Billy Collins, Roger Markwell, and Ken Takos. In fact, were it not for the union's strong support working in concert with company management of TFI in the elimination of the incentive system and the installation of gainsharing, the survival of the company would have been doubtful.

But as is often the case, the relatively new management exhibited a more cooperative attitude. Although more senior members of management were still fairly autocratic or paternalistic, they started adopting a more consultative frame of reference. They desired to move toward a more participative style as indicated in the original managerial survey. The survey indicated they truly believed in employees' abilities to contribute to the company. However, change often occurs slowly, as was the situation with the implementation of gainsharing. Management initiated various education programs in the period between February and May to help with these changes. These sessions are discussed later in this report. The union's management participated fully in the design and execution of these activities.

United Steelworkers was also deeply involved in the gainsharing plan development through its participation on a Steering Committee to help design a draft of the plan. In addition, the union provided a coordinator and helped in educating the employees on the shop floor level.

How Gainsharing Was Started—The Steps Involved

In most situations, gainsharing systems are kept separate from the union contract. In this situation, the separation became blurred at best because the individual incentive system was eliminated and gainsharing was installed at about the same time (June, 1985). The union vote was overwhelmingly in favor of the change even though many employees took cuts in pay.

Step 1: Late 1984. Discussions with union/management of the approaches to gainsharing, of reading materials and of visits to other gainsharing companies.

Step 2: Early 1985. Started a permanent Gainsharing Steering Committee to oversee the development, implementation, and monitoring of gainsharing. The union selected three members, as did management, and continued to meet monthly to monitor performance. The group developed a draft of the plan including the following features:

a. Purpose/goals,
b. Involvement system after implementation,
c. Method of calculation of the bonus,
d. Policies and procedures.

Step 3: March–May 1985. Started a Development Task Force made up of a cross-section of generally elected members from the entire organization (around 25 members) to prepare a final plan document. Volunteers from this group also participated in making the presentation of the final plan to all employees in early May.

Step 4: March–May 1985. Education started. A series of education sessions were started for all managers/union officials on various aspects of the plan and on managing in a nonincentive environment (approximately 15 hours of classroom education). Education was also conducted for all the team representatives (6 hours). As part of the work force education, the Development Task Force activities/decisions were made available to all employees. In early May, the Development Task Force also made an hour and a half presentation to all employees and the entire plan document was distributed to all employees. The all-employee survey discussed earlier was also administered. Two full-time coordinators were selected, one by the union and one by management. The union coordinator was a vice president of the union.

Step 5: June 1, 1985. Implementation of the plan.

An Outline of the Plan Itself

The plan consisted of ten major sections, each of which is discussed below.

Section 1: Identity Statement (history and expectations) and Purpose. Key items include the need to change, need for involvement, success orientation, performance improvement, and so on.

Section 2: Goals. Thirteen items were listed here such as high quality ratings, on-time deliveries, best reputation, best return on investment and good employment opportunities.

Section 3: Objectives. These were much more specific and included such items as attaining a General Motors Spear I rating by X date, eliminating premium freight by X date, reducing fixed costs by X percent, developing comprehensive involvement systems by X date, and so on.

Section 4: Policies and Procedures. This section discussed such items as the continuing role of the Steering Committee, how changes are made in the plan, taxability of bonuses, and who has final authority in the plan's operation.

Section 5: Decisions Not Affected by the Plan. This section reviewed the decisions that are not part of gainsharing and a statement on nonconflict with anything related to the union contract. The plan would not be subject to grievance procedures. *Note:* Traditionally, as discussed in Chapter 9, gainsharing has not been part of union contracts since separation was thought important by both parties. Where gainsharing is installed in troubled situations and used at least partially as a substitute for a wage increase, this separation will obviously become increasingly more difficult.

Section 6: Involvement System (Departmental Teams). This extensive section discussed the formation (elected by departments/ areas), roles, terms of office, responsibilities, and limitations of the 14 departmental teams made up primarily along normal departmental lines. Some smaller interdependent office groups were combined. Around 75 employees including supervisors were on the teams. The coordinators appointed the first chairpersons, who were normally the supervisors from the area, to develop accountability. The teams were able to implement ideas submitted to them if the total cost was not greater than $200; if all team members agreed; and if they were the only department affected by the idea or could get the other area/ department to also agree. If the idea did not meet the above criteria, it was referred to the Review Board. The teams were to meet at least once a month for approximately one hour, on company time.

Section 7: Review Board Structure. The Review Board served as a link between the teams and top management. Membership consisted of union officials, coordinators, members of top management, and one nonmanagement representative from each departmental team. The coordinators took turns chairing the meetings.

The functions of the Review Board, which met in the second or third week of the month, included reviewing economic conditions, bonus results, and team activities. They had authority to implement those suggestions costing less than $2,000 recommended by the departmental teams; to make recommendations on larger, more complex suggestions; to perform special reviews; and to make sure that the plan was operating efficiently.

Section 8: Responsibilities of All Employees and Management. This section contained a fairly detailed list of responsibilities for *all* employees and specific ones related to management only. Some examples are as follows: being success oriented, being cooperative, helping other employees, and submitting cost reduction ideas.

Section 9: Terms and Calculation. This extensive section covered the technical aspects of the plan including definitions of various terms of the plan such as shipments, the percentage of the bonus going to the employees based on organizational performance, a discussion of the reserve (50 percent of the employees' share of each month's bonus was set aside for year end to protect against normal ups and downs and to reinforce long-run thinking; if positive at year end, it is distributed to the employees, and if negative, absorbed by the company), and eligibility for bonuses.

The calculation decided on was one commonly referred to as multicost. That is, if actual costs were less than the historical 10-year average, a bonus was earned. Some plans are based on a much shorter, more recent performance, and others are based on targeted performance or a combination of past and targeted performance. Some are based on much more specific and narrower measures of performance.

A hypothetical example of the bonus calculation follows:

		Month X
1.	Net sales	$ 3,000,000
2.	Allowed cost (92.46% of line 1)	2,773,800
3.	Actual cost	2,719,800
4.	Bonus pool (line 2 minus line 3)	54,000
5.	Employee share (assume 40% of line 4)	21,600
6.	Reserve for year end (50% of line 5)	10,800
7.	Net bonus (line 5 minus line 6)	10,800
8.	Participating payroll (assume)	800,000
9.	Payout ($10,800 divided by $800,000)	1.35%
10.	Balance in reserve	10,800

Note: Most gainsharing plans are paid as a percentage of wages to comply with the Fair Labor Standards Act regarding overtime.

Section 10: Updating of Base Ratio and Other Activities. This section covered how the most recent 10 years would be used to establish the base ratio (92.46 percent in the previous example). Also covered in this section was an interest adjustment to be used if the interest costs become excessive because of excess inventory and receivables.

Later subsections had to do with responsibilities of teams, coordinators, and other aspects of the plan.

Although it appears complex, the plan document, in reality, developed the structured ground rules as to how the gainsharing plan would operate. Each year, this document is to be reviewed by the Review Board and Steering Committee for applicability and possible modification.

Post-Implementation Activities

A series of post-implementation activity strategies were developed. Some of these are discussed below.

1. A survey of team representatives and managers was conducted every four months to evaluate the proper operation of the plan. These were discussed and corrective/communication efforts were developed as necessary. These provided a wealth of information upon which to give recognition and/or take corrective action.

2. Interviews of samples of employees from various levels were conducted; these provided additional perspectives on improvements being made and problem areas.

3. Follow-up education was conducted at various intervals. This included:

   a. reinforcing principles, practices and operation of the plan along with evaluating performance and jointly developing corrective action (six hours for all representatives and managers two months after plan implementation);

   b. team building—all managers (three hours of education after five months);

   c. changing behavior under gainsharing (three hours after six months);

    d. Statistical Process Control education (after four months with the plan);

    e. various calculation education sessions were held for various groups.

    4. A second all-employee survey was also administered after 15 months experience with the plan.

Some key questions from this survey are listed below. The percentage of improvement over the 1985 results is indicated next to the question.

	Percentage of Improvement From 1985
1. All in all, how satisfied are you with your company?	13%
2. Communications between departments is clear, open, and effective.	32
3. Top management communicates well with employees.	30
4. Supervisors do a good job of listening to their people.	21
5. Departments in the company seem to cooperate with each other well.	26
6. Management usually makes good on its promises to people.	17
7. It is fair to say that the products we make are better than our competitors'.	27
8. We are frequently reminded of the company's objectives.	15
9. To employees of the company, product quality is a big concern.	11
10. This company produces good quality products.	34

These results indicate impressive improvements in employee attitudes toward communications and high quality, two of the key problems indicated in the earlier survey. In addition to the original survey questions, many aspects of the plan itself were also evaluated. Listed below are some key questions along with the percentage of people expressing a combined positive or very positive attitude regarding the questions, along with those who were undecided. The undecided were not negative responses and are disclosed for informational purposes.

	Percent Positive	Percent Undecided
1. Top management is as supportive of the plan today as it was at implementation.	63%	24%
2. Managers have behaved in a more participative manner since the plan was implemented.	56	27
3. Supervisors allow the team representatives and teams time to do their activities.	67	23
4. Team representatives, in general, are committed to the plan.	60	29
5. Most employees feel that the suggestion system is a good way to have input into the company.	70	21
6. Our gainsharing plan encourages us to work as a team.	70	18
7. Our gainsharing plan encourages an individual to use his/her experience and knowledge on the job.	70	18
8. Participation has increased under our gainsharing plan.	66	23
9. Our gainsharing plan is good for us.	66	24
10. Working conditions have improved after gainsharing was put in.	68	18
11. It is important for you to have the opportunity to participate in decisions concerning your job or work area.	88	8
12. You want to help in making your gainsharing plan successful.	85	11

Note: It is particularly important to note the highly positive responses toward the opportunity for employee involvement, a more participative management approach, and positive employee attitudes. With this kind of attitude improvement one would expect significant improvements in performance. This will be discussed under the section on quantitative results.

Many other questions dealt with specific areas of the plan's operation, including knowledge of the bonus calculation. All of these question areas provided a wealth of information for monitoring and corrective action. Monthly meetings were also held with all employees to discuss problems, economic conditions, bonus results, and team activities. Extensive other communication tools were developed or expanded including posted charts, monthly newsletters, daily flash memos, banners, and so on to help develop a productivity or performance commitment.

All of this improvement was accomplished despite the backdrop of wage reductions for some people on incentives and a business contraction because of the previous quality-related business losses. There were, and are still, people with negative attitudes, but they are decreasing in number.

A Review of the Quantitative Results

To date, the results derived, in addition to those concerning attitudinal changes, must be evaluated in relation to the primary intent of installing gainsharing in the first place—survival. Significant difficulties were expected because of known business losses due to the long advance time of contracts with major customers. Nevertheless, the company has shown significant improvement in many areas. Some of these are discussed below.

Quality Improvements

This was one of the primary reasons for installing gainsharing. The past individual incentive system made improvements in quality very difficult. A few of the specific, measurable results occurring after gainsharing was installed are noted below:

1. Product repair costs as a percent of sales dropped from around 4.5 percent (very high) to around 2.0 percent after a year.

2. Percentage of total customer returns decreased on a trend basis from around 2.3 percent to around .5 percent.
3. General Motors Supplier Index increased from around 130 on a trend basis to 143 (145 is perfect). A new Spear II Quality Rating from General Motors allowed the company to start bidding on contracts again.
4. Premium Freight has been reduced from around $20,000 per month to almost zero. (This is the extra freight required by the contract to meet customers' requirements.)
5. The company became the first tubing supplier to be Source Certified by AC Spark Plug. (AC would not have to inspect the incoming product.)

Obviously, these and other improvements indicated that significant progress had been made in quality and customer service areas. These probably were, and still are, the key to the long term survival of the firm and were extensively discussed in the monthly meetings with employees.

Suggestion Activity

By the end of the first quarter, 171 suggestions had been received of which 89 were accepted and implemented, 30 were declined (a fairly high rate but some people were testing the system), and the rest were under investigation. By the end of the first year, 531 had been received with documented savings of almost $800,000. Suggestion totals per month ranged from a low of 27 to a high of 115.

The suggestion rate in the second year declined slightly per month in total but increased as an average per employee (expected since employment had dropped somewhat because of a loss of business). Commitment to the system has obviously continued to be very high.

Other Benefits

As discussed earlier, overall attitudes improved. Additionally, the following results were noted:

1. Absenteeism was reduced from 4.0 percent to 2.9 percent.
2. Employee grievances have decreased significantly.
3. Scrap has been reduced by over 30 percent.
4. Appearance of production areas had improved significantly.

5. Improvement in overall attitudes exceeded 15 percent in key areas, from a pre/post attitude survey taken in a trying situation.
6. Because of improvements, over $1 million of new equipment was purchased to help secure the future growth of the company.

Surveys also showed employees believed that major improvements had been made in the other key goal areas listed in the plan document.

Bonus Results

Although bonuses were not a major portion of the plan, they do provide a benchmark as to how well things are progressing. Obviously, they also help sell the gainsharing concept.

The first bonus was actually earned in June of 1985 (the first month) and amounted to around $3 per person, which generated some "interesting" comments. The first significant bonus was earned in December 1985. Bonuses in subsequent months averaged between 2 percent and 4 percent, but it is important to remember that the plan was not installed primarily on the basis of the bonus. For the first year, bonus money totalled around $400 per employee. Because of the previously discussed loss of business, bonuses in fiscal 1987 have been sporadic, but enthusiasm was still high, as evidenced by the attitude at team meetings and the number of suggestions being made.

Because of the broadness of the calculation, the inclusion of most fixed costs, the decrease in business because of poor quality in the past, and customer service problems, earning a bonus has been difficult. This will change as sales levels improve.

Continuing Union and Management Support

The United Steelworkers officials both inside and outside the plant continue to support the plan. Dan Martin, the USW Subdistrict Director, gives talks supporting the concept. The union was involved in all major decisions and has made major commitments regarding no work stoppages to help obtain long-term contracts.

Some comments by union members are as follows: "The plan

230 Cases and Applications

has helped to improve our quality;" "Things are now getting done;" "Employees now have more input into decisions;" "Employees are taking more pride in the company and products;" "Communications have improved between employees and departments." As Bob Pickering, Vice President and General Manager, recently said, "All employees now feel as though they have a real impact on the company's future. . . . Gainsharing allows for the input of ideas and knowledge from those employees most familiar with the equipment and products, the people themselves."

Summary and Conclusions

Has Tech Form's gainsharing plan been successful? If based solely on the *size* of bonuses, probably not. In fact, because of financial problems at a sister company, bonuses are currently on hold. There are certainly major detractors who can be very vocal. However, the company has survived, attitudes are better, performance has improved, and the company is probably much better off because of gainsharing and is building a solid base for the future. Given the historical circumstances, what more can one say for a system.

Chapter 11

Gainsharing Apprehensions:
A Case Study and Survey

Timothy L. Ross and Ruth Ann Ross

Although gainsharing plans have grown in popularity in recent years, we still need to understand them better. Why do they work or not work? Can they be used to foster organizational change or should they only be installed after changes have been made and employee involvement has evolved? Do managers gain or lose control with more employee involvement, and how does adding a bonus affect the change process? Would managers continue their plans or drop them? Can they work well in both autocratic and participative management situations or only in participative ones? These are a very few of the unanswered questions that concern gainsharing. Without any doubt, the practitioner/innovator has led the researcher in gainsharing development and implementation.

To delve into a small portion of the research questions, we recently surveyed 108 managers in eight firms that have gainsharing plans. We will review the managers' evaluations of how their jobs were affected, how their subordinates behaved, and how satisfied they were with their plans. In addition, we will review other studies documenting the organizational benefits that can be expected from such plans and will present a case example of one company's experience with a plan.

A Short Case Example

Ross Manufacturing (a fictitious name), a 480-employee manufacturing company in Ohio, has operated since 1983 under a gainsharing plan typical of many being implemented today. The plan has two basic features: (1) an idea system that solicits and implements employees' ideas on improving performance, and (2) a bonus formula that measures performance and pays employees a financial bonus when performance exceeds a targeted level.

The idea system is the heart of the plan, because it opens lines of communication, builds team spirit, and channels workers' energy and creativity toward productivity goals. It is a way to get things done and, although different firms use different types of idea systems, Ross Manufacturing's will be used as a typical example.

The process begins when an employee writes down an idea on a simple form and turns it in to the department's team. Ross has 16 such teams. Each consists of a supervisor and from one to four elected nonmanagement representatives. Team members often help employees refine their ideas and prepare them for submission.

The departmental team investigates an idea to determine cost, feasibility, and likely benefits. The team may implement a suggestion if it costs less than $200, does not affect another department, or if it can get another department to agree to implement. If a department is seriously affected or does not agree, the suggestion goes to a plantwide review board, also consisting of management and elected nonmanagement personnel. The board reviews ideas costing more than $200 and acts in an advisory capacity to management.

Ross employees have contributed ideas touching almost every aspect of its business. Employees have made suggestions on ways to simplify jobs, reroute work materials, reduce material handling, eliminate unnecessary operations, reduce set-up time and down time, order office supplies, and other ways to improve the organization's effectiveness. Over 800 suggestions were made during the first two years of the system, resulting in more than $500,000 in estimated cost savings.

In most organizations, involvement systems such as the one just described are designed by both nonmanagement and management personnel. At Ross, a cross section of employees from all levels of the organization met over a two-month period to develop their idea system and design other plan policies.

The second major feature of the plan, the financial bonus, was developed so that employees could share in the gains made under the new system of management. Gainsharing is different from most other worker-participation plans such as quality circles and labor-management committees. The basic philosophy in gainsharing is equity: all employees should benefit financially for their creativity and extra effort just as the company benefits financially.

In simple terms, the company's performance—labor costs, material costs, sales value of production, and so forth—is assessed every two months. When performance for a current term is above the performance for the historical base period of the preceding several years, 40 percent of the improvement goes to the employees and 60 percent is retained by the company. Any bonus is paid to all employees as a percentage of wages earned for that term. Fifty percent of the employee's share is held in a reserve pool to be paid, if positive, at the end of the year. The reserve encourages positive attitudes toward long-term improvements in performance.

It should be noted from previous chapters that this is only one example of a bonus calculation and that most companies will tailor formulas to their specific needs. Some companies pay bonuses more frequently, on a monthly or even weekly basis. Some firms define productivity narrowly, such as work output per direct-labor workhour; other calculations include so many indices of performance that they resemble formulas for profit-sharing plans. A primary distinction is that most gainsharing plans require performance to exceed some historical level before a bonus is paid. This is not so with many profit-sharing plans.

Results at Ross Manufacturing

A successful plan requires adjustment from almost everyone in the firm, and many organizations appoint a full-time coordinator to administer gainsharing activities and facilitate the change process. At Ross Manufacturing, Bob Gibson was plan coordinator during the first two years of their plan. Gibson remembers that during the early period of implementation there was some concern about how staff and middle-level managers would adjust to the more participative management style. Said Gibson:

> I think the middle-level managers felt a little bypassed because suddenly we had an open channel from the bottom of the organization right to the top. Care must be taken not to bypass these managers, but to keep them involved.
>
> We have people with professional degrees—I'll use an engineer as an example—who thought "that guy out there running that machine doesn't know as much about that as I do." We've had to deal with that attitude not to belittle or insult either one, but to bring them closer together. To make them see "By golly, maybe he does

have something to add. And maybe I did overlook this when I designed it." And I think we've gained a lot.

The object is to build teamwork, to get everyone involved. In part, this requires working with managers who may feel threatened when subordinates make suggestions for productivity improvement. Some will see such suggestions as thinly veiled criticism of how they were managing their work units. There is sometimes fear that others will say, "If you are such a good manager, why didn't you think of that idea?"

This may be an especially sensitive issue for first-level managers or supervisors. Some supervisors fear that they will lose their authority, their control over the work unit, when their people are given a say in work decisions. Gibson recalls:

> Initially, the supervisors thought they were going to be undermined. The nonmanagement people had a tool whereby they could go around their supervisor and get something done. I was so anxious to get involvement from the nonmanagement people on the floor that I overlooked the supervisors. I set the departmental teams up with the people from the floor as chairmen. I think I really hurt the supervisors when I did that. They said, "Everybody's talking about my department, but I don't have the say." And that wasn't my intent. I was so anxious to grasp all the involvement I could that I bypassed the supervisors.
>
> Now, however, the supervisors are the chairpersons and the system is working much better. Because they know their way around. They know who to ask and how to get things done.

Ross Manufacturing's experience shows that when more participative management is introduced, it can cause apprehension among managers at all levels. The success of their plan also demonstrates, however, that sensitivity and responsiveness to the managers' legitimate concerns can ease their adjustment and help make a plan even stronger.

A Survey of Managers in Gainsharing Firms

Of course, Ross Manufacturing is only one firm, and its experiences with managers under a participative productivity plan may not be representative. We wanted to learn about the experiences of managers from a variety of organizations with similar systems.

To this end, we distributed a survey to 145 managers in eight gainsharing organizations. Completed questionnaires were returned by 108 (74 percent) of the managers. Of these, 4 percent were upper-level managers, 34 percent were middle-level managers, 59 percent were first-level managers, and 4 percent did not indicate a classification.

All of the organizations were production firms, with products including waste-disposal trucks, industrial pumps, hydraulic equipment, valves, wood products, industrial monitoring equipment, and information processing equipment. Each firm employed between 100 and 450 employees (with an average of 288) and had been managed under a gainsharing plan for between one and six years.

The survey allowed the managers to evaluate various aspects of their jobs. Each area was rated with a five-point scale, ranging from "very poor" to "very good." For each area, the manager made two ratings. The first evaluated the area as it was before the gainsharing plan and the second evaluated the area as it was at the time of the survey (after the plan was in effect).

Managers' Adjustment to Participative Management

One group of questions was designed to assess the managers' perceptions of their own jobs. We wanted to know whether a manager's role becomes more difficult under the participative gainsharing philosophy. Of particular concern was whether managers felt they still had control in the work unit, whether they still understood their role as managers and felt they could get things done.

These questions dealing with role adjustment, along with a summary of responses, are presented in Exhibit 11.1. It indicates that the managers, as a group, perceived improvement under gainsharing in every area.

Items 1, 2, and 3 reveal that, after plan implementation, managers felt that they had greater influence over their jobs, had greater ability to get work done, and were better able to handle crisis situations. This change in their general capacity to make things happen probably has much to do with improved cooperation from the people they directed. As item 4 reveals, the percentage of managers rating such subordinate cooperation as good or very good jumped from 48 percent before the plan to 80 percent after. A later section of this chapter will deal with subordinate performance in greater detail.

Item 5 shows that an alarmingly large number of managers do not consider their work load to be reasonable. Despite this fact, the average manager felt the situation had improved after gain-

Exhibit 11.1   Survey Responses, Managers' Adjustment to Gainsharing

	PERCENTAGE INDICATING "GOOD" OR "VERY GOOD"	
	BEFORE GAINSHARING	AFTER GAINSHARING
1. Your influence over what happens on your job	41%	66%
2. Your ability to get work done	64	75
3. Your ability to deal with "crisis" situations	56	77
4. The extent to which your subordinates do what you want them to do	48	80
5. The reasonableness of your work load	25	36
6. Your understanding of what your job duties are	60	71
7. Your understanding of the goals and objectives of your job	58	84

Note: Percentages are based on 108 completed questionnaires received from managers in companies with gainsharing plans.

sharing was adopted. This perception is especially encouraging in light of the fact that gainsharing adds new tasks to most managers' role: leading meetings, soliciting ideas, and helping to research and implement employee suggestions. These findings may suggest that the increased teamwork in the work unit sufficiently lightened the managers' work load to offset the extra duties required by the plan.

Items 6 and 7 reveal that, under a gainsharing plan, the average manager developed an even greater understanding of his or her job duties, goals, and objectives. The greater clarity of managerial goals and objectives probably results from the new lines of communication and the increased emphasis on goal setting. For example, employees at Ross Manufacturing meet (in groups of 80) once each month to review the company's performance. After opening remarks from the president, the company controller provides a detailed account of the factors influencing company performance. Time is spent identifying areas such as warranty costs or direct labor costs that are helping or hurting the employees' chance to earn a bonus. A question and answer period follows. When the meeting ends, managers and nonmanagement personnel alike leave with a better understanding of the goals that should be pursued in the following month.

These common goals, in large part, contribute to each work unit's sense of teamwork and cohesion. While the monthly meetings at Ross have been successful in this regard, other gainsharing firms choose to post company performance data on a more frequent—even daily—basis.

In summary, the survey presented no evidence that the managers lost control of their work settings or experienced major adjustment difficulties when their plan's more participative management style was adopted. It should be remembered, however, that these changes did not come about automatically. In most of the surveyed companies, the organization supported its managers by giving them a realistic appraisal of what to expect, seeking their input along the way, and providing education and training as to how to manage under the plan. Such positive results cannot be expected when these safeguards are overlooked.

Managers' Evaluations of Subordinates

A second group of questions on the same survey allowed the respondents to evaluate changes in the behavior of the employees they managed. This was necessary to test one of the major assertions of the gainsharing philosophy: that employees behave differently under a plan. That is, a plan should not only open up lines of communication and accelerate the implementation of good productivity ideas, but should also lead to more team-oriented behaviors in a majority of the workers. With common goals, the average worker should be more concerned about keeping costs low and output high. The surveyed managers were in an excellent position to provide these evaluations.

The summary of item responses in Exhibit 11.2 suggests that the managers felt that the average worker showed substantial improvements in all of the areas assessed. Items 8, 9 and 10 indicate that while employee concern about costs, outputs, and quality had been somewhat low prior to gainsharing, major improvements were seen afterward. The remaining items reflect similar gains with regard to employee willingness to accept change, job involvement, and absence rates. In short, most managers believed that their people were performing more effectively under their plans.

It should be emphasized, however, that a gainsharing plan should not be designed as a "speed-up" device. A gainsharing plan should result in a work unit that performs more intelligently, with employees using their know-how to cut waste, shorten delays, and remove obstacles to higher efficiency. When everyone pulls in the same direction, performance improvements follow. Although some

**Exhibit 11.2   Survey Responses, Managers' Evaluations of
Subordinates' Performance**

	PERCENTAGE INDICATING "GOOD" OR "VERY GOOD"	
	BEFORE GAINSHARING	AFTER GAINSHARING
1. Your subordinates' concern for controlling costs	24%	70%
2. Your subordinates' concern for increasing the amount of work accomplished	25	69
3. Your subordinates' concern for maintaining/ improving quality	40	84
4. Your subordinates' willingness to accept change	20	58
5. Your subordinates' feeling of involvement in their jobs	27	72
6. Your subordinates' commitment not to be unnecessarily absent	36	67

Note: Percentages are based on 108 completed questionnaires received from managers in companies with gainsharing plans.

firms encourage gains in output quantity, the company using a plan primarily as a speed-up mechanism is likely to encounter strong and ultimately fatal resistance.

Satisfaction With the Gainsharing Plan

A final group of questions allowed the managers to indicate general satisfaction with their organizations' gainsharing plans. Responses were made on a seven-point scale ranging from "strongly disagree" to "strongly agree," and are summarized in Exhibit 11.3.

It can be seen that over three-fourths were at least somewhat satisfied with their plans, and over nine-tenths felt that their companies should continue under gainsharing. Informal conversations with individual managers revealed that, while they were generally pleased with the gainsharing concept, there was often some specific aspect of their company's plan that they found disagreeable. These "bugs" in the system varied from manager to manager, and comments ranged from "I don't like the paperwork" to "I don't like some of the costs included in the bonus formula." Such individual objections are, of course, to be expected from any diverse work force. On the average, however, managers liked the gainsharing

Exhibit 11.3   Survey Responses, Managers' Satisfaction With Their Gainsharing Plans

	PERCENTAGE INDICATING "SOMEWHAT AGREE," "AGREE" OR "STRONGLY AGREE"
1. You are satisfied with your bonus plan.	77%
2. Your company should continue with the plan.	91
3. Would you advise others to install a plan like yours?	82
4. The plan is good for nonmanagement employees.	89
5. The plan is good for supervisors.	74

Note: Percentages are based on 108 completed questionnaires received from managers in companies with gainsharing plans.

idea, and 82 percent said they would advise others to install a plan similar to their own.

Interestingly, respondents were somewhat more likely to agree that their plan was good for nonmanagement employees (89 percent) than for supervisors (74 percent). This is probably because nonmanagement participation in plan activities is voluntary—workers can be as involved or uninvolved as they desire, and even the disinterested employee will share in the bonus if the plant earns one. On the other hand, supervisors must of necessity put out extra effort, actively participate in the plan to make it work, and assume a broader role as manager. As was discussed earlier, however, this new role should eventually lighten the supervisor's work load, as the work unit develops as a team and assumes more responsibility for managing itself.

The Case of Ross Manufacturing

The impact that gainsharing has on management and nonmanagement personnel can be better understood by reviewing a case example. Ross Manufacturing's experience is useful in that it shows how firm commitment to the plan from top management, along with openness and teamwork, can be effective in turning an unprofitable company into a profitable one. We will review the organization's unfavorable conditions existing prior to implementation, follow the actions taken to maintain employee involvement during the first year when no bonuses were paid, and summarize the improvements in organizational effectiveness that were ultimately achieved.

Declining Profitability

The late 1970s had been good times for Ross. Markets were strong, and plant employment soared to a high of 700. But as the economy declined, cities and private haulers cut back on orders for truck bodies and garbage truck units. By the early 1980s, the company was failing to show a profit in most months. Layoffs followed, trimming employment to around 300 by 1982. Remaining employees listened to the news of the closing of other manufacturing plants in the area, and rumor had it that Ross' closing was not far off. John Miller, president of Ross at that time, agrees: "That's true. . . . I don't think there's any question about that," he acknowledged. "You're on a collision course when management and the hourly personnel—the people who make it happen—don't communicate with one another and refuse to listen to each other's ideas and suggestions. That's really what was causing our problems more than anything else."

Worsening the division between management and nonmanagement personnel was an outdated individual incentive system that served as a constant source of conflict. The company averaged 160 grievances a year, many of them involving rates established under the old incentive plan. Because the old rates had not kept pace with changes in technology, some workers could reach their daily quota in only a few hours' time. Miller saw this as a major obstacle to productivity: "When you put an incentive system in and you are forced to put a cap on it that says an employee can only earn X number of dollars, that says that you have totally lost control. And that's what had been going on here for a long while. Let's face it, we had no incentive system, We had a giveaway system that said 'whatever you want to run, you run, then go sit in the corner or do whatever you want.'"

Turning It Around

Miller arrived at Ross in mid-1982, when morale was at its lowest. Poor product quality and resulting warranty and product liability claims were draining profits. In troubleshooting this problem, Miller wanted input from the employees on the production line. His goal was to reduce the number of inspectors on the payroll, and instead give employees responsibility for inspecting their own work. "You can't inspect quality in," he stated. "I don't care if you put on 50 inspectors. That won't get it done. People in the plant out there know when they're producing a quality part. They know when they're producing a part that will withstand the strains that it's required to withstand. And if you refuse to listen to their ideas, they'll tell you a couple of times and then they'll say 'OK, fine. The hell with it. If that's what you want, I'll produce all the junk you want.' And that's kind of what we were doing."

After buying out the old incentive system, the company began to develop the group gainsharing system that would replace it. From the beginning, it was understood that the new plan would encourage the participation of all employees. Management and nonmanagement personnel worked together on a developmental task force that hammered out plan details: Who would be eligible to earn a bonus? How would nonmanagement members on the departmental teams be elected? What kind of suggestions would be acceptable as being "performance-related?"

The goal was to promote employee ownership of the plan. To this end, management openly discussed the company's bleak situation with the employees and sought the union's input and recommendations. It was understood that without openness and trust, the attempt at participative management would fail.

The implementation was further supported by preparing managers for the transition to the new management style. Prior to the actual plan start-up, and continuing throughout the year, managers (including supervisors) received dozens of hours of education as to how to be more effective under the new system.

Employees were told that the system would not work without their commitment. To ensure this, a vote on the plan was held. The plan was to be adopted only if 80 percent voted in its favor; it was approved by 89 percent.

From the beginning, a variety of factors worked against the plan's success. The market for trucks and truck bodies had dried up, and low sales volume made it impossible for employees to earn a bonus during the first 12 months after implementation. One might have predicted that such events would cause employees to believe that the promise of a bonus was a management lie and subsequently lose all interest in the gainsharing plan, called PEP (Program for Employee Participation). This did not happen, however. President Miller attributes this to the new atmosphere of mutual respect developing in the firm. "It's a matter of trust and communication," he said. "We had monthly meetings where I got everybody together and poured out my soul: 'Here are the problems we're facing, and here are the opportunities we have. Here are the things which have gone right, and these are the things that have gone wrong. Here's where I think we are, and here's how long I think it will take us to get to a bonus. Now what do you think?' And we continued to talk and we saw progress—not a lot of progress—but progress on a monthly basis."

Employees' ideas continued to come in and be implemented. New ways were found to cut costs—from the welders on the shop floor to the secretaries in the office. Finally, in the fourth two-month period, a $92,278 bonus was announced. Bonuses have been earned fairly consistently in subsequent periods, even if they are not always large.

Results for the Company

Ross is quite profitable after six years under the PEP plan. Miller says that the big gains were in the area of quality control, with warranty costs based on sales now about half of what they were the preceding year. Product recalls have dropped to about 3 percent of sales. In keeping with Miller's objective, in-plant inspectors were reduced from sixteen before the plan to two at the present time. Miller further adds, "I had nine service people on the road. And those nine service people were out repairing junk. I mean things that are ridiculous; things that should not happen. Like someone on the production line forgot to put in some bolts or whatever. And that number of service people has now gone from nine to one."

In a recent year, less than 30 grievances were filed, down from an average of 160 annually in preceding years. In a recent year, 98.3 percent of the employees voted to continue with the PEP plan, up from 89 percent at the original vote. Progress continues to be made.

Conclusion

The results of our managers' survey suggested that the majority of managers in gainsharing companies had adjusted well to their new roles, had seen improvement in the behavior of their subordinates, and were generally satisfied with their plans. But, as the

Ross Manufacturing case demonstrates, adjustment problems can occur, and managers must be given understanding, support, and training if they are to adapt to life under a plan. At Ross, this was accomplished in part by recognizing the needs of the managers and adjusting the plan's idea system accordingly.

Winning the support of managers in this way paid off at Ross Manufacturing. The company managers implemented their plan under the worst of conditions and held fast to its philosophy of participative management, even as months passed with no financial bonus. Today the company has turned around and is making inroads in new markets both here and internationally. Many of the managers we talked with, however, felt that the plant would have simply become another entry on the list of unionized midwest companies forced to close had it not been for the PEP plan and the changes it introduced.

Chapter 12

Some Education Recommendations for Successful Employee Involvement

Timothy L. Ross and Ruth Ann Ross

As the use of gainsharing expands into a variety of different situations, education needs for all levels of employees will also expand. For example, if gainsharing is being used solely as a form of contingent or variable compensation, education needs may be minimal. However, if gainsharing is installed to change significantly the way employees are managed or as a replacement for individual incentives, education of employees may be extremely important to the plan's long-term success. Likewise, if gainsharing is installed with significant employee involvement, education may make the difference between long-term success and failure.

Although each organization must evaluate its own needs, internal/external resources, and abilities to pay for such activities, what follows is an outline of perhaps a minimum amount of education that an organization should provide for the typical installation when considerable formalized employee involvement is included in the system. The approach used here is for a more generic, customized approach as opposed to a more "packaged" one. An outline is found on Exhibit 12.1.

Stages of Education

Stage 1

This stage represents preliminary top management education, which is always necessary. In some cases, training could include the union officials if applicable. The purpose at this stage is to investigate whether gainsharing is appropriate for the particular organization. Education may take the form of attendance at a seminar developed internally, which is perhaps most commonly conducted by an outside consultant. It is introductory in nature and frequently covers the topics outlined in Exhibit 12.1. A one-day session can provide a fairly thorough introduction.

Stage 2

This stage includes more in-depth discussions and work on a calculation. This is a key stage of development and, unless major issues are resolved at this point, the rest of gainsharing will not proceed. Material covered on formulas and measurement issues in Chapters 3 and 4 should be of significant help in this stage. Key issues are orientation (broad vs. narrow measure(s)), base periods, reserves, percentage to employees, and so on.

Stage 3

This stage consists of an all-employee survey which is frequently considered optional but should not be. The survey can help assess the need to change, the level of employee knowledge, and the level of trust within the organization and in management, as well as other factors. Standard surveys that assess need to change and an evaluation of current conditions could be used. Feedback could then lead to gainsharing; the whole process is in itself educational provided feedback does occur.

Stage 4

This stage can be a brief half-hour to an hour presentation to all employees discussing what gainsharing is and the need to develop a task force to finalize the plan. One could use the feedback survey mentioned above as a lead-in to the gainsharing concept at this time.

Stage 5

Pre-Implementation Education

If a major increase in employee involvement is desired, general managers'/supervisors' education about gainsharing should

Exhibit 12.1   Recommended Education With Major Employee Involvement

STAGE	AUDIENCE	TIMING	TYPICAL CONTENT
1	Top Management	First session of exposure: public seminar or consultant	Various gainsharing approaches Key decisions Different involvement approaches Different calculations Expectations Study and implementation strategies Evaluation of current system / need to change
2	Top Management	Early in study phase	Decide on calculations Develop a working plan Evaluate comprehension of plan
3	All Employees	Before introduction of gainsharing concept	Typical employee survey assessing need to change; must have feedback. Probably infrequently used in actual practice; some assessment of conditions is needed, however.
4	All Employees	After closure on calculation and after corporate approval; to help develop a task force for completing the plan document	Introduction to gainsharing General principles/philosophy Typical employee involvement Typical calculations (few details) Possible benefits to company and employees Plan of action Need to develop a task force to finalize plan
5	All of Management/ Supervisors	After introduction but before plan is finalized by a task force (3–5 hours)	Principles of gainsharing Implementation steps Typical involvement systems Typical calculations Differences in management styles How to achieve a more consultative/participative environment How to maintain it Common reactions to change and how to overcome

Exhibit 12.1 *Continued*

STAGE	AUDIENCE	TIMING	TYPICAL CONTENT
6	All Employees (1 to 1½ hours), and six hours for all Managers/ Supervisors/Team Representatives	Immediately before implementation	All Employees: How the plan will operate All Managers/Team Representatives Key mechanisms Purpose/goals Involvement system Bonus calculation Policies Calculation simulations Agendas for meetings Mechanics of flow of information/ideas Planning and holding effective meetings Evaluation of meetings Responsibilities of everyone Handling change
7	All Employees	On a regular basis, at least monthly	Bonus results for period Current business/economic conditions Involvement activities Goal attainment
8	All of Management/ Supervisors/Team Representatives	After two or three months with gainsharing	Assessing plan's effectiveness with a simple survey on key issues, brainstorm good and poor areas Highlight plan's principles and procedures Group sensing Dealing with problem situations Key communication responsibilities Getting people involved Handling problem situations
9	All of Management/ Supervisors	Various after three months depending on needs; could be three six-hour modules developed for each topic	Managing in a participative environment/integration processes Planning and organizing skills Delegating Communication effectiveness Motivational systems Identifying and correcting problem situations Creativity/problem solving techniques such as brainstorming, Pareto analysis, cause/effect analysis Team building techniques Special calculation education Specialized statistical and other education

begin shortly after the company announces it is considering gain-sharing. Usually this education takes place while a developmental task force is working out details of the company's plan. Within weeks the company will tell employees what those details are, so managers should be able to answer questions their people are sure to have. Three to five hours of education are usually adequate for this stage.

At first managers who are not used to gainsharing's consultative-participative approach may feel uneasy about its emphasis on teamwork, cooperation, and communication. They'll need to understand the difference between traditional supervision and supervision under a gainsharing plan. To help them develop that understanding, the trainer should introduce the principles of managing under gainsharing early, then assess, reteach, and reinforce those basics at each subsequent stage.

The session should include an initial preview of the plan's implementation steps and should give managers a detailed picture of how gainsharing will influence their jobs and the people in their work units. In addition to items covered in Exhibit 12.1, one could discuss the following:

- a supervisor's typical gainsharing-related responsibilities;
- what will take place in departmental gainsharing team meetings;
- how performance-improvement ideas may be implemented;
- how employees and the company should benefit under the plan;
- how the organization's communication and management systems might change;
- how to have effective consultative or participative management;
- how to motivate workers under group bonus systems;
- reasons employees sometimes resist change and don't want to become involved.

When these sessions are completed, managers will have an idea of what to expect from the plan and of what will be expected from them. Trainers will have the chance to identify managers who may need extra help in adjusting to the new way of life. This additional support can be provided either by a good inside manager or by an outside consultant.

Stage 6

Education for Plan Start-Up

Before implementation, the organization probably needs to conduct a series of meetings to explain the gainsharing concept to all employees, along with the specific plan, now finalized. Managers will soon have to move into this second stage of training. Five to six hours of training will probably be adequate for managers/supervisors and all team members; perhaps an hour should be allotted for the remainder of the employees.

By this time the developmental task force will have completed its work, and managers need to become familiar with plan details decided by that group. This means managers should understand the plan's long-term goals; how production costs and other factors influence the bonus calculation; how bonuses are determined; who is eligible under the plan; and other technicalities of bonus distribution and team operations.

The key word is "detail" because managers must quickly develop an understanding of everyone's individual gainsharing responsibilities as outlined in Exhibit 12.1. These include the responsibilities of—

- managers, supervisors, nonmanagement representatives, and the plan coordinator, if one exists;
- departmental versus plantwide review teams, if present;
- management versus nonmanagement employees' responsibilities.

At the same time, managers should receive instruction as to how they will contribute to plan start-up, including:

- steps they must follow during start-up;
- how to begin with effective departmental meetings, and what they should and shouldn't cover in them;
- how to evaluate gainsharing meetings;
- the importance of giving employees prompt feedback on ideas they contribute.

Stage 7

This stage consists of ongoing education, which may be accomplished through meetings or through written communication or a combination of the two. Activities would include discussions of bonus results, how the involvement is going, problems and possible resolutions, surveys, and so on. Some firms make a major effort in this area, while others offer only limited training at this time.

Stage 8

Problem Sensing and Problem Solving

Two or three months after the plan is underway, managers and team members will have a sense of what is and is not going well. This is the time to review basic principles of gainsharing, identify positive aspects, see what problems have developed, and provide help in solving those problems. Six hours of education are usually necessary.

One good way to begin the problem-sensing process is to review the gainsharing plan objectives outlined by the developmental task force and to assess the company's success in meeting them. Various organizations have also had success by—

- asking managers, representatives, and others to complete surveys to evaluate their plan's success on key areas;
- interviewing managers and representatives in groups to identify problem areas;
- brainstorming about solutions for typical difficulties encountered;
- administering a quiz to test everyone's knowledge about aspects of the plan.

Other possible topics are outlined in Exhibit 12.1.

Groups must spend time discussing each problem and working together to come up with solutions. Drawing on each other's experiences is often useful and helps drive home the message that everyone's "in this" together.

Problems uncovered during these sessions frequently center on supervisory relations with nonmanagement personnel who are uncooperative or apathetic to the gainsharing plan. It can be worthwhile to have managers agree on correct ways to handle such employees and then role-play through several predictable confrontations.

While you'll have to focus a lot of energy on unresolved problems, you also should spend time promoting successes achieved under the plan. This helps "stir the pot" and maintain interest in gainsharing.

Stage 9

Integrating gainsharing concepts with good management practice can be a time-consuming activity. If there has been a major commitment to employee involvement, organizations should plan for an additional 20 to 30 hours of general management education during the first two years under gainsharing. Additional training is particularly appropriate if a major change in management philosophy and practices is to be expected as outlined in Exhibit 12.1. This education will be necessary in part to deal with the system changes already discussed. Education also may be necessary because employees often demand better management under gainsharing. If the plan is successful, employees will be concerned about the organization's performance, and will see the central role managers play in improving it.

At this stage trainers should tailor programs to help managers integrate the plan's structures and mechanisms into their everyday activities. At this point they'll likely appreciate the difference between "just managing" and managing under the gainsharing philosophy of cooperation and common objectives. The goal should be to help managers see how they can use the plan to improve their effectiveness at *planning work, delegating, communicating, motivating, correcting performance problems,* and *handling other management difficulties.* A team building program is often used at this point.

Managers may also find it easier to implement tools such as statistical process control once the plan is in place. The gainsharing bonus provides a common objective for all employees and gives managers a powerful lever for winning employee acceptance of performance improvement techniques. Specialized problems such as elimination of individual incentives may require specialized education in that specific ground rules must be developed as to how to manage in a nonincentive environment.

Conclusions

A gainsharing plan's success or failure depends on managers' ability to adapt to the new approach. If upper management suddenly installs a plan on an unready organization, managerial frustration, resentment, and ill feelings may follow, because employee involvement in work decisions often threatens a manager's sense of control over the work unit. The result may be managers who not only fail to contribute to the plan's success, but even work against it. This problem occurs more often when the work force is unionized.

Eventually most managers do well under gainsharing plans and evaluate them positively—but only when they are adequately prepared for the change and receive support and encouragement during the transition. When a plan succeeds, it's a safe bet that the foundation was a thoughtfully designed and responsive management/employee education program.

Chapter 13

Gainsharing Application in the Service Sector

Timothy L. Ross

Will gainsharing be applied increasingly in the service sector as predicted by a 1987 American Productivity Center Study? Certainly so, but the pace may not be as rapid as predicted. Contrary to some individuals' perceptions, there are often fewer measurement problems in service sector firms than in some manufacturing organizations, although there may be fewer options. Actual applications are more limited, however, because of lack of interest in productivity improvement, less competitive pressures, and the lack of awareness of the various systems. In this chapter, the types of service industries are discussed, then the different gainsharing formulas as applied in the service sector are reviewed. The chapter concludes with a gainsharing approach for use in bank branches followed by a discussion of some approaches that have been used by various service sector firms.

Service Sector Classifications

The activities commonly described as services cover a far-ranging group of organizations that share some common characteristics: output that cannot be stored and transactions that usually require direct interaction between an employee and a customer. Some people remove from the services category activities that are capital intensive and large in scale. This categorization divides the economy of the United States into the following three sectors,

253

generally based on the nature of the inputs involved and the resultant outputs:

1. agriculture—agriculture, fisheries, and forestry;
2. industry—manufacturing, construction, mining, transportation, communications, and public utilities;
3. service—wholesale and retail trade; finance, insurance and real estate (F.I.R.E.); professional, personal, business, and repair; and federal, state, and local government including education.

A review of the service group above suggests one common characteristic: labor-intensive operations. When this facet is combined with the need for direct interaction with the customer, it becomes possible to evolve a more precise service classification system that uses the potential for rationalization and control. Such a classification system has been devised by Chase.[1] The following four categories are based on the extent of customer contact, roughly defined as the percentage of the total transaction time that the customer must be in the system:

1. manufacturing—no customer contact during the production process;
2. quasimanufacturing—possible identifiable physical units of output;
3. mixed service—significant exposure to direct customer contact;
4. pure service—maximal exposure to direct customer contact; possible intangible units of service.

These categories become quite useful when managers attempt to use productivity gainsharing as a socially responsible means of achieving improvements in performance.

Measurement for Gainsharing in Service Sector—A General Review

In quasimanufacturing operations within the service sector of the economy, the availability of identifiable physical units of output and the minimal amount of customer involvement in the transaction tend to make productivity measurement relatively easy. (In fact, manufacturing firms with much indirect labor—e.g., engineering, material handlers, and maintenance—may be more difficult to measure.) Within the mixed category such as bank tellers or hospital nurses, who have a fair amount of customer or patient contact, productivity becomes more difficult. One reason for this is the relatively intangible dimension of quality that is included in the teller-customer or nurse-patient relationship. The closer one moves toward pure service organizations, the more difficult it becomes to devise "productivity measurement pure" gainsharing calculations. "Pure" in this sense is a physical output-per-hour calculation such as Improshare as opposed to broader measures such as multicost or even prospective forms of gainsharing, such as beating budgets, which will be discussed later.

Also involved is the customer influence on the level of resources (inputs) required to provide a satisfactory service as perceived by the customer (outputs), as well as the difficulty of identifying and measuring these productivity components. Until recently, another factor that has limited efforts to make effective use of performance measurements in the mixed services category has been the managerial preoccupation with other aspects of the overall operation. For example, managers have been mainly concerned with marketing of services and effectiveness of services, rather than with the efficiency of the service rendered. This obviously will have to change in the future.

Measurement

In attempting to measure the performance of a mixed services unit such as a hospital, it is difficult to separate productivity from other factors because hospital output is so heterogeneous and hospital charges may not be reliable guides to the relative costs needed to develop an overall output measure.

One suggested approach to an output measurement system requires the use of different weights for different illnesses, operations, accidents, and other service requirements. However, hospitals do have revenues, payroll costs, and operating expenses. Reimbursing agencies (third-party payers), which represent the major portion of hospital receipts, require detailed accounting for costs. In addition, statistical records such as MONItrend reports provide administrators with a considerable amount of information about the hospital's operations. Therefore, despite the many problems that exist, the data required for most of the performance gainsharing calculations are available for service sector calculations at a hospital. Gainsharing has been applied at several hospitals and interest is likely to grow in the future.

In banking, there is also significant information to draw on for performance measurement. The proper measure of banking output for use in this case can be narrowed to a choice between two concepts: the liquidity approach, which is based on deposits and the transactions approach, which is based on transactions. The transactions approach is the form most accepted by the banking industry. One can develop factors that might be considered for multiple weighting among different types of activities, such as number of accounts; number of checks handled; value of accounts and checks; savings and checking accounts; loans and size of loans. Some recent research dealing with productivity of bank branches indicated that suitable weights for transactions could be developed from the relative average times required for various logical groupings of transactions. Such times need to reflect the technology in place and any other site-specific factors. The most significant inputs related to these outputs are teller labor and other branch-related payroll and fringes costs, which are discussed later as an example.

Consideration also needs to be given to various other costs that are inputs, such as rent, depreciation, and cash variations and losses. While the decision as to which accounts to consider for inclusion in the calculations must be based on a site-specific review of historical data, it is highly likely that only a few will have significant impact.

The above two examples (medium-sized general-care hospitals and bank branches) represent extremes of the mixed services continuum; that is, organizations oriented to altruism and organizations dominated by finance. It is possible to develop and/or manipulate the raw data needed to evolve one or more alternative measurements suitable for each type of organization. Suitable creative analysis of other industries on the services continuum is very possible. The nature of the useful alternative calculations is described in the following section. The nominal group technique has been found to be extremely useful in developing performance measurements in service sector environments. Regardless of perceived measurement problems, goals and other budget oriented systems can always be used.

Alternative Calculations

The needs of individual service organizations and the availability of data required for various calculations can differ to a considerable degree. Fortunately, the calculations available for use in firms considering the use of gainsharing plans cover a wide range of options. Each of the calculations normally makes use of the total net output for a relatively brief period (such as one month) and makes payments to nearly all employees (including managers and perhaps executives). A review of some of the most commonly used calculations as discussed in Chapter 3 is helpful in understanding the differences as applied to service organizations.

Improshare or Allowed Labor

Both Improshare and the Allowed Labor calculations are based on the use of detailed work measures for each task defining the amount of time required to produce a specific unit of output. These calculations are adjusted upward to allow for related unmeasured work associated with base labor that generates the output. Because of the requirement that detailed time standards be available for use, Improshare and Allowed Labor calculations tend to be more applicable to quasi-manufacturing operations, such as hospital laundries and bank check-processing operations. However, other firms, such as repair shops, general laundries, and schools can use such calculations quite easily and can incorporate considerations for quality. These types of calculations have been used extensively in government situations.

Single Ratio

The single ratio calculation is based on the simple relationship of total labor costs for the period to the total revenue. As shown in Exhibit 13.1, it may be calculated for a typical medium-sized general-care hospital as follows:

$$\text{Single ratio} = \frac{\text{Total labor}}{\text{Total revenue}} = \frac{\$295,000}{\$500,000} = 59\%$$

If the actual costs are less than 59 percent of revenue, a bonus is earned. The major advantages of the single ratio calculation are its ease of calculation and simplicity of understanding. Most manufacturing firms would have an allowable percentage lower than 59 percent. As previously noted, the labor intensity of mixed-service operations permits this calculation to represent a majority of the input costs, which can be broken out separately by department and/or function.[2] Indexing can be used to adjust for the inflationary

Exhibit 13.1   General Care Hospitals: Typical Financial Details for Use in Calculating Performance Gainsharing Ratios

OUTPUT

Gross revenue	$ 527,000	
Loss on medicare	−25,000	
Other adjustments	−23,000	
Net revenue		$479,000
Interest (may be excluded)		15,000
Misc. income (may be excluded)		6,000
Total Revenue (TR)		$500,000

INPUTS

Payroll	$250,000	
Fringes	45,000	
Total Labor (TL)		$295,000
Supplies/fees and materials	$125,000	
Adminis. & Misc. costs	55,000	
Other Costs (OC)		$180,000

CALCULATIONS

$$\text{Single ratio} = \frac{TL}{TR} = \frac{\$295,000}{\$500,000} = 59\%$$

$$\text{Multicost ratio} = \frac{TL + OC}{TR} = \frac{\$295,000 + \$180,000}{\$500,000} = 95\%$$

$$\text{Value-added ratio} = \frac{TL}{TR - OC} = \frac{\$295,000}{\$500,000 - \$180,000} = 92\%$$

impact on revenue and wages. However, the single ratio does ignore the impact of capital and/or energy inputs on changes in output.

For the typical hospital being used as an example, capital expenditures frequently involve the adoption of new technology, which is often embodied in new services that are additions to, rather than replacements for, existing services.

One problem that can occur with the single ratio is a variation in product mix over time. A common method of overcoming that problem is the use of the split-ratio calculation, which is discussed below. The single-ratio calculation could be used in hospitals, appraisal services, consulting firms, distribution centers, government services, security services, restaurants, car washes, educational institutions, and computer service firms, to name a few.

Split-Ratio Expansions

Essentially, the split-ratio calculation is two or more single ratios, which are aligned according to the labor intensity of the services that generate the total revenue. Each of these ratios would include the directly associated labor costs and a rational allocation of the other payroll and fringe costs as shown in Exhibit 13.1. In general, the split ratio has the same advantages and disadvantages associated with the single ratio except that it does help resolve the product mix problem. Many of the other problems that exist can be overcome by the use of a more comprehensive ratio—one that incorporates a greater percentage of the inputs required to generate the total revenue. Organizations that would find the split ratio more applicable include advertising agencies, architectural firms, and insurance firms.

Multicost Ratio

The inclusion of other costs (OC) essentially converts the single ratio into the multicost ratio. As shown in Exhibit 13.1, it is calculated in the following manner:

$$\text{Multicost Ratio} = \frac{TL + OC}{TR}$$

$$= \frac{\$295,000 + \$180,000}{\$500,000} = 95\%$$

While the resulting percentage will vary among service sector industries and depends on decisions concerning the specific costs to be added, the expansion normally results in a ratio that is 70 percent to 95 percent inclusive of the total revenue. This large percentage of the revenue reduces the problems of inflation and product mix. A problem that it creates, however, is a potential conclusion by the participants that they have little control over some of the factors included in the ratio. This calculation does have a major advantage over profit sharing in that management does not have to disclose profits. The more costs are included, the closer one gets to profit sharing.

The multicost formula can be applied to banks, employment

agencies, executive search firms, hospitals, hotels and motels, restaurants, theaters, and many other types of establishments. It has been used in many manufacturing firms with major success when the orientation is toward overall organization performance.

Value-Added Ratio

As suggested above, this ratio is a simple modification of the multicost ratio. Using the data for medium-sized general-care hospitals found in Exhibit 13.1, the value-added ratio is calculated in the following manner:

$$\text{Value-added ratio} = \frac{\text{TL}}{\text{TR} - \text{OC}}$$

$$= \frac{\$295,000}{\$500,000 - \$180,000} = 92\%$$

Research into the use of this ratio—which is the common basis of the Rucker plan—indicates that it does not need to be changed for wage rate increases, changes in charges for services rendered, material cost changes, or variations in the portion of work subcontracted, all of which frequently test the single ratio. It would tend to give erroneous readings, however, following the installation of cost-effective technological improvements. Such changes would undoubtedly require a new or modified calculation for an equitable measure and/or related bonus plan.

This calculation can be used in sites where product mix is a problem, such as retail stores, job shops, theaters, and airlines, or when multicost is not selected for disclosure reasons.

Other Measures

In service sector companies that have a comprehensive set of standard costs, it is possible to make use of a standard labor ratio. This ratio is based on the relationship of labor costs to total standard costs. Its advantage is that it does not require use of total revenue in the calculation. The use of service-specific time and material measurements greatly decreases the problems of product mix, and the use of physical performance-based measurements generally eliminates the effect of inflation.

Even broader-based measures of productivity can be developed. Such ratios deal with the return achieved on assets or stockholders' equity. The calculations required under these measures closely resemble the multicost ratio supplemented by a factor to reflect the contribution of capital assets. Such plans require a major commitment from management, lack a direct relationship to performance productivity, and require a significant communications effort.

Some organizations attempt to overcome these problems by modifying one of the calculations discussed above in a manner that emphasizes one or more important areas of their business rather than very broad-based calculations. The variety of input data and output data available within an organization can be creatively combined to develop a tailor-made hybrid calculation. This can involve the use of a series of weights to give recognition to levels of service quality, generation of incremental revenue (cross-selling of available services), or other important factors for the long-term success of the firm. Multiple pool approaches discussed in Chapters 3 and 4 can also be used. Budgeted performance is sometimes used. The exact nature of the service sector industry and the site-specific, time-related situation will guide the choice of the best calculation for use by individual mixed-services firms.

Numerous governmental units have used gainsharing in a variety of situations. Most of the applications have used specific measurement formulas such as Improshare. The U.S. General Accounting Office has published a report describing some of these experiences.[3] Chapter 8 discusses many others at all levels of government.

A Specific Application in Branch Banks

The Problem

There are more than 50,000 banking offices in the United States, most of which employ fewer than ten persons. Control of the associated cost has become an increasingly important factor since extreme variations in interest rates and deregulation efforts of the federal government have made the improvement of earnings more difficult. Concerned managers have adopted various strategies, such as automatic teller machines (ATMs), have used the teller simulation model developed by the Bank Administration Institute, or have increased the use of part-time tellers. The focus of these efforts has been to improve productivity by holding a key input (employee expense) to the lowest level possible by unilateral man-

262 Cases and Applications

agerial action. Despite these endeavors, earnings are still dangerously low and in serious need of improvement.

Gainsharing As a Solution

For over fifty years, many American firms have met similar problems by installing gainsharing plans to encourage employee identification with corporate goals and to enlist their participation in efforts to improve productivity and quality.

Illustrative data for a typical branch bank is shown in Exhibit 13.2. It also includes a variety of base calculations of the gainsharing formulas which can be easily used.[4] Based on the calculation depicted in Exhibit 13.2, a bonus example is shown in Exhibit 13.3. Normally an extended past period is used to develop a base period ratio in order to reflect the gainsharing concept of beating past performance. Exhibit 13.3 illustrates the bonus percentage calculation if we assume that the historical analysis indicated that $0.27 would be an acceptable base ratio for the single ratio (a labor-only calculation).

Each gainsharing calculation will be somewhat different. One could use an Improshare version of allowed time minus actual time to yield the bonus pool. All of the commonly used performance and financial-based calculations have certain advantages and disadvantages that would have to be considered by each bank. Broader calculations could obviously be applied to higher levels of banking activities. In some instances, budgets and forecasted goals are integrated into the gainsharing system. Such approaches are being used today.

Application—Actual and Potential

Many different calculations have been used by service organizations. Unfortunately, the calculation is often perceived by managers or owners as more important than behaviorally oriented variables. This is seldom true, but this misperception works against gainsharing success. From a purely pragmatic standpoint, the objectives of the measurement system are more important than its form. For example, if one wants an overall improvement in performance (such as return on investment or return on sales) to coincide with bonuses, then one should adopt one of these measures or, preferably, the multicost or value-added formulas. Looking at

Exhibit 13.2. Typical Bank Branch's Operating Data and Productivity Measures/Formulas

OUTPUTS

TRANSACTION TYPE	NO./MO.	WEIGHT	TIME/ COMPLEXITY WEIGHTED TRANSACTIONS
Credits	16,600	1.0	16,600
Cashed Checks	10,400	1.0	10,400
Savings	3,700	2.0	7,400
Other	1,200	3.0	3,600
Total Transactions (TT)			38,000

INPUTS

ACCOUNT NAME	AMOUNT	DEFLATION*	DEFLATED AMOUNT
Salaries	$ 9,130		
Overtime	66		
Benefits	2,090		
Total Labor (TL)	$11,286	1.10	$10,260
Depreciation	$ 800		
Losses-teller differences	720		
Losses & Depreciation (LD)	$ 1,520	1.00	$1,520
Rent	$ 1,700		
Maintenance	400		
Stationery	200		
Taxes	1,500		
Credit Reports	130		
Travel	50		
Insurance	600		
Other	1,006		
Other Costs (OC)	$ 5,586	1.05	$ 5,320

SAMPLE FORMULAS

$$\text{Single ratio} = \frac{TL}{TT} = \frac{\$10,260}{38,000} = \$0.270$$

$$\text{Multicost ratio} = \frac{TL + LD}{TT} = \frac{\$10,260 + \$1,520}{38,000} = \$0.310$$

$$\text{Expanded Multicost Ratio} = \frac{TL + LD + OC}{TT}$$

$$= \frac{\$10,260 + \$1,520 + 5,320}{38,000} = \$0.450$$

*Deflation indexes are developed to adjust each financial figure to constant dollars representing a base period. This procedure may or may not be required. Another simple approach would be to compute annually a new base ratio.

Exhibit 13.3 Bonus Example—Month X

Allowed costs (43,000 total weighted transaction times $0.27/transaction)	$11,610
Actual costs (assumed)	10,300
Bonus pool	1,310
Employee share (assume 50%)	655
Reserve for deficit periods (assume 25%—depends on variability and long-run attitude reinforcement)	164
Net monthly pool (varies from a moving weekly average, from monthly to quarterly)	491
Participating payroll (assumed)	9,000
Bonus % (normally paid as a % of wage for everyone): $491/9,000)	5.5%

other options, gainsharing can always be based on reduction in budgeted costs or a whole range of targeted performance.

In actual practice, gainsharing can be applied in many service organizations, as the partial list given below indicates. Many service organizations also have profit-sharing programs, which in a very broad sense could be considered gainsharing. Some gainsharing plans that have been brought to our attention as actual or potential applications include the following:

1. allowed labor/Improshare: repair shops, laundries, schools, government applications;
2. single ratio: appraisal services, consultants, distribution centers, government services, security services, restaurants, car washes;
3. split ratio: advertising agencies, architects, insurance firms;
4. multicost ratio: banks, employment agencies, executive search firms, hospitals, hotels and motels, property management firms, publishing firms;
5. multiple pool: various pools for day labor, other costs, quality customer service; can be applied about everywhere;
6. value-added ratio: dental clinics, retail stores, funeral homes, nursing homes, photographic studios, restaurants, theaters, printers;
7. standard labor ratio: captive service operations, data processing services, dry cleaners, libraries;
8. profit sharing or return on investment: TV and radio broadcasting, newspaper publishing, investment companies, law firms, accounting firms, medical clinics;

9. budgeted or goal oriented systems: normally based on improvements in these variables rather than just a percentage of profits.

In the years to come, we expect many other service firms to install gainsharing.[5] Gradually, more firms will become familiar with its principles and with both behavioral and measurement data shown from real-life experiences. These service firms will normally start with the simpler calculations based on the criteria of understanding, administrative ease, and so on, and will move to increasingly more complex calculations. In fact, much of gainsharing's future growth will probably center on service sector firms because of limited past interest and applications and because of the increased emphasis on employee involvement in service oriented firms.

Notes

1. B. Chase, "Where Does the Customer Fit in a Service Operation?" *Harvard Business Review*, November–December 1978.
2. W.C. Hauck, "Measuring Effectiveness in Banks and Hospitals," *Industrial Management*, 28, March–April 1986, 26–27.
3. "Gainsharing—DOD Efforts Highlight an Effective Tool for Enhancing Federal Productivity," No. 86–143 BR (Washington, D.C.: U.S. General Accounting Office, 1986).
4. W.C. Hauck, "Measuring Effectiveness," note 2, above.
5. B.E. Graham-Moore, "Productivity Gainsharing in the Service Sector" in *Personnel Management: Compensation Service* (Paramus, N.J.: Prentice-Hall 1987).

Chapter 14

Attitude Change Versus Performance Improvement: One Look at the Long-Term Results

Timothy L. Ross, Larry L. Hatcher, and Ruth Ann Ross

Gainsharing case studies typically emphasize the role of the average worker in reducing costs, increasing production efficiency, and improving product quality. Often a system of teams throughout the organization solicits and acts on employees' suggestions and subsequently develops goals.

Gainsharing plans have traditionally been discussed in terms of their impact on productivity, and many published case studies describe the resulting improvements. This emphasis on productivity is understandable since many of the early plans were implemented to save companies in serious financial difficulty.

In addition to productivity, worker attitudes have also received major attention in the gainsharing literature. Various authors have suggested that a successful gainsharing plan can result in higher levels of cooperation, participation, and job satisfaction. The majority of the evidence regarding attitudes, however, is more qualitative in nature. Many of the case studies providing quantitative information on improvements in productivity provide only anecdotal evidence regarding changes in employee attitudes.

Representative of such studies is one reported by the U.S. General Accounting Office.[1] Financial data were obtained from 24 firms with gainsharing plans, and it was reported, for instance, that companies with annual sales of less than $100 million averaged work force savings of 17.3 percent. Savings averaged 16.4 percent at those firms with sales in excess of $100 million.

In contrast, the report provides data regarding attitude change which is more subjective. It discusses interviews held with plant employees, concluding "climate between labor and management was said to have improved over what had existed before the productivity sharing plan was implemented." The conclusion is interesting, but without information on the sampling technique used, the interview format used, or the procedures used to analyze the responses, it is difficult to evaluate the accuracy of the finding.

Bullock and Bullock[2] report the results of a survey which was administered to employees before a gainsharing plan was installed and then again one year later. Improvements were reported in work-group functioning, openness, trust, communication, goal setting, and a number of other areas. Unfortunately, statistical significance was not reported. The research reported in this chapter is based on longitudinal survey data in an attempt to begin filling this void in the literature.

A survey was administered to employees of a manufacturing company before a gainsharing plan was implemented, and again after 18 months under the plan. Care was taken to insure the reliability of the scales, which assessed employee satisfaction with the company, satisfaction with the work itself, cooperation, opportunity for participation, productivity, satisfaction with supervisor, and satisfaction with working conditions. Observed changes in attitudes were tested for statistical significance.

Ashley March: A Case Study

Background

Ashley March (a fictitious name) is a medium-sized midwestern company producing industrial equipment, with sales of around $30 million annually. Nearly two thirds of the 200 or so employees are in a union, and three-fourths are male.

The years 1984 and 1985 were particularly bad for the firm. Inventories reached an all-time high in 1984, and high interest rates subsequently caused a substantial drain on profits. Production was cut to lower inventories, and layoffs resulted.

In addition to these difficulties, relations between management and nonmanagement employees were strained. Mutual mistrust and poor communication existed throughout the organization. Many employees were resentful of the layoffs and felt that favoritism was a problem. There was little, if any, sense of teamwork, and productivity suffered accordingly.

Gainsharing seemed an appropriate choice since it would address Ashley March's most pressing problems: lack of cooperation, low productivity, and poor worker attitudes. The need to change was very evident since survival was at risk. As is often the case, gainsharing was to be used to lead organizational change.

Details of the Gainsharing Plan

In developing a gainsharing plan, a company must deal with two basic questions: (a) How much employee involvement is desired? and (b) What type of bonus calculation is best? The system at Ashley March was designed by a developmental task force comprising a cross-section of employees from all levels of the company. The task force met over a three-month period to design the objectives, involvement system, rules, and policies and procedures, and to critique the calculation. In other organizations, the time period for this process has been shortened. Both a departmental and a higher level team system discussed earlier helped to ensure that actions and communications occurred as necessary.

Research Questions

Much has been conjectured regarding the impact of a gainsharing plan on worker attitudes, but little has been demonstrated with carefully developed measures and statistical analysis of longitudinal data. Hypothesis testing is difficult in this area, because predictions made are often broad and nonspecific. For example, Frost, Wakely, and Ruh,[3] Moore and Ross,[4] and O'Dell[5] have each suggested that a plan can result in improved job satisfaction, but do not note which aspects of job satisfaction will be influenced: satisfaction with the company, job, work environment, and so forth.

The present study was designed to assess employee satisfaction in several areas and identify those showing a significant improvement under the plan. Question 1 stated that postimplementation satisfaction with the company, with the work itself, with the supervisor, and with working conditions will be significantly higher than preimplementation satisfaction in these areas.

There is less ambiguity in predictions made regarding other aspects of change. All three sources discussed earlier predict improvements in cooperation, employee participation, and productivity under a successful gainsharing plan. Although the chapter does not report behavioral indices, it is possible to assess the change as perceived by the employees. Accordingly, Questions 2, 3, and 4 state that there will be a significant improvement in employees perceptions of cooperation, opportunity for participation, and productivity, respectively.

Development of the Attitude Scales

Approximately one month before the gainsharing plan began, an attitude survey was administered to all company employees. This 78-item survey assessed their satisfaction, needs, and perception of various attributes of the company. Eighteen months later, another survey was administered. Forty-one items were common to the two instruments. Scales were constructed from these common items.

On an *a priori* basis, items dealing with similar constructs were grouped together. The homogeneity of these items within scales was assessed and questions displaying poor item-total correlations were sequentially dropped. All item analyses were performed using data from the preimplementation survey.

Seven scales were developed. These scales, and their items, are presented in Exhibits 14.1 and 14.2. All items used a 5-point response format, with 1 the most negative and 5 the most positive response. An employee's responses to the items were averaged to obtain his or her score on each scale for discussion purposes here.

Results

If employees had identified their surveys so they could be paired from the first and second administrations, the most appropriate analysis to use on the data would be a repeated measures t-test. It would allow each respondent to be treated as his or her own control. Although not done in this fashion, other alternative tests were used to test reliability and significance levels.

Exhibit 14.1   Items Comprising the Satisfaction Scales

SCALE AND ITEMS	SURVEY RESULTS	
	PRE-MEAN	POST-MEAN

Satisfaction with company
1. All in all, how satisfied are you with your company?
2. How do you feel about your future with your company?
3. How are employee complaints dealt with by the company?
4. Your feeling of loyalty to the company (is now). . . .
5. Your feeling of trust and confidence in management (is now). . . .

	PRE-MEAN	POST-MEAN
Average (1–5 scale)	2.96	3.39

Satisfaction with the work itself
1. All in all, how satisfied are you with your job?
2. Your interest in the work itself (is now). . . .
3. Your being informed about performance measures for your job (is now). . . .

	PRE-MEAN	POST-MEAN
Average (1–5 scale)	3.22	3.46

Satisfaction with supervisor
1. To what extent do you have confidence and trust in your supervisor?
2. How well does your supervisor know your work record?
3. How well does your supervisor do the planning and scheduling of your work?
4. How well does your supervisor do the people side of his/her job (giving recognition, building teamwork, giving feedback, etc.)?
5. To what extent is your supervisor free to take independent actions that are necessary to carry out his or her job responsibilities?
6. To what extent does favoritism exist in the treatment of employees at your level?

	PRE-MEAN	POST-MEAN
Average (1–5 scale)	3.46	3.61

Satisfaction with working conditions
1. Overall, how would you describe the physical working conditions (noise, lighting, temperature, etc.) of your location?
2. How do you feel about the equipment and materials available to you to get your job done?
3. How well does the company minimize safety hazards to you on the job?

	PRE-MEAN	POST-MEAN
Average (1–5 scale)	3.14	3.26

Exhibit 14.2   Items Comprising the Cooperation, Participation, and Productivity Scales

SCALE AND ITEMS	SURVEY RESULTS	
	PRE-MEAN	POST-MEAN
Cooperation 1. How would you rate cooperation between departments in general? 2. How would you rate communication between departments in general? Average (1–5 scale)	2.20	2.69
Opportunity for participation 1. Is management willing to accept suggestions you make? 2. Does your supervisor ask your opinion when a problem comes up that involves your work? 3. Your opportunity for participating in the setting of goals, methods, and procedures (is now). . . . Average (1–5 scale)	2.83	3.23
Productivity 1. How would you describe the level of productivity in this plant compared to what it could be? Average (1–5 scale)	2.42	3.05

Responses to Research Questions

Question 1: Satisfaction

Employee satisfaction with the company was significantly higher on the postimplementation survey than on the preimplementation survey. The preimplementation mean average for this scale was 2.96, while the postimplementation average was 3.39.

Similarly, satisfaction with the work itself improved significantly under gainsharing. The scale average on the initial survey was 3.22, while the average on the later survey was 3.46.

Although the score on the satisfaction with supervisor scale was more positive postimplementation than preimplementation, the difference was not significant. Similarly, the increase in satisfaction with working conditions was also insignificant; this fact was surprising to everyone since major improvements had occurred (their feeling was that expectations had increased after the installation).

In summary, the scales measuring satisfaction with the company and satisfaction with the work itself reflected significantly more favorable attitudes after gainsharing had been implemented. There is, however, no evidence that employees were more satisfied with their supervisors or with their working conditions after 18 months under a plan.

Question 2: Cooperation

From Exhibit 14.2 the mean for this scale increased from 2.20 to 2.69 after 18 months under a gainsharing plan. This improvement was statistically significant.

Question 3: Opportunity for Participation

Before the gainsharing plan began, the average for this scale was 2.83. After 18 months under the plan, it increased to 3.23, which represented a significant change.

Question 4: Productivity

The most powerful effect in the study was seen with regard to this single-item scale. Employees felt that their plant was much more productive after the gainsharing plan was implemented, with the scale average increasing from 2.42 to 3.05. The improvement was significant.

Discussion

Satisfaction

A considerable number of studies have demonstrated a positive relationship between employee involvement in decision making and overall satisfaction. In the present investigation, however, improvements in satisfaction were demonstrated only with regard to the company and the work itself.

One possible explanation for significant results in these two areas relates to a discussion by Bowers on control. He outlines numerous benefits resulting from employees' increased sense of control over their jobs. Under gainsharing, employees' sense of control over their jobs is expected to increase as the worker assumes a more active role in eliminating inefficient procedures and redesigning less effective aspects of their jobs. Bowers found that as control increased, so did satisfaction with both the company and the job.[6] These results suggest that gainsharing may provide one appropriate setting for researching such control techniques.

Unexpectedly, employees' satisfaction with supervisors did not significantly improve under the gainsharing plan in this one example, although the pre-average of 3.46 was already quite high. Previous research has shown that employees in a participative environment tend to be more satisfied with their supervisors than those in a more authoritarian situation; perhaps the change was not that major in this situation.

What remains is the present finding that employees did not become more satisfied with their supervisors after the gainsharing plan began. Subsequent longitudinal studies may provide an explanation for these unexpected results. Perhaps expectations have also increased in this area.

The lack of a significant improvement in the results measuring working conditions was unexpected by many employees at Ashley March. When this finding was presented at a meeting of the overview team, some workers and managers disputed it, arguing that the physical appearance of the plant had improved dramatically since the plan had been in operation. They felt that the employees had more pride in the company and were making an effort to keep walkways clear, dispose of scrap properly, and keep the area cleaner. They were convinced that expectations had increased since gainsharing had been installed.

Cooperation

Employees' perceptions of cooperation improved significantly under the gainsharing plan. This improvement probably was due to the work of department teams and other teams, work which involved meeting, discussing issues, solving problems, and working together. The formal structure of these teams and the suggestion process strongly encourages cooperation.

Opportunity for Participation

To evaluate the employees' perceived opportunity for participation involves little more than looking at actual results: if workers do not feel they are participating more, then the plan is not doing what it is supposed to do. In this case the employees did indicate on the postimplementation survey that they had a greater opportunity for participation since it was certainly true (i.e., team activities, meetings, submitting ideas).

Productivity

Evaluations of productivity made after 18 months under the plan were significantly more favorable than those obtained prior to implementation. While the scale measured overall performance, objective data gathered at the time of the survey revealed the specific areas of company performance showing improvement. For each of these measures, the 12-month period preceding implementation of the plan was used as a base, and was compared to the 18-month period following implementation.

Analysis revealed a 17 percent improvement in efficiency. Indirect labor was down 6.6 percent, scrap costs were down 49.0 percent, and warranty costs decreased 14.5 percent. Annual sales volume was approximately the same across the preimplementation and postimplementation time periods.

Virtually all personnel who were interviewed at Ashley March attributed these improvements to the plan. Unfortunately, research to date has been unsuccessful in determining which components of a gainsharing plan were most responsible for the improvements in company performance, a frustrating situation in organizational research. One line of reasoning attributes these changes to the motivating influence of participative decision making (PDM).

At least three processes may account for improvements in performance obtained in a participative environment. It may be that under a gainsharing plan, employees make more effective use of goal setting. In the departmental meetings at Ashley March, team members reviewed the ideas of their peers and set deadlines for either obtaining additional information or actually implementing the acceptable suggestions. Because these assignments were made in a participative manner, a team member was accountable to his or her colleagues for meeting deadlines. In this way, the participative structure of the plan provided the opportunity to set goals as well as a mechanism for monitoring success in reaching these goals. Research has shown that goal setting typically leads to higher levels of performance than admonishing people to do their best.[7]

With this in mind, goal setting is incorporated into many aspects of the plan. Goals are set regarding the number of suggestions to be obtained, reductions in warranty costs, and other areas affecting organizational performance. It should also be stressed that this goal setting is done in a participative manner. Studies have shown that goals arrived at in this way can be more difficult than assigned goals but sometimes lead to higher levels of performance.[8]

Another process which may explain the observed performance improvement is the cognitive component of participative decision making. This refers to the way a gainsharing plan taps the knowhow of the average employee. It assumes that the employee operating a machine for a long time is in an excellent position to contribute ideas on how to cut scrap, improve output, streamline operations, and so on. By allowing this worker the opportunity to participate in job-related decisions, more intelligent decisions can be made. The result is improved operations and higher productivity.

Unfortunately, little is known about this cognitive aspect of participation. Many studies in the area of participation have subjects performing simple or unfamiliar tasks which do not lend themselves to employees working smarter. Future research should involve settings in which the contribution of worker knowledge in participative decision making (PDM) is given a more fair test.

In addition to PDM, it is likely that productivity improvements at Ashley March may be attributed to the presence of a financial incentive. During eight of the first eighteen months of the plan, employees earned a bonus for having improved performance.

Although much has been written regarding the impact of financial incentives on performance and satisfaction (see Lawler[9]), a number of questions remain regarding the motivational attributes of a gainsharing bonus: Do employees see a relationship between their performance and the bonuses earned? Is it necessary that they understand the bonus calculation? How frequently must bonuses be paid in order for them to have a motivational impact? How large a bonus must be earned for it to be motivational?

The answers to these questions will have major implications as to how future gainsharing plans will be structured.

Conclusion

It can be seen that the success of a gainsharing plan presents more questions than it resolves regarding organizational outcomes. Conditions at Ashley March improved, but why? Future research should identify those components of a gainsharing plan which most directly affect worker attitudes and performance. Researchers cannot keep up with the practitioners/innovators.

With regard to employee attitudes, these components may include the improved levels of communication between management and nonmanagement, the recognition of employees as an important resource in improving operations, and the increased amount of control employees are given. While it may be that some of the above components are more important than others, the possibility that their combined influence is responsible for the change should also be considered.

With regard to performance gainsharing, companies should provide useful sites for addressing some of the issues under debate in the motivational literature. Research should be directed toward understanding whether participation in decision making results in employees working harder, working smarter, or both. Work should also be done in understanding whether the financial bonus motivates performance, how its motivational attributes may be enhanced, and how it affects nonproductivity-related outcomes such as worker attitudes. These questions will become increasingly important as an even wider range of firms, from the troubled to the highly successful, install gainsharing.

It is hoped that more attitude- and productivity-oriented studies of gainsharing plans will follow. When larger numbers of studies documenting successes and failures from a behavioral point of view are accumulated, we will be in the best position to guide organizations toward the type of results enjoyed by Ashley March.

Notes

1. U.S. General Accounting Office. *Productivity Sharing Programs: Can They Contribute to Productivity Improvement?* (Document No. AFMD-81-22; Gaithersburg, Md.: U.S. General Accounting Office, 1981).
2. R.J. Bullock and P.F. Bullock, "Gainsharing and Rubik's Cube: Solving System Problems," *National Productivity Review*, 1982, 1, 396–407.
3. C.F. Frost, J.H. Wakely, and R.A. Ruh, *The Scanlon Plan for Organization Development: Identity, Participation, and Equity* (East Lansing, Mich.: Michigan State University Press, 1974).
4. B.E. Moore, and T.L. Ross, *The Scanlon Way to Improved Productivity: A Practical Guide* (New York: John Wiley & Sons, 1978).
5. C.S. O'Dell, *Gainsharing: Involvement, Incentives, and Productivity* (New York: AMACOM, 1981).
6. In A.S. Tannenbaum, *Control in Organizations* (New York: McGraw-Hill, 1968).
7. D.L. Dossett, G.P. Latham, and T.R. Mitchell, "The Effects of Assigned Versus Participatively Set Goals, KR, and Individual Differences on Employee Behavior When Goal Difficulty is Held Constant," *Journal of Applied Psychology*, 1979, 64, 291–298; G.P. Latham, T.R. Mitchell, and D.L. Dossett,

"The Importance of Participative Goal Setting and Anticipated Rewards on Goal Difficulty and Job Performance," *Journal of Applied Psychology*, 1978, 63, 163–171; G.P. Latham and L.M. Saari, "The Effects of Holding Goal Difficulty Constant on Assigned and Participatively Set Goals," *Academy of Management Journal*, 1979a, 22, 163–168; G.P. Latham, and L.M. Saari, "Importance of Supportive Relationships in Goal Setting," *Journal of Applied Psychology*, 1979b, 64, 151–156.

8. Latham, Mitchell, and Dossett, "The Importance of Participative Goal Setting," note 7, above.

9. E.E. Lawler, *Pay and Organization Development* (Reading, Mass: Addison-Wesley, 1981).

Chapter 15

Gainsharing and the Future

Brian Graham-Moore and Timothy L. Ross

Throughout this book, we have attempted to encourage the serious reader to critically evaluate the theory and evidence underlying productivity gainsharing. Its theoretical development is still extremely limited, but we are hopeful that this book will provide a significant new contribution upon which to build. In the years to come, the country urgently needs more work in both basic and applied theoretical gainsharing research.

Little doubt exists that many firms will find it difficult to adopt gainsharing. Quite simply, some firms shouldn't try it. Some organizations will explore contingent gainsharing which is a new area requiring more research. This book, however, is concerned with traditional gainsharing. Chapter 1, Understanding Gainsharing, provides a basic introduction necessary for comprehension of gainsharing. Many of the conditions and variables associated with gainsharing success and failure are delineated in this book.

Any decision maker who wishes to pursue gainsharing may find the path difficult. What follows is our discussion of attitudes and opinions of managers who revealed some of their deepest concerns about adopting gainsharing.

Impediments to Gainsharing

As part of a small study project, we asked top plant, group, and corporate managers in two firms knowledgeable about gainsharing why they did not believe more of their peers were actively studying gainsharing as a formalized strategy. Their response is condensed in the following nine sections. We believe these opinions are indicative of true managerial concerns and probably illustrate why gainsharing will not be applied in all firms.

1. Why Pay for Something We Can Get From Good Management? If everyone had this view, it might explain why the country's productivity growth has been so dismal. Clearly, there are many good ways to manage.

2. Union Resistance. Unions traditionally have not been strong advocates of gainsharing, probably because they lack knowledge, fear loss of control, or fear the program will be used in lieu of wage increments. This resistance is slowly being eroded, and gainsharing is being discussed in union negotiations.

The United Auto Workers' union has long sought industrywide profit sharing as a wage supplement and has accepted performance gainsharing in many locations. Obviously, union leadership must be heavily involved in most situations for a plan to be successfully implemented.

3. Risk of Failure. The risk of failure is perceived as a particular problem for some firms. Firms of this type often focus only on the bonus aspect of gainsharing and, if conditions are not right, bonus earning opportunities may be limited or even nonexistent for some time. Unless a significant need to change exists because of poor performance or unless a very successful firm wishes to share the fruits of that success with employees, these firms are unlikely to be drawn toward traditional gainsharing.

4. Lack of How-To Knowledge. The relative lack of knowledge of gainsharing has been a problem, particularly in systems in which measurement is difficult (e.g., pure service organizations). Until experiences are more widely shared and research expands into new areas, there won't be any ready answers. Nevertheless, the major improvements which have been made in accounting and information systems in recent years, should help in this area. Electronic spreadsheets are a significant tool in gainsharing calculation assessment.

5. Management Style. The type of management found in a firm can have a positive effect on installations of some systems, while it can hurt others. For example, control-oriented firms might look upon Improshare very favorably but may reject a Scanlon orientation because of discomfort with employee involvement systems. Many other managers, although they do believe that employees at all levels contribute more to organizational success, do not believe that they do so unless forced into such a position. Supervisors often feel most threatened by gainsharing when employee involvement is required. This fear can be overcome through education and when favorable experiences result from gainsharing programs. Changes in supervisors are sometimes required. Many supervisors will come to view gainsharing favorably when a better departmental team is the result and they have not lost control.

6. *Lack of Divisional and Corporate Support.* Lack of support is a major problem in some firms. These firms do not wish to establish a precedent for other units by allowing one to install gainsharing. Other firms, however, actively encourage the installation of these systems with white papers, corporate task forces, staff support, seminars, references, and so on. Very few have a corporate position paper on gainsharing, but more are developing such a document. Some firms require several layers of approval, making it difficult for lower units to propose such plans.

7. *What to Do With Existing Incentive Systems.* These can range from individual, factory incentive systems to sales commissions or managerial bonus systems. Generally, upon the installation of a gainsharing system, these individual incentive programs are eliminated through some form of buyout. Sales commissions and managerial bonuses are continued, although bonuses are typically not paid on the incremental portion or, alternatively, a cap may be placed on sharing.

Individual incentives are thought to be somewhat inconsistent with gainsharing because they emphasize what the individual can do for himself or herself; gainsharing systems, in contrast, are designed to emphasize what can be gained by working better together as a team. Rarely are individual incentives equitably maintained. If part of a union contract, the union must obviously be involved and committed to the elimination since it normally negotiates part or all of the incentive system. If they exist at the time of installation, these systems can at times present thorny issues to resolve, but some firms do mesh the systems without major difficulty.

8. *Inadequate Preparations.* Still weak in our research methodology is the way to establish whether a firm is a good candidate for installation and ultimate success. The ideas presented in this

book should help significantly in this evaluation process. But what about the firm that considers itself inadequately prepared but still wants to proceed? How does it prepare for installation? Each of the major problem areas addressed in this book must be carefully reviewed, including the broad areas of management commitment, employee identification with problems, financial system sophistication, or any others. The review of each of these areas may require considerable time and resources.

Frankly, many managers are unwilling to make such an investment and consequently will drop investigation. The full implementation time is probably around one to two years, with impatient managements losing interest before the preparatory work is completed. Time lags of this duration are not required, but they normally occur. If a shorter time period for installation is necessary, the reasons for this rapid implementation must be fully understood before gainsharing is undertaken.

9. Difficulty with Devising Calculations. Obviously in some situations calculation alternatives will be limited. Rarely is it impossible to develop a viable calculation if management is determined. The first six chapters offer more total information on gainsharing than exists anywhere else. An optimal calculation will normally result if key decision makers pursue organizational goals compatible with those discussed in this book. The key is to accept the relevant behavioral philosophies found in the gainsharing optimal conditions listed at the end of this chapter.

The Future and Gainsharing

Even given the present level of theory development, we believe that the current growth trends in gainsharing will continue and perhaps accelerate in the near future. We note several reasons for this trend. Many business and government leaders publicly proclaim the great importance of productivity growth in maintaining a satisfactory standard of living without major inflation. In 1982, President Reagan formed a blue-ribbon National Productivity Council to address the question of the declining productivity growth rate. Gainsharing became part of the Council's long-term matrix of endorsed systems. No other system incorporates the behaviorally intrinsic variables of employee involvement, recognition, problem identification, and accountability with extrinsic rewards as does gainsharing. This reward system will undoubtedly play an increasing role in helping to reverse the trend of productivity decline simply because it will make more managers behaviorally attuned to employee involvement and motivated toward sharing the financial benefits of any productivity increase.

Better reference works are available today. In the past, there were few articles on gainsharing and virtually no books. Fortunately this is no longer true. The notes at the end of each chapter indicate a vast and ever growing literature. The nation's need to increase productivity is one reason for this growth, coupled with an expansion of the principles that underlie most long-term successful applications of the various systems. Many more researchers are becoming involved in gainsharing. International exposure and application of these systems are bound to grow as other industrialized countries become aware of the fairly elaborate system that the Japanese have for sharing productivity improvements with employees. We are, however, perplexed by the large numbers of managers who have not yet heard of gainsharing, considering the references that are available.

More flexible gainsharing formulas are now available. In earlier years, many managers perceived the need to establish fairly common productivity-sharing calculations. Today, calculations can suit varying conditions, and most organizations custom design one to fit their own needs at a particular time. Calculations have been designed or are being developed for processing and job order manufacturing concerns, engineering firms, banks, hospitals, insurance companies, state and city organizations, to name a few. They may be based on performance productivity measures, such as physical measures of output and input, or on financial productivity measures, such as profit and return on investment. Some calculations approach the problem from a prospective or targeted productivity performance. We believe that this expansion of calculations will create gainsharing applications for many more different types of organizations.

Our knowledge and experience with these processes have grown tremendously in recent years. More gainsharing systems have been installed during the past five years than in its entire previous history. The expansion that Joe Scanlon thought would develop in the 1950s seems to be happening 30 years later.

Organizational culture is changing fairly rapidly. Confrontation within organizations is giving way to a more cooperative environment. Both unions and managements perceive much to be gained

from developing a more cooperative culture because they are identifying competitors, both domestic and foreign, as the enemy rather
than the forces within the organization. Management is now starting to indicate a willingness to spend the time and money to develop
employee-oriented systems which will serve to meld individual
goals with corporate goals. This current emphasis is further indication of an increased focus on cooperation.

Comprehensive organizational development systems make more
sense today as companies become more interdependent, auto-
mated, and as they constantly change. Slow-moving organizations
will be left by the wayside in the 1990s, and increasing numbers
of managers will likely perceive the goal-oriented, employee-
involvement gainsharing plans to be desirable systems toward which
to move. Many firms using Quality Control Circles will probably
evolve toward the use of gainsharing because of pressures to share
the financial benefits of performance improvements. Quality Control Circles, labor-management committees, and other committee
structures can be redesigned to become gainsharing involvement
teams.

Aside from the trend toward high acceptance of employee
involvement systems, more gainsharing systems are successes today. Plans seem to be better installed, monitored, and evaluated.
Although this figure is not well substantiated, the long-term success
rate is probably 65 percent. Some of the firms that drop their
systems because of economic conditions would actually prefer to
manage in a participative style and eventually reconsider this decision. Obviously, some firms do eventually drop their gainsharing
plans. Most observers believe that a long-term success rate of 65
percent is outstanding considering some of the situations surrounding installation and some of the monitoring techniques used.

Richard Pascale and Anthony Athos, in *The Art of Japanese
Management*, express the belief that the superiority of Japanese
management is explained by its managerial beliefs, assumptions,
perceptions, style, and skill.[1] These authors maintain that involved
workers are the key to productivity. In view of this assumption, if
some Japanese managers can be said to be ahead of some American
ones, then traditional gainsharing managers must be considered to
be ahead of both these groups. New scholars also maintain that
Japanese managers practice interdependence. That is, the human
resource of a Japanese corporation is regarded as a collaborator—
not merely an extension of a machine. Indeed, employees are
usually called associates in order to stress this new work role. If

managerial style is a functional factor in Japanese firms, then traditional gainsharing firms with high involvement reflect a kind of style that is open, oriented to problem-solving, and conducive to positive working relationships in the future, with no win/lose or face-saving forms of interpersonal competition.

Where does this leave us? We indicated that some newer forms of gainsharing are evolving and are currently being designed. These new forms are a logical extension of the development of gainsharing since the 1930s, and it is very likely that we will see examples of them in the 1990s. The American work force is continually getting older, wiser, and more skilled. The forces that produce high-quality workers and managers will inevitably produce newer and better forms of gainsharing, with the ultimate goal being a self-managed work force.

While the practices of some gainsharing firms may foster pseudo participation other than a true enhancement of the quality of work-life, a few firms are starting to adopt what might be considered new and different forms of gainsharing. Two commonly cited examples are the companies Donnelley Mirrors and Herman Miller. Both firms use innovative and advanced calculations. These companies have also developed involvement systems and work force commitment that are likely to set the standard in the future for newer forms of gainsharing.

Exhibit 15.1 illustrates results collected by the U.S. General Accounting Office in a survey of gainsharing firms.[2] Of note is the fact that many gainsharing firms recognize that nonmonetary benefits are clearly associated with successful experiences. Better teamwork, increased job satisfaction, less resistance to change, and closer identification with the firm go hand in hand with improvement in productivity, as shown by the findings of the GAO survey. It is not surprising that improved labor-management relations, fewer grievances, less absenteeism, and reduced turnover are associated with gainsharing firms.

We are enthusiastic about and encouraged by recent growth in gainsharing research and application. As the General Accounting Office study concluded, "[w]e have found that when properly implemented and administered, productivity sharing plans can effectively contribute to improved productivity." We agree with this statement and believe that the future is bright. We hope this book will help those who wish to conduct research in and/or implement productivity gainsharing.

Lastly, we end this book with a list of conditions that reflect

Exhibit 15.1 Nonmonetary Benefits of Productivity Sharing Programs

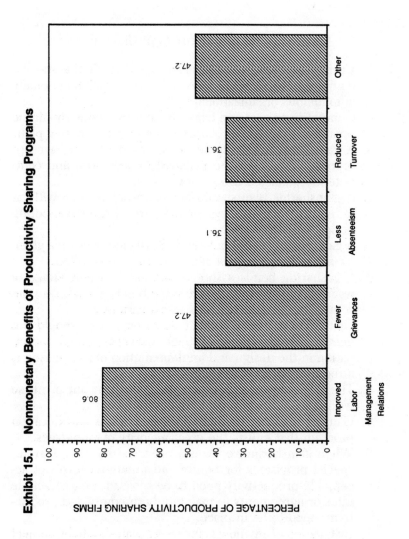

normative beliefs surrounding this important reward system. We hope that each of these can challenge policy makers within high commitment organizations to meet or exceed *optimal* conditions for traditional gainsharing.

Optimal Conditions for Gainsharing

1. Each plan must be custom designed to fit the specific culture, technology, and environment of each functionally autonomous organizational unit.
2. Competitive wage and fringe benefit programs should be operative prior to any consideration of a gainsharing plan.
3. A gainsharing plan should not be used as a "salvage operation" but should be installed in successful and competently managed companies.
4. A gainsharing plan should not be installed along with an individual incentive system because of their competing philosophies.
5. A gainsharing plan should include all employees at a given facility—from the least skilled to the most skilled.
6. Gainsharing bonuses should be paid as a percentage of wages for time worked during the bonus period, i.e., the actual bonus co-varies with actual earnings.
7. Gainsharing, because it is paid to everyone, should not be a part of the union contract. However, union participation in the design and implementation of gainsharing is a requirement for an acceptable plan.
8. The gainsharing plan year should be kept out of phase with the union contract termination date.
9. Gainsharing plan implementation requires an education program that enlists the great majority of employees.
10. When gainsharing replaces a previous incentive system, special provisions for equity and minimum levels of acceptable productivity need to be secured, i.e., red-circle rates or agreements to maintain both equity and productivity need to be in place.
11. Installation of any new gainsharing plan should be subject to a significant majority affirmative vote of all employees.
12. The first year of gainsharing should be a trial period after which future continuation of gainsharing should be contingent on one additional favorable vote by employees.
13. Termination of gainsharing should be subject to 90-day

notice by management or by any significant group, such as a union.

14. Everyone involved should have an understanding of the gainsharing formula, at least in terms of its connection to performance.

15. The gainsharing formula should be monitored regularly and carefully to ensure equitable results for both the company and the employees.

16. Discussion of the labor contract and of fringe benefits is inappropriate in departmental and organizationwide meetings.

17. Initial gainsharing success depends on the dedication, enthusiasm, and competence of a "champion," such as the highest ranked manager at the facility.

18. The role of catalysts in developing, disseminating, and educating the operating facts of gainsharing are very important in the building of trust and confidence.

19. Managerial succession requires that a thorough training and indoctrination as to gainsharing principles be conducted for any new manager taking charge of a gainsharing assignment.

20. All suggestions, as well as minutes of the involvement system, should be open, public, and distributed so that maximum employee recognition is achieved.

21. Quality of the product should be improved as part of a plan to achieve total organization productivity.

22. A certain percentage of the bonus should be reserved for covering during deficit periods. This strategy will serve both to protect the company's interests and to encourage employees to think in the long-term.

23. The plantwide committee is a consultative or advising body and not a decision-making one—management manages, the committee advises.

24. Rapid follow-up on the disposition of suggestions encourages employees to make more suggestions.

25. Foremen and first-line supervisors must be involved in the plan; otherwise, they may choose to undermine it.

26. The productivity-sharing calculation, or any changes to it, must establish the bonus at a level which does not jeopardize the company's ability to compete in the marketplace.

27. Bonus earnings should be paid separately from normal earnings, i.e., employees should receive a separate check.

28. Since teamwork is the key to success, do not reward one group of workers at the expense of other workers.

Notes

1. R.T. Pascale and A.G. Athos, *The Art of Japanese Management* (New York: Simon and Schuster, 1981).
2. U.S. General Accounting Office, *Productivity Sharing Programs: Can They Contribute to Productivity Improvements?* (Document No. AFMD-81-22; Gaithersburg, Md.: U.S. General Accounting Office, 1981).

Glossary of Gainsharing Terms[*]

Allowed labor formula. A calculation similar to the Improshare formula. The base ratio equals the allowed labor activity multiplied by the allowed wage with a provision for all indirect labor costs.

Base Productivity Factor. The relationship in the base period between the actual hours worked by all employees and the value of the work-hours produced by these employees. This value is determined by the measurement standards used in the base period, or:

$$\text{BPF} = \frac{\text{Direct labor hours } + \text{ indirect labor hours}}{\text{Total standard value hours (Improshare)}}$$

Base ratio. The total personnel costs divided by the sales value of production (sales $+/-$ change inventory valued at cost or sales price). The original single ratio of Joseph Scanlon, often referred to as the single ratio of labor.

Bonus reserve. A portion of the gross bonus set aside to compensate for deficit months. At the end of each gainsharing year, any reserve is distributed. Any year-end deficit is absorbed by the firm.

Buy-Back principle. Workers receive a cash payment for productivity gains they achieve over established ceilings. For this bonus, management has the right to change the product standard.

Ceiling. A productivity limit. Productivity exceeding the ceiling can be banked and eventually brought back to the employees in the form of a cash payment—e.g., the buy-back.

---

[*]Adapted from: B. E. Moore, *Sharing the Gains of Productivity* (Scarsdale, N.Y.: Work in America Institute and Pergamon Press, 1982).

Fixed payroll. On a current basis, the total employment costs for the human resources whose time does not vary directly with annual production volume.

Gainsharing. A generic term used to describe a broad range of sharing systems usually based on some difference between actual costs and an equitable standard.

Improshare®. Invented by Mitchell Fein, the name is an acronym for *Im*proved *Pro*ductivity Through *Shar*ing. Past average productivity determines the Base Productivity Factor (BPF). The BPF is multiplied by standard hours to produce Improshare hours. The actual hours required to produce acceptable results less the Improshare hours can create a bonus that is split 50–50 by the company and all employees.

Incentive. Motivating action toward the expectation of a reward; inducement, influence.

Involvement system. Ranges from a type of suggestion system that emphasizes involvement to facilitate productivity-related suggestions to elaborate self-managed teams.

Memo of understanding. A document that defines the gainsharing plan—especially in regard to defining the bonus calculation and any involvement system responsibilities. Often used in a union environment.

Multi-Cost formula. A calculation that includes some costs in addition to labor, but can include most or even all costs which are then generally divided by the sales value of production. While based, like profit sharing, on success of the firm if most costs are included, it has many advantages over profit sharing since it is productivity (or output/input) related.

Participating payroll. Those employees sharing in the bonus payout—typically all employees (managers and workers) less the sales force and probationary employees.

Production (or departmental) committee or team. A committee composed of employee and management representatives that considers productivity-improving suggestions from its area. It refers all suggestions not within its realm of responsibility to the screening committee or larger plant board for review and, perhaps, for broader implementation.

Production value. The difference between the market value of goods and the material cost and services used in producing these goods equal to the value added by the firm.

Profit sharing. A system under which the firm pays compensation to employees in addition to their regular wages, based upon the profits of the company. While not output/input related, it is usually based on a definite formula specifying how much of the profit is to be distributed and how it is to be computed, usually at the end of the fiscal year. Some people consider profit sharing to be one form of gainsharing if paid more frequently than once a year.

Quality circles. This team-building concept involves small groups of departmental work leaders and line operators who have volunteered to spend time helping solve various departmental problems. The groups are taught problem-solving techniques and how to present their solutions to management. These circles are similar to Scanlon production committees.

Rucker committee. These committees are composed of nonmanagement and management representatives whose purpose is to improve communication between workers and management about suggestions, problems, and solutions.

Rucker plan®. A productivity gainsharing program that measures economic productivity as the index of the overall effectiveness of a work group. Its goal is to maximize the output value of production (value added) for a given input value of payroll.

Rucker Standard. The percentage of the production value paid out in wages and benefits to nonexempt employees. It is calculated by dividing variable payroll costs by the production value (revenue minus outside purchases):

$$\text{Rucker Standard} = \frac{\text{Payroll costs included}}{\substack{\text{Production value} \\ \text{(revenue} - \text{outside purchases)}}}$$

If costs are less than this standard, a bonus is earned.

Sales value of production. The actual period's sales, plus or minus the inventory.

Scanlon plan. An organizationwide performance improvement plan designed to increase productivity through greater efficiency and reduced costs. The basic elements of the plan are the philosophy and practice of cooperation, the involvement system, and formulas to measure increased productivity and distribute bonuses.

Scanlon single ratio formula. One of the original productivity gainsharing formulas, the base ratio is often expressed as:

$$\frac{\text{Labor costs}}{\text{Sales value of production}} = \text{base ratio}$$

The base ratio is the expected relationship between labor costs and the sales value of production. Actual labor costs are subtracted from expected labor costs to create a bonus or deficit.

Screening committee. Composed of representatives from employees and management, it reviews and disposes of suggestions from the production committees, reviews bonus results, and discusses the economics of the firm.

Split ratio formula. A calculation composed of two or more base ratios of payroll costs divided by value of production, with each calculated for a product line to help cope with product mix issues.

Standard time. The time, usually established by a time and motion study or some other method, required for an employee to perform a specific operation without undue fatigue. Incentive earnings are gained when the worker produces in less than the standard time.

Suggestion systems. Employee involvement programs that provide employees the opportunity to give ideas to management that can increase the effectiveness and efficiency of the firm.

Value-Added formula. A formula that is similar to the Rucker formula. The value of production (sales plus changes in inventory) less outside purchases (materials, etc.) multiplied by the historically determined base ratio to equal the allowed labor cost. Then, the allowed cost minus actual cost equals the increase or decrease to productivity.

Variable payroll. Total employment costs on current basis, for people whose time input varies directly with annual production. Also, these are costs that one may want to control on a directly variable basis with current volume.

Variable purchases. Costs to procure goods and services that are consumed during production. These vary with the level of production. Management wants employees to try to conserve them by seeing their impact on the bonus; especially applicable to the Rucker Plan.

Work-Hour standard. The average number of work-hours required to produce a finished product as calculated by dividing the total work-hours by units produced. May also be based on accounting or engineered time standards.

Index

A

Accountants, correlates of gainsharing success ranked by, 104–107
Adamson Company, 24
Administration, of gainsharing plan, 53–54, 72, 79, 84
Alanis, R. S., 45
Allowed hour formula, 25
Allowed labor formula, 25, 51, 55, 65–67, 87. *See also* Improshare
  definition of, 289
  effect of, on behavioral and emotional factors, 68–70
  federal sector's use of, 186, 188–189
  service sector's use of, 257, 264
American Productivity and Quality Center, ix
American Productivity Center, 36, 253
Anderson, A., 46
Anderson, Richard, 139
Army Materiel Command, Arlington, Virginia, gainsharing plan, 188
Ashburn, A., 114–115
Athos, Anthony G., 283, 289
Atlas Powder Co., 31
Autonomous work groups, 116, 123–124

B

Bank Administration Institute, 261
Banking
  gainsharing in, 261–264
  performance measurement in, 255–256
Barker, Jim, 148, 159–160
Base productivity factor, 29–31, 65–66
  calculation of, 67

definition of, 289
Base ratio
  definition of, 289, 291–292
  moving vs. static, 89–90
Behaviors
  changes in, under gainsharing plan, 237–238
  knowledge of, and institutionalization of organizational change, 119
  performance of, and institutionalization of organizational change, 119
  preferences for, and institutionalization of organizational change, 119–120
Bell, C. H., 41, 47
Bell, L., 192
Berg, D. N., 134
Black, Elizabeth, *174*
Bluestone, Irving, *vii*
Bonus
  accounting for, 93
  amount of, 52
  calculation of, 4, 17, 21, 24–26, 233. *See also* Gainsharing formulas
    constructed by Scanlon, 24–25
    measurement aspects, 81–99
    and unions' attitudes toward gainsharing, 204
  financial, definition of, 4
  and gainsharing success, 106–107
  knowledge of those earning and contributing to, 107
  motivational attributes of, 275–276
  payment, frequency of, 98–99
  percent vs. flat amount, 96–97
  size
    and bad times, 92
    caps on, 91

Note: Page numbers in italics indicate contributions to this volume.

Highland, Bob, 150–151, 160, 168
Hood, Arch, 215
Hooker Chemical Co., 31
Hospitals
    gainsharing formulas used for, 257–
        260
    performance measurement in, 255–
        256
Howell, W. J., Jr., 46
Human resource costs, 141–142

I

Identity, 21–22
Improshare, vi, 3, 19, 25, 27–33, 41,
        72, 87, 91, 261, 279–280. *See
        also* Allowed labor formula
    acceptance of, 31–33
    Allowed Labor/Improshare calcula-
        tion, 29–30
    definition of, 290
    evaluation studies of, 35
    federal gainsharing plans' use of,
        186, 188–189
    formula, simplicity of, 29–31
    frequency of payout, 67
    installation of, 32–33
    key factors in, 29
    policies of, 67–68
    in service sector, 257, 264
Incentives, 280. *See also* Individual
        incentives
    definition of, 290
    elimination of, 95
Indirect work, in base productivity
        factor, 31
Individual incentives, 95, 280. *See
        also* Tech Form Industries
    and gainsharing, 95
Individual recognition. *See* Employee
        recognition
Inflation, 26, 72, 260
    effect on public-sector gainsharing
        plan, 179
Information, sharing, with unions,
        210
Ingersoll-Rand, 31
Institute of Public Performance, 192
Institutionalization
    definition of, 118
    degrees of, 119–120
    of organizational change, 118–121
        empirical findings on, 122–126
        factors affecting, 121–122
        importance of understanding,
            117–118

International Association of Machin-
        ists, 202, 204
International Brotherhood of Boiler-
        makers, 202
International Ladies Garment Work-
        ers Union, 202
International Union of Bricklayers and
        Allied Craftsmen, 202
International Union of Tool, Die, and
        Mold Makers, 202
Interpersonal skills, 172
Inventories, 92–93
Involvement system, 4, 41, 72, 222,
        232
    acceptance of, 282–283
    analogs to, in organizational devel-
        opment, 43
    critiques of, 33–34
    definition of, 3, 290
    and gainsharing success, 106
    institutionalization of, 38
    opportunity for participation in,
        272–274
    in Scanlon plan, 33–34
    as structure and process, 146–151
Irritants, 152–155, 170
Ivancevich, J. M., 123, 134

J

Japanese management, 283–284
Jarrett, James E., *174*, 180, 192
Jarrett, Marion, *174*
Jehring, J. J., 39–40, 45–47, 114
Job-enrichment program, public-
        sector, 124–125
Job satisfaction, 8–9, 164, 268, 271–
        273
Job security, 206, 209
Job switching, 116, 124–125
Johnson, R. B., 39, 47
Johnson, R. H., 46–47
Jones, G. M., 45, 114

K

Katz, H. C., 38, 201, 213
Kochan, T. A., 38, 201, 213

L

Labor costs
    historical standards of, 20–21
    leverage effects of, 91–92

Labor force, and success of gainsharing, 8–9
Labor-management committee, 32–33, 68, 283
Labor-management cooperation, Scanlon's belief in, 23–24
Labor-management problem-solving groups, 116
Labor/management steering committee, 211–212, 220–221
Lake Charles, Louisiana, 175
Latham, G. P., 276–277
Lawler, E. E., III, 17, 36, 38–39, 45, 47, 124, 134, 275, 277
Leadership abilities, of employees, identification of, 161
Lefcowitz, J. J., 39, 46–47
Lesieur, F. G., 22, 40, 44–47, 139, 146, 173
Lester, Tom, 139–140, 144, 148, 159, 167–168, 172
Levine, A., 128–129, 135
Lincoln, J. F., 44–45
Lincoln Electric, 25, 32–33, 52, 95
Literature
  on correlates of gainsharing success, 102–104
  on gainsharing, 9–10, 282
  review of, 19–47
Livernash, E. R., 46–47
Locke, E. A., 124, 134
Loftus, P. J., 26, 45
Loveland, Colorado, gainsharing plan, 183–185

M

Majerus, R., 206, 211, 213
Management
  challenge to, in gainsharing, 158–160
  integration of gainsharing into, 251
  reward-oriented, 93
  type of, and gainsharing, 279–280
Management by Objectives, 123
Manager surveys, 234–239, 242–243, 278–281
Managers
  education of, about gainsharing, 244–251
  evaluation of gainsharing, 281
  evaluation of subordinates, 237–238
  expectations of, and gainsharing success/failure, 102
  satisfaction with gainsharing plans, 238–239

Manufacturing, 254
Markwell, Roger, 215, 220
Martin, Dan, 215, 220, 229
Massachusetts Institute of Technology, 19, 34, 36
McAdams, J., 17, 47
McClellan Air Force Base, gainsharing plan, 187
McDowell, Amy M., 163, 167, 173
McGraw-Edison, 31
McKersie, R. B., 46, 152, 173
Measurement, 81–99
  conceptual framework for, 82
  of government service outputs, 191
  in service sector, 253–255
Memo of understanding, definition of, 290
Metzger, B. L., 45
Michigan State University, 34
Miller, E. J., 129, 135
Mirvis, P. H., 134
Mitchell, T. R., 276–277
Mix problems, 93–94
Mixed services, 254–255
Mohrman, S. A., 129, 135
Moore, B. E., 12, 14, 18, 23, 25, 28, 36–37, 42, 44–45, 47, 49–50, 57, 61, 64–65, 71, 80, 154, 173, 268, 276, 289. *See also* Graham-Moore, B. E.
Morrison, J. C., 45–46
Motivation and learning theory, 38–39
Mower, N. R., 38, 201, 213
Multicost ratio formula, 25–26, 55, 59, 72, 88, 223
  definition of, 290
  and fairness, 74
  in service sector, 259–260, 264
Multicost split ratio formula
  determination of, 62–64
  and ease of administration, 64–65
  effect of, on behavioral and organizational factors, 62–64
  implementation of, 65
  monthly report for, 64
  reinforcement value of, 62, 65
Multiple pool, in service sector, 264

N

Nassau County, New York, 175
National Productivity Center, 281
New Hampshire, 181
New York City, 175
New York State, gainsharing plan, 175

About the Authors

Brian Graham-Moore is a professor of management at The University of Texas at Austin, where he has been since 1972. He received his B.A. (1961) from Northwestern University, his M.A. (1967) and Ph.D. (1971) from Washington University, Saint Louis. From 1964 to 1966 he was on the corporate personnel staff of Helene Curtis Industries, Chicago. From 1968 to 1972 he was on the faculty of the Graduate School of Business, The University of Chicago. Author of *Sharing the Gains of Productivity*, a monograph for Work in America, he has co-authored two previous books on gainsharing: They are *The Scanlon Way to Improved Productivity: A Practical Guide* (1978) and *Productivity Gainsharing* (1983). His primary research interests are reward systems, job analysis methods, and human resource information systems.

Timothy L. Ross is Director of BG Productivity and Gainsharing Institute at Bowling Green State University where he earned two degrees. He received his Ph.D. from Michigan State University (1969). He is co-author of *The Scanlon Way to Improved Productivity: A Practical Guide*, published by John Wiley and Sons, and *Productivity Gainsharing* published by Prentice-Hall. In addition, he has had numerous journal articles published on various aspects of gainsharing. Dr. Ross also consults with organizations throughout North America and Europe on all aspects of gainsharing.

Ruth Ann Ross is President of R.A. Ross and Associates, Inc., a consulting firm that specializes in the implementation, evaluation and monitoring of gainsharing systems in organizations throughout North America. She has published numerous articles on various aspects of gainsharing.

Paul S. Goodman is professor of industrial administration and psychology in the Graduate School of Industrial Administration at Carnegie-Mellon University, where he is also the Director of the Center for the Management of Technology and Information. He received his B.A. (1959) from Trinity College in economics, his M.B.A. (1961) from Amos Tuck School of Business Administration at Dartmouth College, and his Ph.D. (1966) from Cornell University in organizational psychology. His primary research interests are in the effects of technology and social systems on organizational structure and effectiveness. He is author or editor of many books on organizational behavior including *Assessing Organizational Change: The Rushton Quality of Work Experiment* (1979) and *Designing Effective Work Groups* (1986), both published by Jossey-Bass.

James E. Jarrett is Director of Research at the Texas Advisory Commission on Intergovernmental Relations in Austin, Texas. Formerly he was Director of the Productivity Center at the national Council of State Governments. He holds a doctorate in political science and public administration from the University of Pennsylvania.

James W. Dean, Jr., is an assistant professor of organizational behavior at Pennsylvania State University, as well as Assistant Director of Pennsylvania State's Center for the Management of Technological and Organizational Change (CMTOC). He received his M.S. and Ph.D. degrees from the Graduate School of Industrial Administration, Carnegie-Mellon University, and his B.A. in psychology from Catholic University in Washington, D.C. Professor Dean's research interests include the management of advanced manufacturing technology, innovation, and strategic decision making. He is the author of *Deciding to Innovate: How Firms Justify Advanced Technology* (1980), published by Ballinger Publishing Company.

Larry L. Hatcher is an assistant professor of psychology at Winthrop College, Rock Hill, South Carolina. His main areas of research include employee attitudes, participative management, and gainsharing. He received his Ph.D in industrial and organizational psychology from Bowling Green State University.